Interpersonal Communication

How do people communicate with each other in their face-to-face meetings and conversations? Can we trust our first impressions of people, or should we be more cautious? What evidence is there that our gestures and facial expressions reveal to others what we 'really' mean?

Interpersonal Communication provides a framework for understanding how we communicate with others in everyday situations. Peter Hartley explores the key features of the skills we use in communicating with other people, and provides a comprehensive introduction to the hows and whys of interpersonal communication.

This expanded and revised second edition

- outlines the main components and distinctive characteristics of interpersonal communication
- offers detailed analysis of communication processes, considering their everyday applications and implications
- includes new material on contemporary issues in communication studies such as race and gender
- explains the debate over differences between male and female communication
- looks to the future of the subject, introducing new areas such as computer-mediated communication

Peter Hartley is Senior Academic in Communication Studies at the School of Cultural Studies, Sheffield Hallam University.

Interpersonal Communication

Interpersonal Communication

Second edition

Peter Hartley

LONDON AND NEW YORK

First published 1993

Second edition first published 1999
by Routledge
11 New Fetter Lane, London EC4P 4EE

Simultaneously published in the USA and Canada
by Routledge
29 West 35th Street, New York, NY 10001

Routledge is an imprint of the Taylor & Francis Group

Reprinted 2001(twice), 2004

Typeset in Janson by Routledge
Printed and bound in Great Britain by TJ International Ltd,
Padstow, Cornwall

British Library Cataloguing in Publication Data
A catalogue record for this book is available from the British Library

Library of Congress Cataloging in Publication Data
Hartley, Peter, 1946–
Interpersonal communication / Peter Hartley – 2nd edn.
Includes bibliographical references and index.
1. Interpersonal communication. I. Title.
BF637.C45H35 1999 98–47600
153.6–dc21 CIP

ISBN 0–415–20793–2 (hbk)
ISBN 0–415–18107–0 (pbk)

Contents

SECTION C
Issues and controversies in interpersonal communication 161

SECTION D
Going beyond interpersonal communication 203

Illustrations

Figures

Tables

Acknowledgements

Thanks to many colleagues who helped me get the first edition off the ground, especially to Guy Fielding, Gary Radford, Andrew Beck and Jane Weston.

Thanks to the colleagues who gave me support, ideas and inspiration for this second edition, especially to Mark Neath, Caroline Dryden and Jonathan Grove.

Special thanks to Kathy Doherty who produced the original outline and research for Chapter 11 and then helped to develop it.

Thanks to all the students whose interest and questioning helped me develop my ideas.

Thanks to Chris Cudmore and Rebecca Barden at Routledge for their support and patience.

And special thanks to my primary group – Julia, James and David – for their perseverance while I huddled over and, more recently, talked to the word processor.

Introduction

If you have picked up this book to flick through the contents, then I probably do not need to convince you that face-to-face communication between people is an important part of everyday life. Our relationships at work, home and at play are critical to our psychological well-being. My telephone company is also convinced of this – it quotes a recent survey which 'showed that 60% of the British public would like to be better at communicating with their friends and family'.[1] Of course, you might not be surprised that a communications company wishes to promote the fact that 'it's good to talk', but we can find plenty of evidence from other sources to support its views on the value of communication.

The way we communicate also influences our life opportunities in situations such as job or course interviews. The importance of interactive or interpersonal skills at work is frequently emphasised and this has led to a corresponding increase in training, seminars, workshops and publications which focus on these skills, across a *very* wide range of organisations. One British example is the 'Good

Practice Guide to Officer Safety' published by the London Metropolitan Police in 1995, which includes recommendations on the body posture which should be used in different situations. It advises officers to respect cultural differences and 'mirror' certain body signals when talking to people from different ethnic groups. You will find similar advice in the manuals and handbooks issued by many commercial and service organisations.

We cannot change our interpersonal behaviour just by reading a book. So what is the value of a textbook like this, apart from helping some students get through their course assignments? Can a book like this make any difference to your everyday situation? Before I try to answer that last question, I'll spell out the main aims of this book.

The main aim is to provide a basic introductory text on interpersonal communication, i.e. face-to-face communication between two people. So I have tried to:

- explain the special or distinctive characteristics of interpersonal communication
- identify the component parts of interpersonal communication
- explain how these components relate to one another
- explain the most important features of the skills we use when we communicate with other people
- contrast the characteristics of interpersonal communication with other forms of communication

All of these aims are *directly relevant* to our everyday situations because we cannot just rely on specific behaviours or techniques to communicate effectively – we need to *understand* the process and adjust what we do to suit the context. And this is *not* as easy as it sounds.

You may have been invited to seminars or workshops which claim to give you 'simple tips on the power of eye contact with strategies that work for even the largest audiences' or show you the 'special body positions to use in dealing with specific kinds of difficult people'.[2] Or perhaps you have seen the correspondence course which will give you 'everything you need to quickly and enjoyably acquire mastery of speaking and writing skills in the shortest possible time'.[3] And what about those books in your local bookseller which claim to 'change your life' or help you to 'read the (body language) signals and find love, wealth and happiness'?[4]

There is plenty of advice on how to communicate 'better', but is this advice based upon sound principles? Is the advice always consistent? Can you apply it in every situation? For example, can you believe the author who promises to explain 'the simple but powerful piece of body language which virtually guarantees that your audience will remember the key part of your message, weeks and months later, without having to take a written note'?[5] What do you believe and what do you act upon?

As you may have gathered from the tone of the last few paragraphs, I am sceptical of many of these claims. This book is based upon the idea that you must try to *understand* the process of communication as well as the way people behave. And there are a wide range of social and cultural factors which can change both the process and the behaviours when we communicate. After reading this book, I hope you will have a much clearer picture of the richness and complexities of human communication, and will have a few ideas which you can apply to your own behaviours and feelings.

In the rest of this introduction, I will explain how this book is organised. But first I will give a few examples which introduce major themes of the book:

- the importance of understanding how we communicate
- the dangers of oversimplified analysis
- the impact of specific behaviours and techniques

How can understanding interpersonal communication help?

In one sense, we all spend a lot of time working on this already. When was the last time you talked to work colleagues or college friends about 'why person X said that'? Or when you talked with your partner about your relationship with the neighbours, or why the kids do not seem to be talking to you as openly as they used to? If we are involved in everyday communication which seems to be 'going wrong' then we try to work out why. This book will hopefully give you ideas which approach these problems from a fresh angle. Consider the following conversation between A and B and then decide who they might be:

A: 'What's the matter?'
B: 'Nothing.'

A: 'What's the matter?' *(said with increased volume and more emphasis on the word matter)*
B: 'Nothing!' *(said slower and with increased emphasis)*
A: 'OK!'
B: 'OK!' *(One or both people then leave the room)*

Remember who you thought A and B were? We'll return to that in a minute.

I have shown this extract to many people. They have all been able to recognise it from their own experience, often in several different contexts: parent/child communication; communicating with a work colleague; communicating with a fellow student; communicating with a flatmate or partner; and communicating with a husband/wife/partner. To take the parent example, I have experienced this conversation from both sides, as child and as parent. If you are a parent and you have just had a conversation like that with your son or daughter, how do you feel about it? What are you going to do next? What has this conversation done to your family relationships? Do you feel that you have done everything you can sensibly do as a parent? Or do you feel that you have failed as a parent in that encounter and go away feeling depressed that you have not got to the root of the problem?

You can reflect upon and analyse that conversation from a number of different angles which are presented in this book. For example, one analysis would suggest that, if this is a regular conversation in the family, the parent and child have played a 'game' (using concepts I discuss in Chapter 10). This game is designed to satisfy their subconscious feelings about their relationship without having to take any more positive action about it. Both parties can feel that they have acted 'as they should'. But this disguises the fact that there may be underlying problems in the relationship, which remain unsolved.

This analysis is one of several possibilities. Another way of examining the conversation would be to look at the non-verbal communication between A and B. For example, have you assumed that the conversation was serious? Could it be a game in the more usual sense of having fun? Are A and B indulging in verbal play, using the *Simpsons* as role models? Assuming it is serious, you could also investigate the way A describes their relationship with B and vice versa; and investigate how A and B see their respective roles; and so on. But this begs the important question – how do we decide which method is the most appropriate? And there is another complication – all of these methods could give misleading results without more detailed background knowledge of the situation. For example, what was your visual image of A and B? Were they partners, or parent/child or what? Were they both white or black or of different ethnic background? Were they both middle class, working class or from different class backgrounds? You would have to consider all these possible differences before arriving at a sensible analysis of the situation.

So the most sensible strategy must be to use various forms of analysis and consider a range of possibilities. This book will give you a range to select from.

Can understanding interpersonal communication save your life?

A well-known American security consultant, Gavin De Becker, suggests that many victims of personal violence fail to recognise the warning signals which would enable them to withdraw from a dangerous situation before they become trapped.[6] He argues that attackers typically use certain communication strategies to gain the confidence of their victims. They can then lure them into a situation where the attack can take place with the least chance of being noticed or interrupted. These strategies are all designed to communicate trust and innocence. A couple of examples will illustrate the point.

One of the strategies is what De Becker calls 'forced teaming', where the attacker tries to establish a relationship with the victim by suggesting that they are both in the same boat. Supposing you are waiting to catch a bus, late at night, in a lonely bus depot, where there are few people around. A stranger approaches you and says: 'So your bus is late as well. You just can't trust these timetables nowadays.' Is this an innocent comment to pass the time of day? Or is the stranger deliberately trying to establish a relationship with you by showing that he is in the same boat as you?

Another strategy is what De Becker calls an excess of 'charm and niceness'. Again, this could be perfectly innocent but may also be deliberate strategy. De Becker's third strategy is what he calls 'too many details'. The stranger in the bus depot may start to tell you a very interesting story about why he is visiting the city, or why he must catch that bus, or about the unfortunate experiences he has had trying to catch buses late at night.

All of these strategies can lull you (the victim) into a false sense of security. On their own, each of these strategies may of course be perfectly innocent. When they are used deliberately by a prospective attacker, and when they are used in combination, then they can signal that the situation is not as innocent as it may seem. De Becker notes that many victims do have an uneasy feeling, an intuitive danger signal, about their attacker. These intuitive warnings are often because the strategy used by the attacker seems slightly false or unnatural.

De Becker's thesis is that people can learn to analyse the communication they receive, recognise danger signals and withdraw or seek help before it is too late. His book is based upon his organisation's fairly extensive experience of dealing with risk. It is also interesting to note that it is endorsed by a wide range of commentators, ranging from lawyers and prosecutors, to representatives of bodies who are involved in work with victims, such as the American Domestic Violence Council, through to celebrities such as Meryl Streep and Carrie Fisher. The book offers considerable anecdotal evidence, both of the strategies used by attackers and the recommended avoidance strategies.

I also found some anecdotal evidence to support his views in one of my recent lectures. After I had used one of De Becker's accounts to illustrate his list of strategies, I noticed that one of my female students seemed particularly interested. After the lecture, she told me that she had experienced almost exactly the same conversation while she was waiting for a flight connection in an American airport quite late at night. Before she had a chance to accept the offer of help from the stranger who approached her, a police officer intervened to warn her that the stranger had a record of violent crime.

But De Becker's book does not offer systematic research data and he does not explicitly investigate all the different examples of potential danger. Perhaps there are some factors which are more important in certain situations. Can we simply accept his views without more evidence from different sources? All his examples are American – do the same principles apply in other cultures?

What should we believe about interpersonal communication?

We all have a set of beliefs about social life and about our society. These beliefs may be based on quite flimsy evidence. For example, would you accept the following propositions about modern society?

- nowadays families tend to eat more snacks
- modern families no longer sit down for family meals in the way that they used to
- this decline in family meals is 'symptomatic of a wider breakdown in family structure and values'

Of these three propositions, we have ample evidence from the food manufacturers and retailers to support the first. The second and third do seem to have been accepted by some sociologists and journalists – but on what evidence? Recent work by Anne Murcott suggests that reality in the UK is/was more complicated.[7] The stereotypical family meal which fostered communication and harmony may have been a middle-class ideal which was not always the norm. Interesting though this is, the main point for this book is that we may have 'false' beliefs which not only shape the way we see the world around us but also influence our behaviour. How many parents have pressurised their children to eat round the table on the understanding that this was both the norm and would promote family harmony?

A more specific example of how our beliefs affect how we communicate is the way many managers act as if communication were 'one way' and 'linear' and ignore any other possibilities. This is discussed in more detail in Chapter 1 when we look at models of communication.

What do the media tell us about interpersonal communication?

Talking about our beliefs about society inevitably raises questions of media influence. We have all probably seen at least one TV chat show which probed into the communication and relationships between two or three 'ordinary' members of the public. Many American chat shows now seem to thrive on difficulties in relationships by allowing the participants to bare their souls and feelings to millions of viewers. As I took a break from word processing this chapter, I noticed Jerry Springer talking on his own TV show to John about his best friend, Marcia, who was sitting beside him. Marcia then revealed that she was harbouring a secret crush on John. Springer then developed the conversation by asking how John felt about it, and then brought in his current girl friend to see how she reacted to this revelation (of course, I have changed these names to ensure anonymity!). The audience was now focused on John, absorbing his every movement. Does his averted gaze mean good or bad news for Marcia? Naturally, these exchanges are always sensitively handled without any consideration for the ratings advantage that a sensational confession might bring!

Some critics argue that TV has become almost obsessed by these conflicts and tensions in everyday relationships, perhaps because they make for rather cheap programming which nonetheless attracts large audiences. The latest variants on this obsession are the programmes which 'eavesdrop' on everyday interaction. Recent examples on British TV include the series of programmes looking at battles between neighbours, and the various programmes looking at people in their everyday jobs and activities such as working in a hotel or taking driving tests. The unwitting stars of these programmes can go on to become minor celebrities in their own right. Another variant uses hidden cameras to spy on real tourists who are forced to confront situations which test the validity of the popular national stereotypes. What will we learn from discovering whether the German tourists will share the sun-beds?

It is not just television which seems to have become increasingly interested in people's everyday relationships. There are numerous examples of this fascination in the newspapers. One major British daily newspaper reassures me that 'body language is the key' to success at my next job interview and so 'improving your body language is vital'. The Saturday issue of this same paper always includes a column which analyses a photograph of celebrities in terms of what their body language is *really* telling us.[8]

As well as observation and analysis, we can also find plenty of advice on how to improve our communication and relationships. Every day (or at least it seems like every day) I can find feature articles which explain how to create/mend/improve my relationships with others. The newspaper agony aunt continues to thrive, usually concentrating on sexual problems but also offering many more comments to do with repairing relationships. And this is often augmented by more general advice on how to behave. For example, the Saturday edition of the *Daily Mail* includes a column by a Drusilla Beyfuss who is described as 'Britain's premier etiquette expert'. She also responds to readers' questions and 'guides us through the maze of modern manners'. Recent examples have included how to use first-name terms in the workplace, how to decline loan requests, and analysing whether it is 'bad form' to prop up your juicy invitations on the mantelpiece.[9]

The flood of advice is also promoted by media 'crossover' where one channel works to promote and feed off another: TV chat shows interview authors; newspapers often use new books to create feature articles; and so on. Two recent examples from the British press will illustrate. An article in the 'career' section of one daily newspaper started with the observation that 'touching your colleagues could ease your path to the top at work'. This then developed into a series of quotes and thoughts from Alan Pease, the Australian author and trainer who has delivered widely advertised seminars and also written on body language. The article simply quoted Pease's views without any hint of analysis or criticism.[10]

Another British daily described one recent American best-seller as 'a DIY therapy guide that tells you all about yourself'. The article explained that the book has been 'touted as the world's cheapest therapy', claiming that it can combine all the secret revelations you can obtain from a personal diary with the sort of advice you will get from a good therapist.[11]

Throughout the book you are invited to fill in the blanks on a series of questions. These start with fairly innocuous personal details but then move quickly on to fairly deep revelations about a person's history, including for example the moment you are most ashamed of and the last time you cried uncontrollably. Not only does this book invite you to spill out your secrets on to the printed page, but the author also suggests that the answers should be shared with friends or even the new neighbours. He also suggests that couples embarking on a long-term relationship should swap their copies of the book before becoming too committed.

Why worry about media portrayals of interpersonal communication?

There are several serious difficulties with much of this media advice:

- it offers very simple 'slogans' which are supposed to apply to everyone regardless of cultural or social background
- it often ignores individual differences in behaviour
- it offers 'quick-fix' solutions to communication problems, again usually ignoring the social context

Unfortunately, these concerns are not new. While researching for this edition, I came across a paper by Judith Hall Koivumaki, in which she analysed five accounts of body language from the most popular best-selling books in the USA in the early 1970s.[12] She made some very powerful criticisms, including:

> findings are often over-simplified, hypotheses and truisms are stated as facts, and the reader is often in the dark as to whose research is being reported.
>
> These books encourage, quite literally, the exploitation of one person by another.

My reading of popular books over the last few years suggests that these criticisms are still very relevant. For example, consider the following five quotes. Are they all saying the same thing? Which quote do you think is the most accurate?

1. 'Over 90 per cent of what people communicate to each other is nonverbal.'[13]
2. '93% of communication relies on aspects other than the words we use.'[14]
3. 'According to recent research done by Kodak the visual impression someone makes accounts for 55 per cent of the information we take on board from that individual.'[15]
4. 'Research suggests that we obtain around 75 per cent of information about other people from their body language, 15 per cent from their tone of voice and only 10 per cent from the words they use.'[16]
5. 'of the messages received in a conversation, 7 per cent are verbal, 38 per cent are vocal (paralanguage) and 55 per cent are facial and non-verbal.'[17]

I shall return to these quotes in Chapter 9 after reviewing major studies and theories on the impact of our non-verbal communication. My conclusion is that *all* these quotes are potentially misleading!

So can you believe this book?

This book tries very hard to avoid the criticisms reported above. There are extensive references so you can check the research and my interpretations. And I have also tried to highlight controversial areas and problems with some of the studies. For example, some research on interpersonal communication has tended to ignore broader cultural and social factors.

I always invite my students to be critical and I extend this invitation to all my readers. If you feel that I have got something completely wrong then you are invited to contribute to the Web site which supports this text (and if you change my mind then you might earn a credit if there is a third edition!). After all I also draw my students' attention to the research which suggests that textbook accounts are prone to offer:

> a sanitized vision of history and life, where important societal conflicts are homogenized and made to seem less severe.[18]

How is this book organised?

The major sections

In Section A, I try to establish a coherent framework for understanding interpersonal communication. As well as offering a definition and a model of the process, I discuss the major skills involved and show how these different approaches to the subject are related. Section B provides a more detailed analysis of the major components of interpersonal communication.

Section C looks at three topical issues which highlight major practical, social and theoretical issues in interpersonal communication. In this section, I try to apply approaches and concepts introduced in Section B to issues which have relevance to everyday life. These are:

- the debate over male/female differences in communication
- whether one of the most popular training methods in interpersonal communication really works (assertiveness)

- whether we can 'use' popular models of interpersonal communication

This section also highlights the practical and theoretical difficulties of establishing what are the 'real facts' about human communication.

Section D concludes the book by discussing situations which involve other people but where there are processes over and above the ones outlined in Section B. For example, communication in groups is not the same as communicating with one other person – there are different influences at work. In the final chapter, I speculate about future research trends in interpersonal communication, and briefly review emerging research on computer-mediated communication – is this a new form of communication which will have a major impact on human experience?

Within chapters

Each chapter is subdivided into major sections which are listed at the beginning of each chapter. Each major section focuses on one important question or issue. At the end of the book, there is a list of notes for each chapter which includes:

- details of references cited in the text
- further comments for anyone wishing to explore the topic in more detail
- references and suggestions for further reading

What is the best way to read this book?

This may seem a nonsensical question. Surely you simply read any book from beginning to end. I disagree. That may be the way to read a novel on a train journey but it is not the way we read many books. This text will be read by different people for different purposes and so you may wish to choose a different approach. For example, if you are reading this simply from general interest in the topic, then I suggest that you:

- read Chapters 1 and 2 fairly quickly

- concentrate on the aspects that interest you in the remaining chapters
- ignore the footnotes unless anything strikes you as particularly interesting
- look at the Web site if you want further details on any particular topic

If you are reading this as a student on a course, then I suggest that you:

- read Section A first
- read subsequent chapters in the order in which they crop up in your course
- skim through a chapter when you first read it before going through it more slowly and checking the footnotes
- look at the Web site after you have worked through each chapter as this will give you further details and updates on each topic

Whatever your approach, I hope you find this book helpful and interesting, and that you find some ideas which you can use to make your own communication more satisfying and effective.

Language and sexism

In my own teaching, I warn students to avoid sexist language and expressions. So here I have tried to practise what I preach. In this book, 'he' is always male and 'she' is always female, except in a few of the direct quotes from other authors who have obviously not read Miller and Swift.[19]

Section A

Understanding interpersonal communication

Chapter 1

Defining what we mean by interpersonal communication

In this chapter, I shall:

- introduce the definition of interpersonal communication which is used throughout this book
- discuss propositions about interpersonal communication which can be developed from this definition and which have important practical and theoretical implications

How can we define interpersonal communication?

Most books which can be used as textbooks start with a chapter which tries to define the subject matter and approach. This is an obvious place to start if you are completely new to the subject. But what about a text on communication? Surely we all know what communication is? Isn't it major part of all our daily lives? One writer has gone so far as to say that: 'all social interaction is necessarily communicative and any social process presumes communication processes'.[1]

In other words, anything we do with other people must involve communication. If communication is so 'universal', then perhaps we can assume that everyone knows what it is, and move straight on to the next chapter! Unfortunately, things are not so straightforward. If you read a number of textbooks on communication, you will find a variety of definitions which emphasise different things. You will also find considerable practical differences in everyday life. Some people seem to regard the essence of communication as 'being able to speak and write proper English', whereas others would argue that 'good communicators are good listeners'. This debate also has political implications – it has been highlighted in recent discussions of the quality of the British educational system. One recent front-page headline in the British press proclaimed that 'standards of spoken English have plummeted in the last two decades'. A senior government minister expressed her concern about 'inarticulate school-leavers who rely on "communication by grunt"' and announced a new initiative to 'revive the use of the English language'.[2] This sort of polemic is based upon views of language and communication which I shall challenge in later chapters.

So, both practically and theoretically, it is important to clarify what I am talking about.

To return to the academic debate, I can easily produce a list of fifteen general definitions of communication which represent rather different ideas or emphases! A similar variety of definitions also exist for interpersonal communication. As well as verbal definitions, there are many models of interpersonal communication, typically expressed as diagrams involving numerous boxes and arrows.[3] In this book, I have attempted to synthesise as many of these ideas as possible to highlight the fundamental processes.

This concern for definition is not just for academic reasons. If you adopt (perhaps subconsciously) a particular definition of communication, then this will influence your behaviour. For example, Clampitt suggests that managers tend to believe in one of the following definitions of communication:[4]

- The arrow approach where communication is 'rather like shooting an arrow at a target' and is 'seen as a one-way activity based primarily on the skills of the sender'. This approach is often represented by the linear model diagram which I discuss later in this chapter. The fundamental belief is that 'Effective Expression = Effective Communication'.

- The circuit approach where communication is seen as a two-way approach and which stresses 'feedback over response, relationship over content, connotations over denotations, and understanding over compliance'. The fundamental belief is that 'Understanding = Effective Communication'.

He then suggests that both views have fundamental weaknesses – the arrow approach sees listeners as too passive. It assumes that the words we use are much less ambiguous than they actually are. Both these issues are discussed later in this book. His main criticisms of the circuit approach are that it assumes that understanding will lead to agreement, and that it can be misleading to see understanding as the only goal of communication. He suggests a third 'better' point of view:

- Communication as dance. This uses the analogy of a dance where partners have to coordinate their movements and arrive at a mutual understanding of where they are going. There are rules and skills but there are also flexibilities – dancers can inject their own style into the movements.

Managers who use this model will be much more sensitive to the different perspectives and interpretations which people place on their communication, and be much more aware of the problems of coding I discuss in Chapters 8 and 9.

In some recent research, we found evidence to support Clampitt's views.[5] A sample of managers from various sectors favoured either arrow or circuit definitions. None provided a definition which resembled the notion of dance. This bias towards arrow and circuit approaches was also reflected in the other part of the study – a review of a representative sample of best-selling management texts on communication. All favoured arrow and circuit approaches and made no real attempt to explore their limitations.

This book is broadly sympathetic to Clampitt's model of communication as dance. But I also need to draw distinctions between different types of situation. I can best introduce my approach by comparing events which obviously involve people communicating with one another in different contexts:

(a) two friends discussing their recent holidays over a cup of coffee

(b) an argument between a married couple concerning the behaviour of their teenage son
(c) a discussion between a lecturer and one of her students
(d) a telephone call to a local store to enquire about the availability of a particular product
(e) a letter from a daughter to her parents about her experiences of working abroad
(f) a trader touting his 'never to be repeated' bargains in a street market
(g) Martin Luther King addressing 100,000 demonstrators at the Washington Memorial in 1968
(h) the Queen's Christmas Day broadcast
(i) sitting in a cinema watching a film
(j) sitting at home watching the news on TV
(k) reading a daily newspaper

All these examples involve communication and they all involve people. But they are very different experiences because of the different processes involved. For example, they can be grouped in terms of major differences as follows.

The nature of the audience

Items (f) to (k) all involve large audiences ranging from the crowd in the market (f) to potentially the whole society ((h) or (k)). Thus, the receivers of the communication are not known as individuals to the sender. In some cases the sender is an individual but in others the sender is a group or organisation, or an individual acting on behalf of an organisation (e.g. the newsreader in (j)).

Relationship

Items (a) to (e), in contrast, all involve events where the participants are specific individuals who are known to one another. This knowledge of the other person is a very important aspect of the interaction.

Medium or channel of communication

Items (a) to (c) are purely face to face whereas items (d), (e) and (g) to (k) all use some medium of communication in between the senders and receivers. Item (f) may use some form of medium, e.g. a public address system, but this will depend on the size of audience and the strength of the trader's lungs!

Interpersonal?

Only examples (a), (b) and (c) in the above list are 'pure' examples of what this book defines as interpersonal communication, which has the following characteristics:

- communication from one individual to another
- communication which is face to face
- both the form and content of the communication reflect the personal characteristics of the individuals as well as their social roles and relationships

Table 1.1 summarises the different forms of communication which I have mentioned. It does not cover some forms of communication which I shall discuss later in the book, namely within and between groups.

Only the box containing (a), (b), (c) fully satisfies the definition of interpersonal communication used in this book. All the other boxes are situations which involve other factors. For example, speaking to a large audience and using devices like a PA system demands techniques of voice control and projection. You may also need to control your gestures in this situation and perhaps exaggerate some in order to ensure that they are visible.

What does this definition involve?

Any textbook definition will have number of practical and theoretical implications. The most important implications which can be

Table 1.1 Different forms of communication

	Individual to individual	*Individual to mass audience*	*Group to mass audience*
Face-to-face communication	(a), (b), (c)	(f), (g)	
Technologically-mediated communication	(d), (e)	(h)	(j), (k), (l)

developed from this definition of interpersonal communication are contained in the following seven propositions.

Face-to-face meetings

Interpersonal communication involves face-to-face meetings between two participants.

I have excluded any communication which I would call 'mediated', such as telephone conversation, where some artificial medium carries the conversation between the participants. This is because any medium has particular characteristics which can have implications for communication. In everyday life, we may not be aware of these characteristics or may never consider them. As a result misunderstandings can occur. For example, there is considerable research on the way people use the telephone which suggests that phone conversations have a very different character to face-to-face meetings. People tend to use the phone in very particular ways and will choose the phone over face-to-face meetings to express specific types of messages. There also seem to be different national norms in terms of how people pick up the phone.

So that we do not avoid these sorts of issues completely, Chapter 14 looks at the evidence on computer-mediated communication, such as email and computer chat lines, and examines the argument that this is a 'new form of communication' with different norms and values attached to it.

This proposition also excludes situations where one person is addressing an audience for some reason, e.g. giving a lecture, or an after-dinner speech. Again this calls for some special principles which are not covered in this book.

Roles

Interpersonal communication involves two people in varying roles and relationships to one another.

I shall discuss the concept of role in much more detail in Chapter 6. For the moment I am using the concept to cover both formal positions such as policeman, teacher, etc., and the more informal roles which we may take on in some situations, e.g. the person who always intervenes to try to alleviate conflict in a group of friends – the 'harmoniser'. This emphasis on roles and relationships may seem blindingly obvious but some writers do talk of interpersonal communication in a rather more specialised sense. For example, consider the following quote from John Stewart:[6]

> Interpersonal communication happens between PERSONS, not between roles or masks or stereotypes. Interpersonal communication can happen between you and me only when each of us recognizes and shares some of what makes us human beings AND is aware of some of what makes the other person too.

Stewart, in common with many American authors, is concerned that people *should* communicate with one another in a particular way. He advocates that we should communicate in order to develop personal relationships of the following sort:

- where there is a high degree of trust
- where each person is prepared to discuss openly their feelings and personal history (often referred to as self-disclosure, which I discuss in Chapter 3)
- where there is genuine and mutual liking or caring between the participants

Thus, Stewart also talks about 'non-interpersonal' communication where people simply communicate 'what they have to'. An example may make this clearer. Have you ever been in a situation where someone whom you do not know well but who is in a position of authority over you (such as a temporary teacher) has asked 'how are you?' You may have been feeling down but answered 'fine' or 'OK'. Without thinking about it, you recognised that the original question was simply a social gesture – it was not a genuine enquiry about your well-being. The person was asking because they felt obliged to do so rather than because they really cared about you. So you replied with a polite but dishonest reply – to use Stewart's definition, you communicated 'non-interpersonally'. What would have happened if you had blurted out all your woes and tribulations – would the other person have been able, or willing, to cope?

Another example would be the 'have a nice day' farewell which you seem to encounter in every American restaurant and in every British outlet of the major American chains. How do you respond to this? Is it a nice gesture? Or a meaningless ritual? Or depressing further evidence that society is moving towards even more predictability and rationalisation of customer service?[7]

John Stewart's book is very clear on how people should communicate interpersonally. There are other American texts which also focus upon two-person interactions (often called 'dyads') but which have a less direct way of promoting a particular style of communication. In these texts, the message that we develop positive relationships with others may simultaneously 'neglect to examine the nature of the society to which individuals are encouraged to belong'[8]

This book does try to raise the ethical questions of how we should (or should not) communicate to others – but I leave the resolution for you to discuss and decide for yourself. My overall approach is to use a broader, more descriptive and more 'neutral' definition of interpersonal communication. But it is important to emphasise that any discussion of interpersonal communication must consider moral and ethical issues at some point.

Two way

Interpersonal communication is ALWAYS two way.

The so-called linear model of communication is one of the most popular ways of representing communication. This model suggests that our communication is linear and one way. In other words, it consists of messages which flow from sender to receiver along particular channels, although there may be some interference (noise) along the way. This model is fundamental to Clampitt's arrow approach discussed earlier and is usually expressed in a diagram as in Figure 1.1.[9]

Unfortunately this model neglects one of the fundamental points in this book: in interpersonal situations there is *always* a two-way flow of communication. For example, imagine a conversation where A is telling B about the good time he had on holiday. A does most if not all of the talking. Does that make him *the* sender? He is also able to observe B's reactions to what he is saying – receiving information from the way B is acting as an audience. In this sense A is also both receiver and sender. He may grunt, nod, look attentive – all *may* be acts of communication which are interpreted by the other person. It is no accident that one of the social skills which psychologists have recently focused attention on is listening, one aspect of which is giving feedback to the other person. You can train people to become better listeners and this is a very important social skill (see Chapter 3).

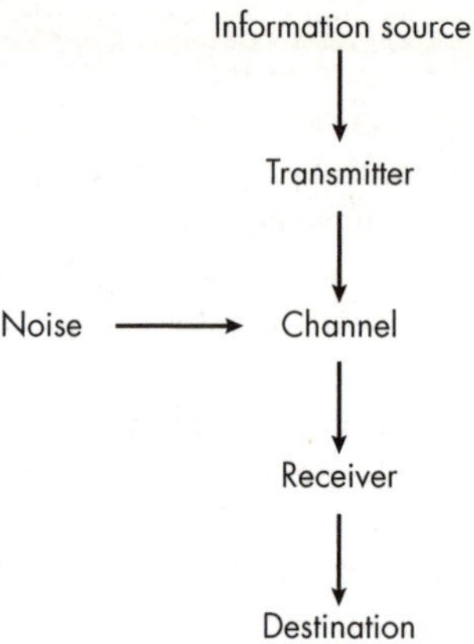

Figure 1.1 Linear model of communication

Meaning

Interpersonal communication does not simply involve the exchange of messages. It essentially involves the creation and exchange of meaning

One important implication of the linear model of communication follows from its concern with 'the message'. This implies that we can arrive at an accurate and unambiguous statement of whatever was communicated. And it also suggests that we shall be able to verify that statement by checking with the participants as well as any observers present. In fact, this is extremely difficult if not impossible to achieve. Whereas we might not agree that 'all human behaviour is ambiguous',[10] just about anything anyone says could be interpreted in a number of ways. Luckily this does not happen all of the time or we would live in a chaotic world. For example, how would you interpret the following question from neighbour A: 'Did you have a good time last night?' This could be a casual, friendly gesture. But what could it mean?

- Is your neighbour behaving genuinely? Perhaps he is being cynical and deliberately trying to 'soften you up' so that he can come and borrow something from you?
- On the other hand, is it a subtle accusation of rowdy behaviour? Is it a warning to be less intrusive next time you have a party?

- Is it a deliberate play on the fact that A was not invited, designed to make you feel uncomfortable?
- Is it a more dejected expression of A's loneliness?

All of these are possible interpretations of A's message. Some of them may seem very unlikely but this depends on the meaning which you and A attach to your encounter. And this will depend on a number of factors discussed later in this book, such as the state of the relationship between you and A, or any of your perceptual biases which might influence your reactions to A. So, this analysis suggests that we must look very carefully at the meaning which people attach to particular events before we can really understand the communication which is taking place. On the other hand, we can learn a great deal about communication without delving very deeply into personal beliefs and interpretations. For example, there have been a number of studies recently which have examined how teachers in schools communicate to their pupils, often using some method of classifying the messages that teachers send, e.g. do they ask questions, encourage pupils, etc.? Thus the messages are classified in terms of their 'obvious' meaning. There is no attempt to study in detail the possible interpretations that pupils place on their teacher's behaviour. Nonetheless useful and interesting results emerge. One fairly typical finding, which comes rather as a shock to teachers, is that they do not always do what they think they do. For example, teachers who claim to be equally fair to boys and girls may still be directing their attention towards the boys when they expect boys will do better in that subject.[11]

The issue I have just raised is one aspect of a very deep-rooted argument within social science, i.e. whether people are mainly passive responders to external stimuli or whether they adopt a more active approach to interpret and make sense of the world. I favour the latter position which suggests that, when we try to understand communication fully, we must be aware of the meaning which people attach to events and surroundings. Thus, in order fully to understand communication, we need to look at how individuals make sense of the situation they are in.

But does this mean that we cannot generalise from situation to situation? If we accept that everyone is unique, does this mean that everyone will interpret events differently? And does this then mean that all communication can only be understood with reference to the specific individuals involved? Is all communication totally personal? I cannot go along with this line of argument. There must be some shared meaning for there to be any communication at all! If we all lived in completely unique and idiosyncratic 'perceptual worlds' then we could not talk to one another. There would be no basis for any language system to work. It may be difficult for you to understand how I interpret particular events (and vice versa) but I *can* explain my interpretation to you, given sufficient time and patience.

Intention

Interpersonal communication is partly or wholly intentional:

> All would agree, for example, that measly face can be INFORMATIVE to qualified onlooker. But is it useful to speak of the sufferer himself (who may be unaware of it) as COMMUNICATING this information? Is there no distinction to be made between the passive manifestation of a symptom and the deliberate (even if instinctive) production of words or non-verbal behaviour (including perhaps pointing to the spots) CALCULATED to inform the observer?[12]

It is not very useful to think of someone 'communicating' that they have measles because their face is lumpy or spotty, and this book concentrates on situations where participants do have purposes or intentions which they wish to communicate. On the other hand it is often very difficult in practice to draw a precise distinction between informative and communicative behaviour, and this is a major theme of Chapter 7.

Process

Interpersonal communication is an ongoing process rather than an event or series of events.

When you think of an event, you usually think of something very definite which happens, and which has a definite start and a definite finish. It can be misleading to think of interpersonal communication in this way. There are a number of more academic arguments which emphasise the importance of understanding interpersonal communication as a continuous unfolding process but for the moment I shall take a practical example – the selection interview. Imagine you are a candidate, sitting in the waiting room. At what point do you start to communicate with your interviewers: when you arrive in the reception area; when you answer the first question; when you walk in the interview room; when you stand up to greet the member of the selection panel who has come out to collect you? Your behaviour at all these points could have an important bearing on what happens because of the ongoing process of communication. There is also the complication that you have already communicated to the interviewers through your application form: what stereotypes and preconceptions are already there in their minds? There may also be more subtle social influences – at least one boss I have known took very serious notice of how his assistant showed prospective job-hunters into the room. The way the candidate was introduced always included very subtle opinions on his or her suitability.

Time

Interpersonal communication is cumulative over time:

> You cannot erase a remembered pain.[13]

Whatever person A says to you today will be interpreted on the basis of what they have said to you in the past and also what you expect them to say. If you are trying to understand communication between people who have communicated before, then you need to take into account the history of their relationship as this might well affect how they interpret each other's remarks at the moment.

Conclusion

This chapter should have clarified what this book is about. Hopefully it should also have convinced you that interpersonal communication is not as simple or straightforward as many people seem to believe. Although this may have seemed a fairly theoretical chapter, the issues raised have important practical implications. For example, we often act as if communication was linear – as if there was an unambiguous definition of the message and that feedback was unimportant. We do so at our peril, as will be demonstrated in the following chapters.

Chapter 2

The process of interpersonal communication

In this chapter I shall:

- discuss how we can best understand interpersonal communication
- outline a model of interpersonal communication, using examples to illustrate the components

How can we understand interpersonal communication?

Social scientists interested in interpersonal communication have usually adopted one of the following approaches:

- developing a model of interpersonal communication – trying to identify the components of the process

- identifying the behaviours which are associated with effective interpersonal communication – defining the skills of interpersonal communication

Some authors seem to treat these approaches as separate and discrete, which I think is misleading. In practice these approaches are inevitably linked. For example, you cannot really identify skills without a good understanding of the process, and I shall say more on this later. In this chapter I shall concentrate on the first of these approaches. I shall briefly discuss what this involves and then explain my model of interpersonal communication.

In the next chapter, I shall discuss what it means to explain interpersonal communication as skilled behaviour and give a few examples to illustrate the value of such an approach. I shall also explain how the two approaches depend upon one another. To understand interpersonal communication fully, you need to integrate both approaches.

What does understanding interpersonal communication involve?

If you say you understand something then you should be able to answer specific questions about it. For example, suppose you say that you understand what a minidisc is – could you answer the following questions about it?

- How were minidiscs first developed?
- How is a minidisc made?
- How do minidisc recorders and players work?
- What are the main differences between a minidisc and other digital music media like CDs?
- How, when and where are minidiscs used?

You may be able to answer some of these questions. So there are *degrees* of understanding depending on how much you know. But there are also *different types* of understanding depending on your purposes. For example, you may be able to operate a minidisc recorder without being able to answer any of the questions above – so you may feel you understand minidiscs because you can use them correctly. This is rather different from understanding their electronics and such intricacies as digital–analog conversion, compression algorithms and the joys of error correction. You may not want to explore these details because you really only want to listen to or record the music!

Applying this type of analysis to communication brings out similar points. Your understanding of interpersonal communication will depend on how much you know, based on what you have observed and the breadth of your experience. Your understanding will also depend upon your purposes and whether you want to enquire further. For example, later in the book there are some examples of sales techniques. Sales representatives may use interpersonal techniques very expertly without fully understanding (or even partly understanding) how they really work. An example I shall use in Chapter 10 is the car salesman who tried to use transactional analysis on me. This also illustrates the other side of the coin – you may be able to defeat any unwelcome attention from sales representatives if you understand their methods, ploys and tactics.

The aim of this book is to provide understanding of how interpersonal communication 'works' by exploring the 'mechanics' of the process, looking at its various components and how they relate to one another. One way of doing this is by asking questions, and you may have come across one classic definition of communication which uses a question approach:[1]

> Who says what
> In which channel
> To whom
> With what effect

This definition can be criticised – it does not take account of the different meanings which participants can perceive in the same situation. It also neglects the more subtle processes of communication – communication is not just talk! Finally it has limitations in that it does not take account of the social context in which the communication takes place.

These limitations could perhaps be overcome by adding additional questions. But then you could end up with a rather unwieldy list:

> When and where does communication occur?
> Who is involved?
> How do the people communicate?

How does the communication develop over time?
What roles are people adopting?
How do they relate to one another?
What is the physical setting?
What do people say and do?
What are they trying to achieve?
How do people interpret each other's actions?

You can probably refine and add to this list. But a list of questions does not give a very clear idea of how the different factors are related to one another. So rather than pursue this approach further I shall develop a model of interpersonal communication which attempts to specify what is involved and how the components relate to one another.

What is a model?

A model is quite simply a scaled-down representation of some thing or event. You can identify the major characteristics of a good model by thinking about physical models. For example, if I built a model of a car out of old toilet roll tubes and then showed it to you, how would you judge it? Apart from wondering why this presumably sane person is wasting his time this way, you could ask a number of questions to test the quality of the model:

- Does it look like a car?
- Does it have all the important bits on it? For example, are there four wheels, engine, exhaust, etc.?
- Does it work in any way? For example, does the engine make the wheels go round? What happens if you turn the steering wheel?
- Could we market it?

The better the model, the more accurate and detailed it will be. But with any physical model, such as a building, you usually have to reach some sort of compromise – you have to sacrifice some detail in order to make the model easy to build in the time available or easy to operate.

These same considerations apply when you try to develop a theoretical model:

- the model should contain the major components
- it should show how these relate to one another
- it should be reasonably detailed

So I am aiming to provide a model for interpersonal communication which can satisfy these criteria.[2] Remember that this is an attempt to *describe* the main factors which influence the way we communicate. It is *not* saying that communication should happen this way, or that it always does happen like this. A model (like any good theory) is there to be used – to see how far it helps us to understand what is going on, and also to highlight what we may not understand.

A model of interpersonal communication

My basic model of interpersonal communication is summarised in Figure 2.1. The major boxes represent major components of the process.

Once you have read all this book and perhaps done further research, you may like to return to this model and criticise it: does it live up to the following characteristics?

- Does it highlight the most important characteristics of interpersonal communication?
- Is it sufficiently detailed to be a useful basis for analysing everyday situations?
- Does it show how the different processes relate to one another?

As this text is designed to be introductory, you should be able to pick some holes in the model once you have become more familiar with some of the relevant theories and research.

How does this model help?

Using the model to identify the components of the communication process should help us to understand what is going on in practical situations. So this section applies the components of the model to specific examples as follows.

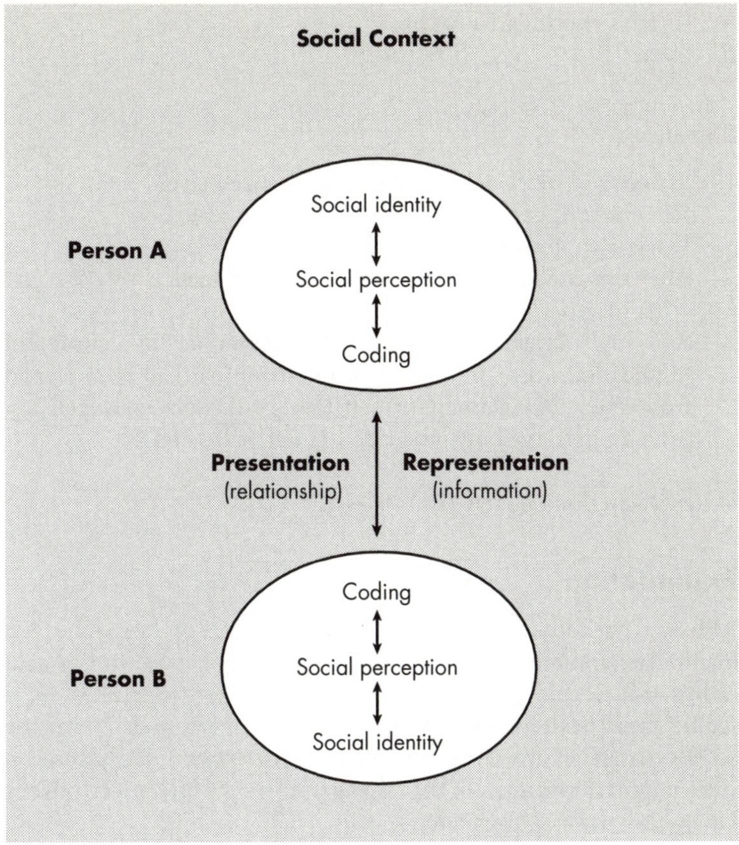

Figure 2.1 Hartley's model of interpersonal communication

The case of Dr Poussaint

Consider the following real conversation between two people (A and B). If you want to test your understanding of communication you can think of your answers to the questions below before you read my explanation.

The conversation

A: 'What's your name, boy?'
B: 'Dr Poussaint. I'm a physician.'

A: 'What's your first name, boy?'
B: 'Alvin.'

Questions

1 Where and when did the conversation take place?
2 What sort of person was A?
3 What sort of person was B?
4 After this conversation, B described his feelings:

> As my heart palpitated, I muttered in profound humiliation....For the moment, my manhood had been ripped from me....No amount of self-love could have salvaged my pride or preserved my integrity....(I felt) self-hate.

Why do you think he felt like this?

Explanation

This conversation is a very vivid example of how someone can manipulate communication in order to serve their own, in this case rather sadistic and racist, ends. The conversation took place on a public street in the USA in 1967. The 1960s was a period of major social change in the USA and racial tensions and readjustments were important features of that change. A was a white police officer, Dr Pouissant was a black doctor.

In order to understand the impact of this conversation you need to understand the following several factors which are identified in the model.

Social context

You need to understand the social context – how the time and the place influenced the actions and reactions. Dr Pouissant felt he had to answer the questions because of his social obligations and the power relations in a public place. A police officer is usually 'allowed' to ask personal questions in public without necessarily explaining why.

Social identities/perception

You also need to know how the two participants saw themselves (their social identity) and each other (social perception). Dr Pouissant saw himself as a respectable citizen and a professional person who normally received some degree of respect. He felt humiliated when this sense of identity was ignored. He saw the police officer as occupying a role of authority. As a result he had no choice but to act according to his obligations as a respectable law-abiding citizen. He would also be very aware as a black professional man of the general social climate of the time.

Codes

The police officer had quite different intentions and you can deduce these from his use of codes. His style of speech was no accident – he must have been aware of these codes.

I shall provide a more detailed definition of codes later on. For the moment, I shall talk about a code as a particular way of expressing a message which has a special meaning to a certain audience. I shall also leave aside the notions of presentation and representation which I shall explain later in this chapter.

As an example of the use of a special code, consider how the police officer first addressed Dr Pouissant. He used the term 'boy' in a very deliberate way to make Dr Pouissant feel inferior. Obviously, he was not using the word in its literal meaning as he could see perfectly well that the doctor was a grown man. He probably also used visual codes to reinforce the cruel and dismissive message, e.g. not looking directly at Dr Pouissant while he was talking. You can see how 'successful' he was in his aims when you read the interpretation which Dr Pouissant put upon his comments.

This conversation has been very thoroughly analysed by Susan Ervin-Tripp.[3] She concluded that the police officer deliberately used racial insults no less than three times in the course of the conversation, simply by breaking the rules of address which people normally obey in these situations.

A rule of address is a social rule which governs how you address the other person. For example, do you call the other person sir, or by their first name, or by their last name? These rules can be quite different in different societies. Social rules are discussed in more detail in Chapter 5 but as an example you can think of how you respond to different people in different situations in terms of the names you call them. And what names do they call you? But let us return to Dr Pouissant and the three insults.

First of all the police officer used the term 'boy'. He would never have used this expression if the doctor had been white. Secondly he ignored the perfectly reasonable answer he received from Dr Pouissant and asked for his first name without any justification. Thirdly he repeated the term 'boy'. He rubbed salt into the wounds quite viciously. So while he showed a degree of 'skill' in the use of communication to suit his purposes, the police officer blatantly demonstrated serious deficiencies as a human being.

The parking meter conversation

For another example to illustrate the model, try this short extract from a real conversation:[4]

A: 'Dana succeeded in putting a penny in a parking meter today without being picked up.'
B: 'Did you take him to the record store?'

This conversation is very difficult to decipher unless you happen to know a number of things over and above the actual words spoken, as follows.

Social context

This conversation took place between two parents in their home just after the husband (A) had brought their son Dana home from nursery school.

Social identities

The couple see themselves as responsible parents who are both interested in the welfare and development of their son.

Social perception

The couple see each other as caring and responsible parents. They regularly share information about the activities and progress of their son. Dana is now big enough to put a coin in a parking meter without help.

Codes

The term 'picking up' is ambiguous unless you know that Dana is young and small. The husband is carrying a record and this prompts the question from his wife.

One important implication of this model is that the various components must be compatible for the communication to be effective. When I say 'effective', I mean that the two parties interpret the interaction similarly, *not* that their opinions on whatever is being discussed necessarily agree with each other. Where the two parties do not interpret the interaction similarly, then misunderstanding or conflict is inevitable.

The final components

This leads me to the final two components of the model: representation (information) and presentation (relationship). I have borrowed this distinction from Kurt Danziger.[5] He makes the important point that whenever we communicate we always do the following two things simultaneously:

1 *Representation* We represent some information – in other words, we make some statement about the world around us. When I refer to this concept in this book, I have added '(information)' as the term 'representation' is often used in different ways in communication studies.
2 *Presentation* We present the information in a particular way, which will then define our relationship with the other person in a particular way. When I refer to this concept in this book, I have added '(relationship)' to show that I am referring back to Danziger's concept.

To take a practical example: it is the morning of 23 June. Suppose we are standing under a shelter at a bus stop and it is raining outside. We do not know each other but we have seen each other in the bus queue before. How would you react if I said one of the following:

(a) 'Nasty rain today.'

(b) 'The weather forecast says there will be two inches of rain today.'
(c) 'Summer has finally arrived then.'
(d) 'Fair pissing down, ain't it?'

The representation (information) in all these four statements – the facts about what is happening – is not all that different. But the presentation (relationship) is very different. Which presentation would you be most likely to respond to? Are they invitations to conversation? To decide on this you also need more details: who are we in terms of age, gender, class, etc., and how was the phrase spoken? (What was the non-verbal message?)

An example which Danziger uses is the salesman trying to clinch a sale. Consider the following interchange between him and Mrs Jones:[6]

> 'You like the special action brush then?'
> 'Oh yes.'
> 'And you understand how all these other features (points) will help you?'
> 'Sure.'
> 'You said you appreciated the ease of operation particularly?'
> 'That' s right.'
> 'So you're convinced that a Hoover will make your work easier?'
> 'Hm hm.'
> 'And you do admit that buying later won't help you now, don't you?'
> 'I guess so.'
> 'In fact you owe it to your family to get one now, isn't that right?'
> 'Yeah.'
> 'So you have decided to take this model then?'
> 'O.K.'

Danziger analyses not just what the salesman says (representation–information) but also how he says it (presentation–relationship). The salesman has a sequence of points which he makes. Each point is skilfully phrased so that when she answers Mrs Jones is 'compelled' to present herself in a particular way. The salesman is laying a trap for Mrs Jones. Firstly, he recognises that Mrs Jones will wish to be seen as caring, considerate and reasonable. He starts by pointing out that Mrs Jones has seen aspects of the product she likes and progressively builds these up to become more significant. Mrs Jones is carried along by the logic, and the speed and loaded phrasing of the questions make it difficult for her to object 'reasonably'. Then the salesman brings in her 'obligations' to her family to clinch the deal. Having gradually committed herself to the benefits of the product and not wishing to appear inconsistent, she is unable to escape this final invitation.

We can also develop this analysis using the other components of my model. The salesman takes great care to present himself as competent, trustworthy and friendly so that Mrs Jones does not become suspicious (social perception). The salesman makes very skilful use of language and non-verbal behaviour (codes) to put pressure on Mrs Jones to act in line with her feelings about herself as a responsible and caring housewife (social identity).

This one example could be dismissed as simply an illustration of the 'gullible housewife' stereotype. But it is far more fundamental than this. It illustrates a crucial question raised by Danziger which we can apply to *every* interpersonal encounter: 'Whose definition of the interpersonal relationship is to prevail?'[7] In this example, the salesman is using all the techniques at his disposal to reinforce *his* definition of the relationship which puts Mrs Smith very firmly in the compliant customer role. And this notion of how we use communication to define the relationship is important in *all* social situations.

Danziger illustrates this importance with the extreme example of torture and interrogation:

> the skillful interrogator will attempt to maneuver the prisoner into a position where the desired confession is a necessary part of the self the prisoner is trying to present.[8]

Accounts from prisoners (often political prisoners) who were able to resist prolonged interrogation support Danziger's analysis. They adopted strategies to maintain some degree of self-esteem and psychological control in the situation. These strategies varied from using particular forms of language to seemingly trivial gestures like always putting on a suit before meeting the interrogator.

In everyday situations, we do similar things in much less dramatic ways. We try to present ourselves in the way we wish to define the situation. And we try to manoeuvre the other person into the role we wish them to play.

There is another reason why the vacuum cleaner example is important – men are *equally* susceptible to these sales techniques! I can testify to this from bitter personal experience at the hands of double-glazing and vacuum cleaner salespeople! And the strategies can be very powerful. Even if you know what sales representatives are trying to do, you can still be caught up in the emotions that they are trying to tap.

If you want to resist these strategies, knowing what is going on is the first step to handling the pressure. Then you need to redefine the situation. You must make it quite clear that you are *not* a customer! Mrs Jones could have dealt with the salesman rather differently if she had recognised how she was being manipulated and if she had been prepared to turn the tables on the salesman. She did *not* have to accept the social identity which the salesman was relying upon. Danziger offers another example to illustrate this process. Suppose Mrs Jones had been confronted by a salesman for a new line in children's food and decided to adopt a different style of presentation. Note how the salesman starts with a question which he thinks no one can refuse to answer the way he wants. Then see how Mrs Jones immediately goes on the attack:[9]

> 'You are interested in better nutrition and health for your family if it's possible to get it aren't you, Mrs. Jones?'
> 'No.'
> 'No?'
> 'They're too healthy now. They're running me ragged. I'm going to start feeding them less. They've had too many vitamins, that's the trouble. They're going to burn themselves out.'
> 'But surely you want them to be properly fed?'
> 'That's been the problem – too much food. I'm cutting them right off milk next week, soon's I use up the box of crystals. Maybe that'll help quieten my husband down nights.'

The salesman's opening remark is based on the quite reasonable assumption that no respectable mother will deny that she is interested in her family's health. Once he has established this very small area of common ground and commitment then he can develop it further. If Mrs Jones refuses to present herself in this way then the salesman's pitch is completely undermined.

Conclusion

That completes my general description of the model. I have suggested that there are a number of components which are present in any and every example of interpersonal communication. These components are of course linked as illustrated in the examples:

- features of the social situation influence our social identities
- how we see ourselves influences how we see others – social perception
- these mental or cognitive processes influence how we act – how we encode and decode our communication

Life is further complicated by the fact that all these components can be subdivided into further processes. For example, your social identity is not a single static entity – it can change and develop and is subject to various influences.

Section B will take each of the four main elements of the model and explore them in more detail.

Chapter 3

The skills of interpersonal communication

In this chapter, I shall:

- explain why it is useful to analyse interpersonal communication as skilled behaviour
- explain the main characteristics of the social skills model, and suggest important practical implications
- describe and analyse behaviours which are used in the skills of interpersonal communication
- show how these behaviours and skills interrelate, using practical examples
- discuss possible criticisms and limitations of this approach
- relate this skills approach to the model described in Chapter 2

Why should we think of communication as skilled behaviour?

We normally use the term 'skill' to refer to physical behaviours (what psychologists call motor skills). We can agree for example that specific sports personalities display certain skills. Greg Rusedski's service in tennis is a pretty formidable piece of behaviour, especially if you are at the receiving end. By using slow-motion film or video we can observe his coordination and rhythm, not to mention the power which many other players cannot equal. We can also observe how Greg varies the shot in order to keep his opponents guessing. In a similar way we can observe a particular social act and try to work out what the participants are doing. And we can observe that some people seem to be far better at handling certain social situations than others.

Think of someone whom you like talking to. What do they do to make the conversation enjoyable? They probably make you feel that they really are listening and interested in what you are saying. They do this by giving you encouragement, perhaps smiling, nodding, etc. Contrast this picture with someone whom you dislike talking to. What do they do to make it unpleasant? Perhaps they seem to ignore you (the boss who shuffles his papers while insisting that he is listening), or perhaps they try to dominate the proceedings.

If you carry on with this sort of analysis you will find that certain behaviours are performed regularly by individuals who are effective or successful in handling social situations and that individuals who are ineffective perform rather differently. And this is the essence of social skills. To put it another way, Michael Argyle makes the analogy between a motor or physical skill like playing tennis and a social skill like having a conversation with someone:[1]

> In each case the performer seeks certain goals (e.g. make others talk a lot), makes skilled moves (e.g. asks closed questions), perceives the effect of this (e.g. short replies) and takes corrective action (e.g. asks more open-ended questions).

Argyle is one of the major British exponents of this social skills model.[2] Interest in this perspective has grown dramatically in the last thirty years in both the UK and USA. The rest of this chapter analyses the social skills model and reviews some of the research on the different behaviours involved.

What is the social skills model?

The model developed by Argyle in the 1970s is probably the most famous summary of the social skills approach – as in Figure 3.1.[3] The major characteristics of this model are still widely accepted. Recent researchers have suggested a few modifications, which I will describe later in this chapter.

This model draws upon the analogy between performance in physical activities and performance in social situations, so you can apply this model very easily to any physical or motor skill. Take the example of riding a bike.

Goal

You can ride a bike for various reasons, ranging from the simple idea of travelling from A to B through to practising elaborate BMX stunts to impress your friends. Having decided your general goal, you will also have more specific objectives, or sub-goals. Whatever the context, one obvious sub-goal is to stay on the bike and avoid falling off. This is the objective you are very conscious of when you are first learning the skill. In order to achieve this you need the following components.

Perception

You need to decide where and how you are going to steer the bike, perceive certain cues from the muscles in your body and also

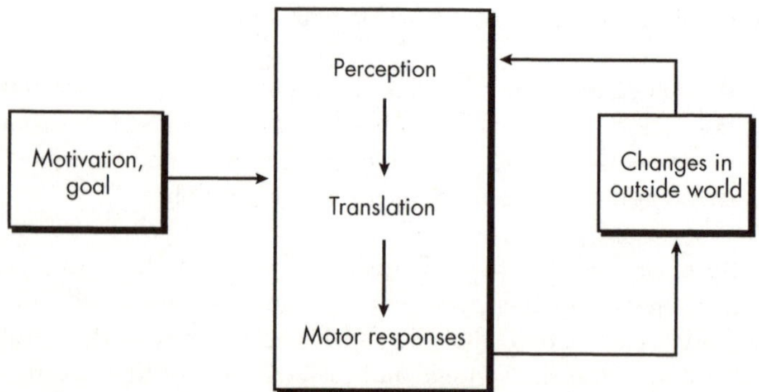

Figure 3.1 Argyle's social skills model

concentrate on the road ahead to avoid obstacles and bumps. One difficulty when you are first learning any skill is the feeling of being overwhelmed by the number of different things you have to pay attention to.

Translation

In order to perform effectively you have to 'translate' your idea of what you want to do into appropriate action. You have to choose the correct action to meet the circumstances. Suppose the road surface changes; does this mean you have to pedal more quickly or more slowly to stay in control of the bike?

Motor responses

Even if you have the correct idea of what you need to do, can your body manage the required muscle movements? Can you do it in time? Have you the strength and power to pedal up that hill which is approaching?

Feedback

If you start to overbalance, do you notice the problem in time to do anything about it? The correct movement (motor response) will bring you back into balance but you also need to recognise the effect of what you have done (the feedback loop). If you overcorrect your balance then you will fall over the other way.

As we learn a motor skill, our actions become more fluent and better timed and more of the action becomes subconscious – we no longer have to concentrate so hard on keeping our balance – our body seems to make automatic adjustments.

How can we apply the social skills model to interpersonal communication?

First of all we can ask whether the same stages apply to our social behaviour.

Goals

We have social goals which may be subconscious – I do not wish to cause offence to any of the people I meet at work every day – but which we can make explicit and think about. Any one of these general goals can also be broken down into subsidiary objectives or sub-goals. For example, suppose I wish to be seen as an interesting lecturer. I can set myself various sub-goals which I need to achieve, including the following:

- assemble material on relevant topics
- use examples and illustrations which are relevant to the audience (which means I must think about who they are and what they are interested in)
- give clear introductions to lectures
- time and pace the material to keep the audience's attention
- maintain good eye contact with the audience (to show them that I am interested in their reactions)
- present information at the right level to match the audience's experience

I could fail on any or all of the above and have to deal with the sleep-inducing consequences.

To take a more personal example, suppose you wish to make friends with someone you have just been introduced to. What would you need to do to achieve this goal? You may like to think about this for a moment and jot down what you think would be the sub-goals you would need to achieve. Then think about how you feel about dissecting your behaviour like this (this self-awareness is an issue we will return to later). Most of the popular guides to 'improving your communication' place special emphasis on this analysis of goals:

> Identifying what you want as the outcome of any interaction is the most important step in the process of learning how to better manage your communication.[4]

Perception

Suppose you have just been introduced to someone at a party. What do you notice about them? Do they appear happy, relaxed, anxious, nervous, bored or what? If you misjudge their mood you may start the conversation in a way which irritates or antagonises them. Are you looking at their facial expression or gestures or posture? And are you aware of the tone of your voice and your own mannerisms? Are you really giving them a warm welcome?

Suppose that you are a young male at a party. You see an attractive young female on the other side of the room. You make eye contact for just under two seconds. She tilts her head slightly to one side, looks down and seems to smile. What do these gestures mean?

Translation

Suppose you notice that someone is feeling upset but is not saying anything about it – what do you decide to do? Do you decide to ignore it and pretend all is well or do you think you should encourage them to talk about the problem? If you decide to ask them about it, do you intend to do it directly or adopt a more subtle approach?

Behaviour

You have decided to ask someone what is bothering them – what exactly do you do? What do you say? Do you try to incorporate some gesture which indicates concern? What do you do – place a hand on their shoulder?

Feedback

What reaction do you get from the other person? Do they seem to interpret your actions in the way you have intended? What if you did place a hand on their shoulder – was this gesture received in the way you intended? Do they respond to your interest as a sincere request or do they react as if you are being too 'nosy'. If they say 'I don't want to talk about it', do you take them at their word? Or do you interpret their reluctance as an invitation to probe further? Do you try again? How you handle this situation depends on how well you have interpreted their reactions.

How has Argyle's model been developed?

As I said earlier, many researchers have endorsed the basic ideas.

One of the leading researchers on this side of the Atlantic, Owen Hargie, has suggested some detailed modifications to cover both people in the interaction, based on the following observations:[5]

- when two people are interacting, both have goals which may differ
- the social context is an important influence
- we gain feedback from our own actions as well as the other person's reactions
- we are influenced by our emotions as well as by our thoughts, and so the term 'mediating factors' is used instead of 'translation'

You may like to compare the diagram of Hargie's model (Figure 3.2) with my model to see if it offers any advantages.

What are the implications of this approach?

If we apply this model to our everyday interactions then we can look at some of its important implications and limitations. Firstly, let us look at some important implications.

Learning and experience

In the same way that we learn motor skills we have to learn how to behave in social situations. And we may be able to learn from experience how to cope with situations which we find difficult. Typical examples of situations which many people find difficult are:

- situations which demand assertive behaviour, such as complaining to a neighbour about noise or taking faulty goods back to a shop
- situations of great intimacy such as sexual encounters
- situations involving some kind of public performance such as giving a speech

Consider a situation which you once found difficult but now find easier to cope with – what was it like on the first occasion? You were probably very self-conscious and very sensitive to what other people were doing. To use the model's terminology, you were probably concentrating very hard on your goals and trying to appear competent. You were looking hard for feedback to make sure you were behaving appropriately. With experience you become more fluent and you are no longer so self-conscious.

Analysing problems and difficulties

You can explain people's difficulties in social behaviour by using the skills model. It has been used extensively with clinical patients who can have extreme difficulty with everyday situations which most of us take for granted. On an everyday level, consider the example of 'George', a person who sometimes tries to be the life and soul of the party and fails dismally. What goes wrong? There are a number of possibilities suggested by the model, as follows.

Goals

Perhaps he does not have a clear idea of what he's trying to do and so behaves inconsistently or erratically?

Perception

Perhaps George is not very good at recognising what is going on round him. So he misinterprets the mood of the party and does the wrong thing at the wrong time – perhaps he tells sexist jokes to a group who find such humour offensive.

Translation into behaviour

Perhaps George can understand what to do but cannot put it into practice. He knows the jokes but his sense of timing is so poor that he ruins the punch lines.

Feedback

Perhaps George does not clearly recognise how the other party guests react to him. If he gets a good response from the first joke he probably launches into a long routine and ignores the increasing signs of boredom from his audience. Like the compulsive gambler, he does not recognise when to stop.

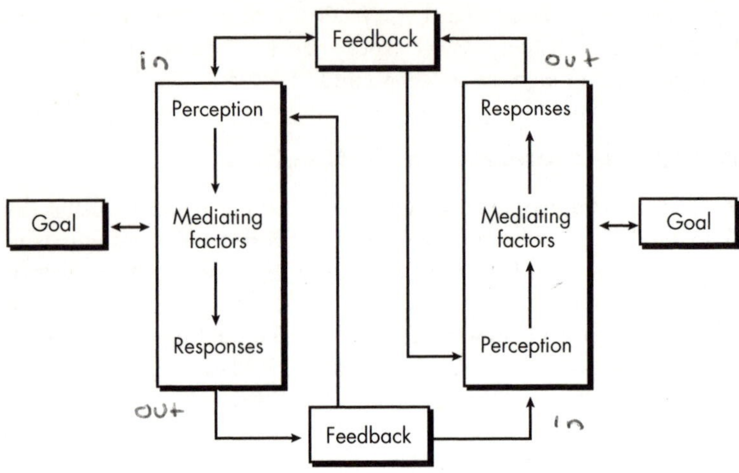

Figure 3.2 Hargie's revised model of social skills

Source: From Hargie, O., Saunders, C. and Dickson, D. (1994) *Social Skills in Interpersonal Communication*, 3rd edn, London: Routledge, page 19

Careful observation of George's behaviour along with discussion of his aims and feelings could highlight which of these problems is the actual one.

You can teach or train social skills

There is now considerable evidence that you can successfully train people to improve their social skills. The success of the training depends upon how well defined the skills are and the quality of the training. I have made this sound very simple and straightforward. In fact the issue of training in social and communication skills is complex for a number of reasons:

- Social skills are not just like motor skills (I shall discuss this in more detail below).
- Social skills can be quite difficult to specify.
  It can be difficult to specify exactly the behaviours which are the necessary components of a particular social skill. This is not altogether surprising as people may have different styles of behaviour which can be equally successful. Leading British

trainers who work on interpersonal skills always insist upon detailed research into the situations where training is required.[6] They observe people at work in these situations, record their behaviour, and then compare the behaviour of participants who are seen as 'effective' and 'ineffective' in that situation. From this they build up a profile of the behaviours which effective participants use. They then train newcomers in these behaviours.

- There are different training methods available.
  For example, you can distinguish methods based upon thinking (using lectures and discussions), feeling (focusing upon the participants' feelings and emotional reactions), and doing (using case studies and role plays). You can also find methods which try to integrate these different approaches.[7]
- It is difficult to measure the outcomes of training.
  It is difficult to measure changes in people's behaviour.[8] Even if you find that someone's behaviour has changed it may not be the direct result of the training – perhaps other people are treating them differently. There is also the suggestion that the success of training may depend as much on the personal qualities of the trainer as on the training method. This may not be too surprising – making significant changes to your behaviour can be an emotional and anxious experience. A lot will depend upon the level of trust between you and the trainer.

Despite these difficulties there is now significant support for the effectiveness of training based on social skills principles.[9]

Motor skills are not exactly the same as social skills

Although the social skills model can be applied in useful ways, it is also important not to lose sight of the fact that social skills are unlike motor skills in many important ways, as follows.[10]

Other people have goals

In motor skills you are dealing with inert objects. Barring accidents and alien or supernatural intervention, my bike is under my control and goes where I direct it. I may have a name for it and I may talk to it occasionally, but I do not have to worry about its aims and intentions. In social situations, the other participants also have goals. If I wish to dominate you and you wish to dominate me, then we are preparing for battle and not constructive dialogue.

The importance of feelings

Argyle comments that, when you ride a bike, you do not have to wonder how the bike is feeling, or whether the bike thinks you are riding it nicely.[10] When you develop a motor skill such as playing snooker, you have to deal with materials and equipment which do *not* react or have feelings.

This is very different in social skills. You cannot predict the reactions of other people in the same way that you can predict that a snooker ball will stop dead if you hit the stun shot correctly.

Metaperception

As well as directly perceiving our own behaviour and the behaviour of others, we can also reflect on how those other people are perceiving us. This has been called 'metaperception' and has been shown to be an important factor in determining how people react to one another.[11] For example, if we are having a conversation and I get the impression that you think I am being too 'chatty' then I might become more reserved to counteract this impression. If my initial impression is wrong then I will probably confuse you or even offend you with my sudden and unexplained change in behaviour.

Situation and personal factors

As I explain later in this book, we make all sorts of judgements about the other people we communicate with and the situation we are in. Even though these judgements can be subconscious they will affect how we communicate.

Some of these complexities will become more apparent as we look at the behaviours which make up our interpersonal skills.

What are the components of interpersonal skills?

I shall discuss specific skills as they crop up later in the book but some examples will illustrate the general approach.

One typical and comprehensive text on interpersonal communication skills included the following topics in 1987:[12]

- non-verbal communication
- reinforcement
- questioning
- reflecting
- opening and closing
- explanation
- listening
- self-disclosure

However, the definition of skilled behaviours is not static. The subsequent version of this same text in 1994 added a few more skills: influencing, assertiveness, and group interaction and leadership. The second edition of a parallel text from the same author in 1997 covered all these skills and added a chapter on humour and laughter.[13]

Many of these topics are reasonably self-explanatory but some need more detailed descriptions to provide a fuller introduction to social skills analysis. I have included more detail on some of the others in later chapters (assertiveness in Chapter 12, and group interaction in Chapter 13).

Non-verbal communication

Non-verbal communication (NVC for short) or bodily communication usually means a range of non-verbal signals, which can include the following:[14]

- facial expression
- gaze
- gestures
- posture
- bodily contact
- spatial behaviour
- clothes and appearance
- non-verbal vocalisations
- smell

As these comprise some of the most significant codes we use, I shall discuss them in some detail in Chapter 9.

Reinforcement

This refers to behaviours which encourage the other person to carry on or repeat whatever they happen to be doing. Various experiments have shown the reinforcing influence of expressions of praise, encouragement, and support, even down to the use of head nods, grunts and the 'uh-huh'. A simple laboratory experiment which illustrated this process was described as follows:[15]

> Subjects in this study were simply asked to produce as many individual words as they could think of. Each occasion on which a plural noun was given, the experimenter responded with 'mm-hmm' while all other types of words were largely ignored. It was found that gradually the number of cases of plural nouns increased substantially.

Questioning

If you have attended a series of job interviews you will know that some professional interviewers are much better than others at extracting information from you. This will be due in part to their question technique – whether they are asking the right sort of question at the right time. For example, texts on interviewing technique usually distinguish between open and closed questions.[16] An open question allows the person to answer in whatever way they like, e.g. what do you think of Tony Blair? A closed question asks for specific information or a yes/no response, e.g. do you agree with Blair's economic policy? Open questions encourage people to talk and expand; closed questions encourage short answers. Inexperienced interviewers often ask too many closed questions and do not get the elaborated answers which they really want.

Reflecting

This is a skill often used by counsellors and other people who have to conduct very personal interviews and who want the other person to talk in some detail about their own feelings and attitudes. As questions can often direct the conversation in ways which reflect the interviewer's assumptions it can be more revealing to use reflections which feed back to the speaker some aspect of what they have just said. This acts as a cue for them to elaborate or extend what they have been saying. You can reflect in different ways and achieve different results. This will depend on whether you are interested in the factual statements that the other person has made or their feelings about what they are saying. The following alternative versions of an imaginary conversation illustrate different forms of reflections and different reactions which they may achieve.

Keywords

This involves the listener identifying a keyword or phrase which will encourage the speaker to say more:

Person A: I have travelled quite a lot over the years and I always enjoy travelling. I did most of it when I worked for ICL.
Person B: ICL?
Person A: Yes, I worked there for 5 years up until the time...

B chose a keyword in what A had said and simply repeated it. A recognised this as a signal to elaborate on this and the conversation develops.

Paraphrasing

This involves the listener summarising what they have heard in their own words:

Person A: I have travelled quite a lot over the years and I always enjoy travelling. I did most of it when I worked for ICL.
Person B: So you have done a lot of travelling?
Person A: Yes, I suppose I must have visited all the major countries in Europe and...

Here B gave a brief summary or paraphrasing of what he had just heard. Again A took this as a cue to develop the conversation in a particular way.

Reflecting feeling

This is where the listener identifies the feelings which the speaker implies in the way they talk:

Person A: I have travelled quite a lot over the years and I always enjoy travelling. I did most of it when I worked for ICL.
Person B: You sound as though you wished you were still doing a lot of travelling.
Person A: Yes I do miss it a lot and I wish there was…

Here B has probably focused on the way A spoke. Perhaps A talked with a hint of regret in his tone of voice. By accurately spotting this and using a reflection B has enabled A to express some of his feelings.

This last form of reflection is perhaps the most difficult and most skilful – you have to sense the underlying emotion accurately and read between the lines. Often quite subtle clues are involved. Consider the following statement:

> 'I worked in the packing department at Hill's. All I did from nine o'clock until five was put tins into cardboard boxes, day after day after day.'

This straightforward description of a job gives several clear clues to the underlying emotion. The phrases 'all I did' and 'day after day' combine to convey the atmosphere of routine and boredom.

However, these different strategies focus on rather different aspects of the other person's communication – the first two relate to the spoken content; the last tends to focus on the non-verbal accompaniment. As a results, David Dickson's recent review of the area talks about 'conceptual confusion, terminological inconsistency, and definitional imprecision'.[17] He suggests that the different impact of the different strategies needs further exploration, especially in naturalistic settings rather than laboratory experiments. However, he also notes the research which shows that reflections can work positively – they do seem to encourage others to self-disclose and also seem to generate positive feelings towards the interviewer.

Opening and closing

This refers to the ways in which we establish the beginnings and endings of a particular interaction. For example, sales staff often receive very detailed training on how to start the interaction with the customer. Often this involves making conversation to establish the sales representative as more friendly and helpful than 'just a salesperson'. Consider all the different possible ways of starting a conversation with someone – some ways would be much more appropriate than others in particular circumstances.

The choice of opening can be very important in more formal situations such as an interview where the opening can establish either a positive or negative atmosphere. One summary of possible opening techniques suggested five different alternatives, including the following three:[18]

- *Social opening* The interviewer makes sure to give the interviewee a positive welcome and spends some time in social conversation – breaking the ice – before getting down to business.
- *Factual opening* The interviewer starts with a clear description of important facts, perhaps by explaining how they see their role, or explaining how they see the goals of the interview, or by summarising what has happened previously.
- *Motivational opening* The interviewer starts with an attempt to encourage and motivate the interviewee, perhaps by introducing some visual aid or gadget to stimulate interest.

There is also a similar variety of tactics available to close or conclude an interaction. The good interviewer will make sure that the interviewee has a chance to clear up any points they have not understood and will make sure that they know what is going to happen as a result of the interview.

Listening

It may seem odd to regard listening as a skill but that is because we tend to think of it as a passive activity rather than being an activity we have to concentrate on and work at. In fact there has now been considerable research into how we listen to each other and this research has identified important factors:

- typical problems or barriers to effective listening
- different patterns of listening behaviour
- behaviours which seem to help the other person express themselves and which therefore help us listen to them

Typical listening barriers

Some problems are fairly obvious, such as problems caused by external distractions or lack of interest. Other problems are more subtle, such as verbal battling or fact hunting:[19]

- *Verbal battle* This is the situation where, instead of listening and absorbing what the other person has to say, we start to debate the ideas in our own head and come up with counter-arguments or criticisms. While we do this we lose track of the other points the person is making.
- *Fact hunting* Instead of listening for the main theme or general points in the argument we concentrate on the detailed facts and lose sight of the overall message.

If you identify these problems you can overcome them. Attempts to train people to become better listeners typically try to get people to identify these 'bad habits'. For example, we can think much faster than we speak and this can either help us listen or add to the distractions:[19]

> The differential between thought speed and speech rate may encourage the listener to fill up the spare time with other unrelated thought processes (such as day-dreaming), which in turn may distract the listener from assimilating the speaker's message. Listening can be improved by using this spare thought-time positively, by asking covert questions such as: 'What are the main points being expressed by the speaker?'; 'What reasons are being given?'; 'In what frame of reference should these reasons be taken?'; and 'What further information is necessary?'

Patterns and styles of listening

Sometimes someone appears to be listening to you but you suspect they are not:

- *Pretend listeners* They appear to be attentive and are making some appropriate non-verbal signals but their minds are elsewhere.
- *Limiting listeners* They only give limited attention to what you are saying. They are focusing on specific topics or comments and may distort or misinterpret other things you say.
- *Self-centred listeners* They are only really concerned with their own views and may be simply looking for your agreement.

Talking to someone who exhibits one of these styles can be very frustrating.

Positive or active listening

Good listening is often described as active listening – not only do you have to absorb and process internally the information you receive but you also have to encourage the other person to talk and demonstrate clearly that you are paying attention. As a result, some authors have subdivided listening into more specific clusters of skills, such as:[20]

- attending skills
- following skills
- reflecting skills

The behaviours which seem to be associated with effective listening involve both bodily communication and internal thinking. Typical recommendations include:[21]

- Be receptive to the other person – show that you are prepared to listen and accept what they are saying (of course, this does not mean that you automatically agree with it). Non-verbal signals are obviously important here and you need to avoid any signs of tension or impatience.
- Maintain attention – using eye contact, head nods and appropriate facial expression.
- Remove distractions.
- Delay evaluation of what you have heard until you fully understand it.

Self-disclosure

When you communicate with other people you tell them various things about yourself. Sidney Jourard coined the term 'self-disclosure' to refer to the process of sharing information about ourselves with other people.[22] So when you self-disclose, you reveal to the other person some aspect of how you feel. Jourard was interested in how people came to reveal aspects of themselves to others and how this process influenced the development of good personal relationships. Perhaps the best way of visualising the process is using a diagram known as the Johari window (Figure 3.3) – so-called after its two originators, Joe Luft and Harry Ingham.[23] The window categorises information that you and others have about yourself into four segments:

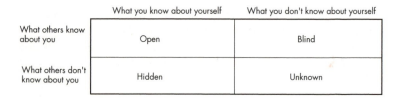

	What you know about yourself	What you don't know about yourself
What others know about you	Open	Blind
What others don't know about you	Hidden	Unknown

Figure 3.3 The Johari window

1 *Open* This contains information about myself which I know and which others know about me, e.g. the fact that I am married with two children.
2 *Hidden* This is information which I know about myself and which I am not prepared to reveal to other people, e.g. specific fears and anxieties which I may feel embarrassed about and which are certainly not going to be published here.
3 *Blind* This is information which others know about me and which I am not aware of, e.g. annoying habits which I do not notice in myself. This blind area can contain very important information: if I see myself as a considerate and approachable leader and others see me as domineering and aggressive then this will inevitably lead to problems.
4 *Unknown* This information is not known to me or others at present but may surface at some future point, e.g. I may have some very deep-rooted unconscious anxieties which are currently under control.

When I self-disclose I enlarge the open segment and decrease the other segments. If I receive feedback from others then I can also increase my open segment and decrease my blind segment.

There are several practical implications of self-disclosure, the most important being its effect on our relationships.

Self-disclosure and relationships

In order to initiate a relationship with someone, you need to self-disclose. What do you tell the other person? How soon do you reveal more personal feelings? Your answer to these questions may well determine how the relationship develops. We are suspicious of other people who become 'too personal too soon'.[24] This issue of how much information we reveal to others is a very real problem for some professional groups. If you are a social worker and a client explains personal feelings which you can identify with, do you share your experience with the client or do you maintain a more neutral stance?

Ideas about the value of self-disclosure have changed over the last few decades, reflecting in part the social values of the time. Jourard recommended that couples should aim for full disclosure, 'where each partner discloses himself without reserve'.[25] More recent research suggests that more moderate levels of self-disclosure are more likely to maintain a relationship over a long period of time.[24]

Conclusion

This account of all the different behaviours which can contribute to skilled performance may seem a rather daunting list. Of course, all of these behaviours are not relevant or appropriate in every situation. You can expect different patterns of behaviour in different situations: for example, in a job interview the interviewer is likely to concentrate on questioning; in a counselling interview, the interviewer is likely to do much more reflecting and reinforcing.

The socially skilled person is the person who can choose the appropriate behaviours to suit the situation they are in, and then perform these behaviours in an appropriate combination and sequence. Of course, this makes it sound rather too easy. Some of the complexities are revealed in the next chapter when we look at how social skills can work (or not) in everyday life.

Chapter 4

Communication skills in context

In this chapter I shall:

- analyse a series of practical examples which illustrate how the social skills model can be applied
- review criticisms and possible limitations of this approach
- relate the social skills approach to the model of interpersonal communication outlined in Chapter 2

Practical examples of communication skills at work (or not!)

We become most aware of social skills in everyday life when they 'break down', i.e. when someone blunders and displays some problem with their level of skills. So to illustrate the workings of communication skills, I shall use examples which range from the fairly light-hearted to the very serious:

- Fred at parties
- chairing a meeting
- the nurse's diagnosis

Fred at parties

In my college days, I had a friend who used to create problems at parties. He was very susceptible to alcohol. After a couple of drinks, his social skills deteriorated. Unfortunately his enthusiasm for social interaction seemed to rise in direct proportion to his intake of alcohol. And this caused the problems. In his enthusiastic/inebriated state, Fred would adopt a particular style of interaction. He would stand very close to people, talk at them very animatedly and would stare them straight in the eye all the time, without blinking very often. This combination of behaviour was interpreted by males as 'aggressive and/or suspicious' and by females as 'too pushy and too macho far too soon'. His group of friends had to rescue him at regular intervals before his victims decided to take evasive or antagonistic action.

The irony in this tale is that Fred would never understand why he was so unsuccessful at parties and we, his friends, could never bring ourselves to tell him in case it hurt his feelings. We could never think of a way of explaining the problem which would help Fred to do something about it. Our subtle attempts to wean him off alcohol all failed. He felt that a couple of pints built up his confidence (which it certainly did) but he did not recognise that this increased confidence was having such a disastrous effect. He was also a victim of unfortunate social pressure: he was very anxious to be 'one of the lads' and show that he could cope with alcohol in the same way that most of us could (or at least thought we could).

How could the social skills approach have helped Fred?

At the very least, a short burst of social skills training with special emphasis on non-verbal communication would have helped Fred both to understand what he was doing and to appreciate the effect he was creating with his style of behaviour. But would this be sufficient? Having recognised the problem could he then resist the temptation to have a few pints before a party? And how confident would he be without the false confidence induced by alcohol? Again social skills training could help. Presumably Fred lacked confidence because he was unsure of how to behave. How do you strike up a conversation with someone at a party in a convincing way? Social skills training could have analysed Fred's present strategies and suggested alternatives which would build his self-confidence. If you already have self-confidence then you do not need the false support of alcohol. And increased self-confidence would have also enabled him to resist the social pressure of 'having to have a few pints'.

This very brief example may seem rather trivial but several surveys have found that many people have difficulty with everyday social situations and this can cause considerable anxiety and loneliness.[1] This example also suggests some of the complexities of social skills analysis – to do it properly you need a lot of information on the person's behaviour and feelings as well as a clear knowledge of the situations which create difficulty.

Chairing a meeting

Most of us have probably attended at least one committee or project group meeting which was chaired badly – perhaps the meeting went on and on without seeming to get anywhere, perhaps the decisions were pushed through without sufficient discussion, perhaps the participants interrupted each other and spoke at cross-purposes. These problems should not occur if the meeting is being chaired efficiently. But what counts as efficient or skilful behaviour in this context?

Despite the pervasiveness of meetings in everyday life and work, there is very little research on what chairpersons actually do. There are several books offering advice but these tend to be based on the authors' personal experience rather than any systematic research.[2] However, there is one systematic study which highlights what a good chairperson actually does.[3] This research also highlights some of the main difficulties in research in social skills:

- identifying the measures of success, competence or effectiveness
- making valid observations of the actual behaviour
- identifying effective behaviour

As the authors comment:

> Apart from satisfaction measures, and these can be misleading, it is difficult to specify the performance criteria which indicate an expert chairman. The measures sometimes used in training evaluation, such as the time taken to complete the meeting or the number of decisions reached per hour, seemed to us naive and inappropriate.

The main criteria used in the research were participants' ratings of fairness and efficiency in conjunction with the experience of the chairman himself (all the subjects were male). The behaviour of chairmen who received the highest ratings was compared with the behaviour of other people in the meeting. Important differences emerged as we shall see later.

Observing behaviour

In order to make a systematic analysis of what someone is doing we need a method of observation. In other words, we need some sort of classification system. The most popular system used by researchers over the years is the system first proposed by Robert Bales.[4] His interaction process analysis uses twelve categories. Every act is classified in one of the categories. Of course every time someone speaks they can perform several acts.

The twelve behaviour categories in interaction process analysis (IPA) are given below (see note 4 for references which provide a more detailed description of the IPA categories and their development):

Shows solidarity
Shows tension release
Agrees
Gives suggestion
Gives opinion
Gives orientation
Asks for orientation
Asks for opinion
Asks for suggestion
Disagrees
Shows tension
Shows anatagonism

An example may make this clearer:

> 'OK, but can we hang on a bit? I think we should proceed very slowly. And I'd like to hear what Jane thinks.'

This contains four acts:

1 OK – shows agreement
2 but can we hang on a bit – gives suggestion
3 I think we should proceed very slowly – gives suggestion
4 And I'd like to hear what Jane thinks – asks for suggestion

Having experimented with this classification and other examples, Rackham and Morgan concluded that different contexts needed rather different classifications depending on what you were interested in. For example, chairing a meeting involves controlling the participation of the members, either bringing people in to make a contribution or cutting them off. These behaviours are not directly registered in Bales' system, so they developed their own system for particular studies, working from a general purpose set of the following categories. The thirteen categories are grouped into four broader categories – initiating, reacting, clarifying and controlling participation:

1 Initiating
- Proposing
- Building

2 Reacting
- Supporting
- Disagreeing
- Defending/attacking
- Blocking/difficulty stating

3 Clarifying
- Open
- Testing understanding
- Summarising
- Seeking information
- Giving information

4 Controlling participation
- Shutting out
- Bringing in

They tested this system to make sure that observers could use it reliably. A classification system is of little help if observers find it difficult to use or if different observers arrive at very different interpretations of the same behaviour. Other researchers have also developed observation schemes for particular situations. For example, Flanders has developed a scheme for classroom interaction which focuses on the different ways that teachers behave to control their pupils.[5]

The effective chair

Applying the observation scheme in a series of meetings led to a series of conclusions. Chairmen who were regarded as effective behaved very differently from chairmen who were rated as less effective. And effective chairmen behaved very differently from other members of the meeting. To quote a couple of examples:

> Testing understanding. One of the most significant differences between chairmen and members was the very high level of testing understanding (15.2 per cent) in the chairmen, compared with 3.1 per cent from group members. Testing understanding, like summarizing, allows a retrospective control of what has been said. It organizes and ties down previous points and people's understanding of them.
>
> Summarizing. The difference here (12.5 per cent for chairman, 0.7 per cent for meeting members) is the greatest on any category. This emphasizes how strongly associated summarizing is with the role of chairman. The association is so strong that if another member of the meeting attempts to summarize, this is frequently seen as a personal challenge to the chairman and his authority.

Other differences included:

- more procedural proposals

- less supporting behaviour (remaining neutral and not expressing support for particular ideas)
- less disagreeing (again this was associated with the desire to remain neutral)
- much more information seeking, but less information giving

Thus, this research did develop a clear specification for the behaviour which can help someone to be an effective chairperson, although the authors are careful to point out that their findings might be specific to the context they investigated. Different types of organisation or different types of groups could demand different combinations of behaviour in skilled chairpersons. And remember again that this study was only concerned with male subjects.

In the context of this investigation, the specification could be used to evaluate the behaviour of the individual chair and also as a basis for training. Training would be based on the following stages:

- *Diagnosis* An individual's behaviour is categorised using the specification from the research.
- *Feedback* The individual is given feedback on how they are doing.
- *Practice* The individual is given time to practice and work on improvements.

The nurse's diagnosis

This example is taken from an article by Peter Maguire.[6] He quotes the following patient assessment which was produced by an experienced nurse. Colostomy involves surgery which creates an artificial opening in the wall of the abdomen so waste is discharged through this opening into a 'bag' which the patient has to change at regular intervals.

> Mrs. T is a 54 year old married woman with three grown-up children. She had a colostomy for rectal cancer four months ago. She called in at the clinic to see me because she was having trouble with her bag. It had been leaking and causing an offensive smell. She had stopped going out much because of it. Otherwise she appears to be coping well. I've given her a new

bag and will call on her in a week's time to see how she is getting on.

This assessment suggests that Mrs T is having difficulties of a fairly practical nature. A very different picture emerged from an independent assessment. This revealed that Mrs T had a number of other problems:

- she had serious sexual problems
- she had become very depressed
- she was sleeping badly and had little energy
- she was feeling both helpless and hopeless

So why did this experienced nurse miss these points? Her next assessment was recorded and analysed. Several problems in communication skills emerged, as follows.

Opening

The nurse would start with a comment like 'I'm here to see if you have been having any problems with your stoma'. She failed to make her role explicit. This rather abrupt opening made the patient feel that the nurse was only interested in any practical problems she was experiencing with her bag. As a result, the patient did not feel she could express her more fundamental problems as this would take too much time and was not appropriate. Of course the nurse would have been very willing to explore these problems if they had emerged.

Questioning

The nurse did not use open questions which would have invited the patient to speak out, such as 'How have you been getting on with your stoma?' Instead she asked leading questions, such as 'Your stoma's been working well, hasn't it?', which encourage short answers, and encourage the patient to go along with the expected answer.

Listening

The nurse was failing to notice signs of worry and distress in the patient's answers.

For example, when the nurse began by asking 'Your stoma's been working well, hasn't it?' the patient said, 'Well, yes, I suppose it has, but I've been a bit worried sometimes...'. The nurse seized on the 'suppose it has' and rightly checked that the stoma and bag were all right. She failed to acknowledge the cue 'worried'.

This example illustrates a problem which confronts many people occupying professional roles in society – nurses, doctors, lawyers, police officers, etc. Their judgements and decisions can have a dramatic effect on other people's lives. Most of their information is derived from interpersonal communication, so the quality of their decision depends upon their communication skills. And yet they may receive very little training in this area. We can hardly blame the nurse for poor questioning technique if she had never been trained in it.

It is perhaps ironic that this example highlights problems experienced by a female nurse (I chose it because it had been so thoroughly analysed). My own experience of the medical world suggests that it is the male inhabitants who have most to gain from social skills training! For example, I think of the doctor who did not initiate eye contact at all during the consultation and never asked open questions. And I remember meeting the consultant who always referred to his patient as 'it' when describing the diagnosis to other medical staff, even when the patient was within earshot.

Many professional groups are now looking at communication skills very seriously and there is much more now incorporated in British medical education. But there is still work to do to make sure that these skills are recognised fully and given the attention they deserve throughout the profession. Not everyone is convinced:[7]

> Many health care professionals (including nurses) feel that...the interpersonal issues involved in practitioner-patient interactions are naturally and automatically understood and acted upon. Many practitioners believe that interpersonal issues do not require active concern and scientific study.

> there is still a common belief that socially skilled action and methods of interpersonal relating are not amenable to training

or education. It is still common to hear nurses at all levels say that social skills just come naturally.

Are there any limitations to the social skills approach?

The social skills approach, and social skills training in particular, has been criticised on a number of counts. There are four lines of criticism that have important implications for this book, as follows.

Is the approach too mechanical?

Does the skills approach present an overmechanical and almost 'demeaning' view of human interaction? Perhaps some texts have created a misleading impression by implying that we all behave very mechanically, and that there are very definite techniques which always achieve certain social results. But this is not the impression you will receive from the more recent and more sophisticated texts.[8] These emphasise the complex nature of human interaction, and also examine a broader set of issues than the specific behaviours involved, which leads on to the second question.

Does the approach really take account of how we think and feel?

Does the social skills approach ignore the way we think and feel (cognitive and emotional factors) and concentrate too much on the observed behaviour? Admittedly Argyle's model does talk about goals and purposes. But are there other factors which are important? You can possess a skill without actually using it – you may not believe that you can perform effectively and so you refuse to try. So a person may actually be able to behave in a skilled manner but may not do so because they lack self-confidence, i.e. they feel that they will be unsuccessful. The importance of a person's feelings and beliefs cannot be ignored and these issues have now been recognised as an important area within the social skills approach.

Where does the social context fit in? (Does social skills analysis ignore it?)

Again this is an issue that is being given increasing attention by social skills researchers.[9] As we shall see in Chapter 5, the social context exerts strong influences on our behaviour. Behaviour that is seen as appropriate in one context will not necessarily be so in another.

Does social skills training simply teach 'modern manners' or what we used to call 'etiquette'?

Does social skills analysis have a hidden political dimension – does it represent a strict adherence to the status quo? Following this line of argument, some critics have suggested that social skills training is highly prescriptive and not as neutral or as scientific as it claims to be:[10]

> The social skills trainer therefore displaces the book on etiquette, which itself eventually replaced the code of chivalry.

The force of this criticism really depends on how the social skills approach relates to other knowledge we have of our social behaviour. And that leads me to the final topic of this chapter: how does the social skills approach relate to the model of interpersonal communication?

Social skill and the model of interpersonal communication

1 Interpersonal communication is an ongoing process with several interrelated components.
2 Whenever people communicate they behave in particular ways which are more or less successful at achieving their goals.

These two sentences reflect the two different approaches which have been described so far. Are these two incompatible ways of understanding interpersonal communication? I do not think so – they must be seen as complementary perspectives. The analysis of ongoing processes must contain reference to the specific behaviours involved and the analysis of skilled behaviour must always look beyond the specific behaviour in order to understand its true significance. Some practical examples may make this point clearer.

Goals and meaning

The social skills approach suggests that people pursue goals in social situations. These goals may not be totally shared by participants in an interaction. For example, Argyle suggests that nurses and patients regard the following goals as the most important when they interact:[11]

Nurse
- mutual acceptance
- taking care of other
- looking after self

Patient
- mutual acceptance
- obtaining information
- own well-being

There is an interesting potential source of conflict here: the patient wants information, the nurse does not see that as an important goal. The nurse's notion of 'taking care' may exclude any possibility of exchanging information. If patients make repeated attempts to quiz the nurse this may cause conflict as the nurse remains unforthcoming. Frustration is likely to build up on both sides: patients become irritated as their goal remains unsatisfied; the nurse becomes frustrated as this constant battle of wits distracts from the major goal of taking care.

But what is important about these goals is not just their implications for specific interactions. These goals represent particular role definitions which have developed in a particular society at a particular point in time. Would patients in previous generations have been so anxious to find out more information? Would they not have placed much greater reliance and trust in the doctors, and perhaps not even seen the nurses as a source of information? Changes in society and the spread of information have weakened the power of medical authority. Patients are much less accepting of conventional medical advice, the growth of alternative medicine being one example of this shift. Of course this more critical tendency will be much more pronounced in certain groups of patients. The percentage of patient–nurse relationships which involve real conflict over goals is probably very small.

The general point I am making here is that the meaning of particular behaviours always involves some consideration of broader features of the situation in which the behaviours occur. So any understanding of skilled behaviour also depends upon a sophisticated analysis of the situation in which it occurs. The social skills approach must depend upon our theories and models of communication or it *will* descend into rather mechanical rules of etiquette. To analyse behaviours and skills we need models of social situations; to develop models we need to investigate the detailed units of interaction.

The case of the skiing student

To provide one further illustration of how different levels of analysis can complement each other we can use a situation described by Gorden.[12] Student A has been invited to join a skiing weekend by some friends. The offer of free transport and accommodation seems too good to miss but it will mean returning to college too late for the Monday morning lecture. College rules do not demand that students report absences, but A decides to find out what will be in the lecture in advance so as to make up the work. A also wants to stay on good terms with the tutor. A goes to the tutor's office and the conversation starts like this:

A: Hello Dr Belden! Could I speak to you for a minute?
Dr B: Surely.
A: I was just wondering if anything important will be going on in class on Monday.
Dr B: Why do you ask?
A: Well, to be frank, I have a chance to take a skiing trip this weekend, and I wanted to find out if I would be missing anything.

If we interrupt the interaction at this point we find an annoyed Dr Belden and a rather confused A, who has not anticipated that his request would cause any antagonism. How do we explain these reactions? And how could A have handled it differently?

A obviously did not recognise certain important details which were significant in this conversation:

- The subtle innuendoes in his second question – the mention of 'anything important' clearly suggests that this class occurs on occasion without anything important happening. This is the first blow to Dr Belden's professional status.
- The question which raised a question – A's question was answered by a question. We accept that higher-status people have a right to do this but it immediately suggests some suspicion towards the first question.
- A's response to the tutor's question – repeating the idea of 'missing anything' and not providing any information which the tutor would find positive. A did not express any desire to catch up with the work, only enthusiasm at the prospective trip – further blows to the tutor's profession!

These are points which you could expect from a social skills analysis. However, they only make sense because of all the social knowledge which we take for granted. Dr Belden's reactions support a specific social identity, i.e. strongly committed to the academic subject matter and working hard to transform students like A into competent and hardworking scholars in an institution which sets fairly high standards. A's rather dismissive comments on the Monday class are a blow to Dr B's individual efforts as a tutor, to the subject area, and to the more general philosophy of the organisation. So the specific behaviours only make sense when you have a fuller account of the social situation.

A different organisational setting would bring different reactions. In a college with a more relaxed attitude to classwork, the typical staff attitude would probably be different. A different social context would also affect things: if Dr B knew that A was an outstanding student who deserved a break, then A's more tactless comments might have been ignored.

Going back to the original conversation, how could A have handled this situation differently? Suppose instead of the first question, A had said: 'I am afraid I may miss your lecture next Monday morning and I'd like your advice on how I can catch up on the work.' This avoids the innuendoes. Would it achieve a more positive reaction?

There is another angle to this example which we can explore. When you read the conversation, what did you assume about the gender of A and Dr B? In Gorden's original text, both are male. Would it make any difference if both were female? Would it make any difference if either one were female?

Any of these permutations would make a difference. The nature and extent of the difference would depend on the college and the subject area, as well as the perceptions and expectations of A and Dr B. For example, how would you feel if you were a female tutor working in an area where female staff and students are in the minority, such as engineering? Wouldn't you feel extremely annoyed by a request of this sort from a male student? You would certainly ask yourself whether that student would make the same request of his male tutors. You might also expect ulterior motives. Could the student be trying to 'set you up' to lever advantages out of other tutors: 'it's OK to skip the occasional class – Dr B has agreed'? Would you expect the student to recognise and anticipate these possible issues? And perhaps acknowledge that the request puts you in a very difficult position? What would the student have to say to assure you that the request was genuine? You might like to consider how many possible permutations of meaning we could obtain from this example just by changing the social identity of the participants.

Conclusion

Perhaps the most important conclusion that emerges from this chapter is that we *can* identify behaviours which are effective in enabling people to understand each other in particular situations. But we do need to consider the context *very* carefully.

This also suggests a point that social skills trainers would wish to emphasise: there is no magic box of tricks which you can apply to each and every situation and guarantee effective communication. And that is why we need both theoretical understanding and practical analysis of interpersonal communication.

Section B

The components of interpersonal communication

Chapter 5

The social context

In this chapter, I shall:

- discuss the meaning and significance of the social context
- define and discuss each of the components of the social context
- discuss how these components interact with one another, using examples from research into the relationships we have with others
- discuss the way these components develop over time, again using examples from research into personal relationships

What is the social context and how does it affect communication?

If you read any number of recent texts about human communication, you will probably find a strong emphasis on the social aspects of communication. Authors are very insistent that communication is a 'social process' and that communication always takes place within a given society at a given time. But what does this actually mean when we come to try to analyse communication?

One reason why modern authors place a strong emphasis on the social context is simply because early authors tended to neglect it. For example, there is little concern for the social context in early models of communication which simply concentrated on encoder–channel–decoder propositions. There is also something of a battle which is carried on within the social sciences between those who regard society as the backdrop against which humans choose to act and those who feel that society creates or determines the ways in which we act. If you follow the first viewpoint then you are likely to believe that there are features of human experience which are universal or common to all races and cultures. If you follow the latter viewpoint then you are likely to believe that all human action is relative to the society in which it occurs, i.e. that there are no universal features of human nature or experience.

These arguments may seem very abstract or remote but you will find that they do have very concrete practical implications. For example, communication between different cultures depends on the different cultures being able to develop a common understanding. If all experience is relative to your own culture then this communication could be impossible.[1]

I have oversimplified this argument simply because I do not have the space to explore it fully. If you want to put me on the spot for an opinion then I will argue that there are some aspects of human experience which are virtually universal. If this was not the case then communication would be impossible. On the other hand I also maintain that you cannot fully understand any process of human communication without understanding the social context in which it occurs. But if I simply say that communication is affected by the social context then that does not take us very far. What we need is a more systematic definition of the social context:

- What are the relevant components?
- What are the specific factors which affect us?
- How do they operate?

Unfortunately many authors have been at great pains to emphasise the importance of the social context but have been rather less painstaking at saying what that means! Thus, my definition reflects a collection of rather disparate areas of research which have yielded important results.

Environment and social structure

Firstly I shall make a distinction between environment and the social structure.

Environment

The environment is the setting or background and has both physical and social elements. For example, one research study found that experimental subjects saw the experimenter as more 'status-ful' if the laboratory was untidy. Another study showed that people judged faces differently depending on whether they were in a 'beautiful' or 'ugly' room.[2]

Social structure

By social structure, I mean the ways in which the particular event we are looking at is organised. For example, if you attend a British wedding you will notice that people behave in fairly predictable ways as if they were following particular rules or codes of behaviour. You will notice that some people are behaving in very specific ways – for example, the best man – as they are fulfilling specific roles. If their performance goes wrong in some way then chaos and embarrassment

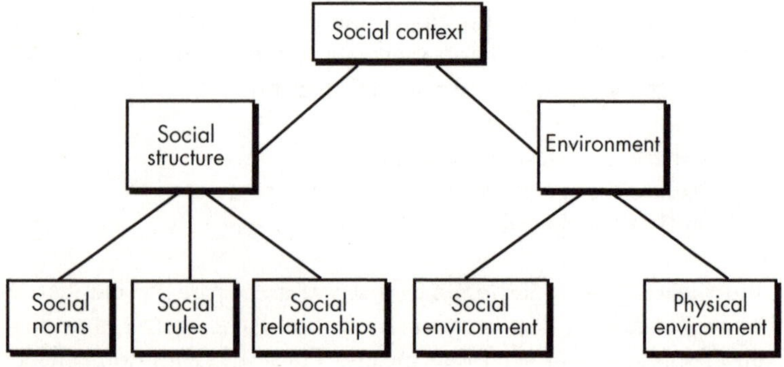

Figure 5.1 Components of the social context

is likely to follow. Consider the best man at a very formal wedding who tried to relax the groom as they were standing at the altar by whispering 'This is your last chance to escape. I'll cover if you want to make a run for it!' This comment was not so well received when the bride's parents proudly played back the tape of the ceremony at the reception. The best man had been standing almost next to the microphone so the comment came out loud and clear.

There is also a very definite sequence of events, e.g. the order of speeches at the reception. All these facts will vary depending on the location and status of the participant: for instance, compare a high-society upper-class wedding with a typical church wedding or with a registry office wedding. In a different culture you will notice even more dramatic differences. But the important point I want to make here is that the participants recognise the invisible 'rules of the game', i.e. they know what is required of them and act out their parts. People can feel very uncomfortable if they are unsure of the proceedings, and a lot of humour is based upon careful observation of the idiosyncrasies or ironies of some of our more formal occasions, e.g. as in the British film *Four Weddings And A Funeral* or the American film by Robert Altman, *A Wedding*.

What are the components of the social context?

I have already distinguished between the environment and the social structure but I need further to subdivide these categories in order to arrive at a more comprehensive definition. This is illustrated in Figure 5.1. I shall now discuss each of these latter categories individually.

Physical environment

The physical environment is the collection of physical objects and factors which surround us, such as the shape and size of the room, colour, lighting, heating, etc. All of these can influence our behaviour in ways we might not necessarily be aware of.[3] For example, different types of neon bulb give off rather different qualities of light and it has been suggested that one type creates a more friendly atmosphere than others. At first sight this may seem a rather unlikely effect but you can easily suggest a chain of events which could lead to such a result. Harsh lighting can lead to eye strain and fatigue – this will make people feel irritable and unsettled; irritable people will tend to be short tempered and grumpy; this will lead to arguments etc.; and this will create an unfriendly atmosphere.

Consider how different physical environments influence you in terms of your mood feelings. And consider how designers try to create a particular atmosphere in buildings:

- the fast food restaurant with a 'bright, cheerful' colour scheme, and fast 'cheerful' music
- the 'posh' restaurant with subdued lighting and very soft background music
- the dentist's waiting room set out like a front room so that you 'forget' where you really are!

The physical environment can affect us in a number of different ways which influence our behaviour and communication, as follows.

Direct physical effects

The environment can have direct physiological effects. If specific neon bulbs, or specific levels of heating, do have predictable consequences upon us, then this could be because these have direct effects on our physiology.

Symbolic meaning

The environment can have symbolic meaning. Manufacturers of products are often very concerned about the colour of packaging because of the way certain colours have certain associations or symbolic meanings. White and blue seem to be associated with cleanliness whereas red and yellow have associations of warmth and excitement. Green is becoming a more widespread colour because of its connotations of 'environment-friendliness'. There is no direct physical effect here – although some types of light may be more arousing to our nervous system, this arousal could be interpreted in different ways. We respond to the different colours primarily because of their symbolic meaning. Thus, the colour of decorations or the feel of different furniture materials can have significant effects on how we feel and how we decide to behave.

Impact on behaviour

The physical environment can make certain behaviours easier or more difficult. In both the UK and the USA, high-rise flats were once regarded as the answer to urban housing problems. They were relatively cheap to build and could accommodate large numbers of people. They were seen as the 'modern' replacement for inner-city slums, with many advantages and no real disadvantages.

Now most high-rise flats either are problem areas or have been demolished. They have a reputation for vandalism, hooliganism, social isolation, etc. Many people put up with much poorer physical home conditions rather than move into one of the flats. And yet these social problems were not characteristics of the housing areas they replaced, where people seemed to suffer mainly from poor physical conditions, such as damp and lack of hygiene.

One major problem with high-rise flats is that they are designed in such a way as to make casual social meetings rather difficult. In the old properties they replaced, you usually met someone the moment you opened your front door. It was easy to have a casual chat over the back fence or on the doorstep. Local shops were at the end of the street where again you would inevitably meet neighbours and local residents. There were often very strong feelings of local community. In contrast, the high-rise developments unwittingly destroyed many of these features. And they replaced them with the worst possible compromise.

Rather ironically the high-rise flat creates problems of social isolation and also lack of privacy. You are surrounded by people you have probably not met but you cannot find a place to be on your own because you are always liable to be disturbed. The partition walls are often very thin so you know exactly what TV channel the neighbours next door are listening to!

Social environment

I can talk about some places which have a warm or cold physical environment because of the way they are designed and built. In the same way I can distinguish different types of social environment or social climate. Just as you might perceive another person as supportive or controlling you may also perceive a social environment as supportive or controlling or any other adjectives which suit. But one important finding is that we do seem to make consistent judgements about particular environments. And particular environments do have measurable effects. For example, a number of studies have shown that a very supportive social climate is associated with a reduction in stress or tension. And there is a good deal of research relating social factors to measurable physiological changes.

One major reason why the social environment can affect our behaviour is simply that we are continually looking for information from our environment which will help us to decide what to do. Schachter illustrated this point with a rather devious set of experiments where subjects were given an injection of what they thought was a vitamin with various explanations about what effect it should have.[4] For my purposes I shall concentrate on those subjects who were not told what physical effects the 'vitamin' would have. The vitamin was in fact adrenaline, which has a number of predictable physiological effects – heart rate increases etc.

Each of these subjects was sitting in a waiting room thinking they were waiting for the real experiment to begin. Each thought that the other person was another waiting subject. In fact the other person was a stooge who had been instructed to act either very angrily or very elatedly. The real subjects experienced the strange physiological feelings brought on by the drug and had no explanation for them. They noticed the behaviour of the stooge and, without being consciously aware of it, they interpreted their own feelings in the same way. For example, the subjects who had been left with an 'angry' stooge reported feelings of anger and hostility. Thus, these subjects were subconsciously influenced by their social environment both to feel and act in a specific way.

Social norms

In most social situations, we have a fairly clear idea of how others expect us to behave – in other words, social norms are in operation. And this demonstrates the most important feature of group norms, namely that a norm acts as a guide on how to behave. If you obey the norms then you are likely to be accepted by others in the situation and your behaviour will be seen as normal. If you break the norms then you may run the risk of being rejected by others and your behaviour will be seen as 'odd' or even hostile. Exactly what will happen if you break a norm will depend upon a whole variety of circumstances. I shall outline a few of these later, but first I shall describe a few examples of norms to make the concept clearer.

The fair day's work

One of the earliest studies on a real workgroup found that members of the group had a very clear idea of what counted as a 'fair day's work for a day's pay'.[5] Each member of the group consistently produced 6,000 units per day even if he could have earned more by producing more. Management continually tried to persuade the men to produce more but this was ignored. The group were suspicious of management as a result of previous events. They felt they would probably lose out in the long run if they did produce more and so they kept to the norm. If a worker did produce more than his target one day then he would adjust the following day's work to make sure he kept to the average.

The collective illusion

Sherif was one of the first researchers to demonstrate a group norm in a controlled experimental setting.[6] He used a well-established visual illusion – the autokinetic phenomena.

If you sit in a completely darkened room and look at a tiny and stationary spot of light at one end of the room then that spot of light will appear to move. Different people see the spot move consistently different distances. For each individual, you can find out the average movement which they perceive. Sherif found that if you then put a group of three people in the room and asked them how far the spot moved then their three judgements would tend to converge and stabilise on a particular value. This group norm would then carry over to the situation where the three people later sat in the room individually. The group norm influenced their behaviour not only in the group but also outside the group.

This norming effect does not happen if the subjects are told about the illusion beforehand, presumably because they then have a rational explanation for their differences. As a result they do not experience any pressure to accommodate to the views of the other subjects. From these examples, you can see that norms exist at different levels. The most important are cultural and group norms.

Cultural norms

These are norms which apply to all members of a given culture. For example, there are very powerful norms of politeness in Japanese culture which mean that it is considered very rude to say 'no' to another person. If you wish to refuse something then you have to do it indirectly, perhaps by simply delaying your answer until the other person has given up! Many foreign businessmen who have failed to do business with the Japanese have complained how much time they have wasted in negotiations. They probably failed to recognise the 'no' signals when they first appeared.

Group norms

These only apply to members of a specific group. For example, teenage gangs often develop strong norms for behaving and communicating. In another of Sherif's experiments (see Chapter 13), two groups of boys from virtually identical backgrounds were observed at summer camp. One group developed norms of loud, aggressive behaviour which included swearing and shouting. The other group developed contrasting norms which emphasised polite restrained behaviour and outlawed swearing.

Unfortunately, the concept of norm is not always as clearly defined or as consistent as it could be:[6]

- Many people do seem constantly to break specific norms and yet this is ignored or even accepted.
- It is very difficult to find any generalisation about how people should behave in a given situation which everybody agrees with. So this leaves the problem of deciding what level of agreement constitutes a norm – is it 70 per cent, 80 per cent, 90 per cent, or what?
- There is often a discrepancy between what people say they will do in a situation and what they do actually do. What counts as the norm?

Social rules

Our social behaviour is guided not simply by group or cultural norms but also by specific rules which seem to apply in specific situations. The distinction between rules and norms is best illustrated by using the analogy of a team game, like football. The rules of football have mostly been written down in formal documents and specify such things as how many players can participate, how long the game is, how you score a goal, what counts as foul play, etc.

Even if every team obeys all the rules, they may still develop different norms. English football fans used to be very critical of 'continental' players for their habits of shirt pulling and overacting when tackled. Judging by the televised footage of the 1998 World Cup, these practices have now become international norms. And televised coverage of the English Premier League shows they are now a regular part of the game over here as well! I shall illustrate this distinction between norms and rules again later in the chapter when we look at studies of our relationships.

Social relationships

Any communication between two people will be influenced by the relationship which exists between them. This relationship can be of different types which reflect different roles (e.g. friend, brother) and of different quality (e.g. close and informal as opposed to distant and formal). The relationship can also be affected by a number of important factors – cultural differences, gender differences, and social class differences. So in order to understand what is going on you need to take all these factors into account.

Social roles

I shall discuss the various components of social roles in more detail in the next chapter. Here I do need to emphasise how important this concept is.

Every social situation incorporates some definition of the roles that are expected of the participants. And these expected roles influence how and what people will communicate. Sometimes the roles will be rather vague or ambiguous and you have to 'negotiate' with the other participants what role to adopt. For example, if you go to a party held by people you do not really know very well, what role will you take on? It is probably unwise to go thundering in as the life and soul of the party in case that violates the norms. On the other hand many a party has died a death because no one was willing to take on an active role in the proceedings.

There are other situations where the role requirements appear to be so strong that they do determine how individuals behave. One rather frightening example of this is Philip Zimbardo's prison experiment.[7] Zimbardo was interested in the effects of prison life on the individual and so he set up a mock prison. All the subjects were very carefully chosen after a series of psychological tests to make sure they were a representative group of intelligent middle-class youths. They were divided at random into prisoners and guards. The guards were equipped with typical American guards' uniforms and hats and were told that they were in charge. The only definite rule was a ban on the use of physical violence. To add realism, the prisoners were arrested by real local policemen and put through the usual signing-in procedure. They were given a uniform – a plain long smock – and left in the care of the guards. Neither group was given any training or instruction in how to behave.

Zimbardo and his colleagues sat back to observe but were soon forced to intervene. In his own words:[8]

> once the experiment began, we, as experimenters, had very little input into the guard–prisoner interaction. At that point, we were simply videotaping, and observing the drama unfold. We had intended it to last for two weeks, but the pathology we observed was so extreme, we ended the study after only six days. By 'pathology' I mean that half the students who were prisoners had emotional breakdowns in less than five days. On the other hand, the guards behaved brutally, sadistically; the only difference among them was their frequency of brutal, sadistic, dehumanizing behaviour. But they all did it to some degree.

These astonishing results were not the product of sadistic or cruel minds. The 'guards' after the experiment were themselves shocked and disgusted at the way they had behaved. And yet during the experiment they had been so caught up in the experience that they had been able to disregard their normal moral values. The roles had 'won'.

The experiment did have one very positive outcome: Zimbardo started to campaign for penal reform in the USA and has since been responsible for a number of worthy developments.

Relationship type and quality

The last few decades have seen a dramatic upsurge in research on personal relationships. Some of this research has focused on different qualities of relationship, e.g. love, friendship, acquaintance, etc. One general conclusion concerns the relationship between certain types or styles of communication and certain types of relationship. For example, self-disclosure has already been mentioned as an important component in developing relationships (see Chapter 3). There have been other important lines of research which relate to themes mentioned in this book, as follows.

Skills

Research has shown that there are a number of social skills differences which are associated with the ability to develop relationships. For example, it has been suggested that lonely and isolated people are not very good at sending non-verbal signals, particularly signals of liking via face and voice.[9] Of course this does beg a very important question: what are the original causes of such deficiency? Do people become lonely simply because they lack skills, or do their skills deteriorate as a result of their experience and feelings?

Rules and social knowledge

As I said in Chapter 4, being able to perform a skill depends on knowing what to do as well as having the ability to carry out the behaviour. People who find it difficult to strike up relationships may simply lack the knowledge and experience of the acceptable ways of doing it (they don't know the rules). For example, one study asked college students how they would try to get to know someone.[9] Their 'plans' were then rated by independent judges on how likely they were to be successful. Students who were more socially isolated tended to produce plans which were seen as less effective. Their lack of social knowledge seemed to be one factor which contributed to their loneliness.

Cultural differences

There are some very important differences in the way different cultures regard different relationships. There are different rules associated with the same relationship and this can have major differences in what and how the participants communicate. I talk about social rules below. To illustrate the influence of cultural background, Argyle reached the following conclusions after a study of differences between British, Italian, Hong Kong and Japanese informants:[9]

> It seems we place more emphasis on expressing emotions, giving opinions on intimate topics, affection and requests for help and advice than our Hong Kong and Japanese

counterparts, at least as far as intimate relationships are concerned. Close relationships, whether spouses, family, friends, or kin by marriage, or even by virtue of heterosexual intimacy (as in dating or cohabitation), are viewed as sources of support, and rules exist about using them as such. We ask for material help, disclose our personal problems and feelings, and ask for personal advice in our intimate relationships. And to a lesser extent, we apply similar rules to our less intimate acquaintances such as work colleagues and neighbours – and also use them as sources of social support. While the Hong Kong informants endorse very similar rules for husbands and wives, Japanese marriages are characterised by less emphasis on the overt expression of intimacy. And the same is true of other Japanese and Hong Kong intimate relationships.

Gender differences

Unfortunately social scientists have not always been very sensitive to differences between men and women. Researchers have assumed that the results from a study using male subjects can also be directly applied to females. Happily, more recent research has been much more careful in examining gender differences. I shall review the number of differences that have been found between males and females in their communication in Chapter 11. However, interpretations and explanations of differences here must be approached with extreme caution for at least two fundamental reasons:

1 *The dangers of stereotyping* Discussions of male/female differences seem to rely on social stereotypes rather than direct observations. This is especially unfortunate at a time when traditional sex roles and stereotypes seem to be in a greater state of flux or change than has been the case for some time. We return to this issue in the next chapter where roles and stereotypes are discussed in more detail.
2 *Methodology* Many of the often-quoted studies in this area are very limited in terms of their procedures and choice of subjects, as we shall see in Chapter 11.

Social class differences

Although class barriers may be changing, we can still argue that social class is one of the main sources of variation in our way of life. There are a wide range of social behaviours which vary in different social classes, covering just about every type of relationship you can mention. As with gender differences, there has been fierce debate over the extent and explanations of these differences. Particular debates which are especially important for interpersonal communication concern:

- *The issue of language* The suggestion that middle- and working-class people use different language codes has received particular attention for its significance to education (where of course most teachers are middle class).[10]
- *Cultural and subcultural differences* Given that different classes live under very different material conditions, it is not surprising if these differences are reflected in their perceptions and expectations.
- *Perceptions and stereotypes* Different stereotypes may well influence 'cross-class' communication in ways which are discussed in the next chapter.

I have tried to refer to the role of cultural, gender and class differences wherever possible in this book. However, these issues could fill a book on their own and do deserve more extended research.

Relating the components of the social context

Although it is useful to identify the separate components of the social context to explain how they work, they never work in isolation in real situations. The best way of illustrating the sorts of interactions which occur is to look at practical examples, so I shall highlight one area of research which has important practical implications for all of us – the nature of social relationships.

I have already suggested that social contact is very important for human beings, yet I can be more specific – it is not just the quantity but also the quality of social contact which is important. There is ample evidence that the quality of relationships we have with other people can influence our health and happiness. Good relationships affect these variables in positive ways; poor or non-existent relationships can have serious harmful effects. One aspect of this is whether we follow the rules which others recognise as important in the particular relationship. There are some important differences here, as follows.

Generality

Rules differ in their general application. For example, Argyle found that:[9]

- there are a small number of rules which can apply to all these relationships (e.g. respect the other person's privacy)
- there are rules which are important to some relationships but not to others (e.g. 'Engage in joking and teasing with the other person' is an important friendship and marriage rule but is not a significant neighbour rule).

Cultural differences

Different cultures may observe different rules for the same relationship. Once again the work of Michael Argyle and colleagues can illustrate this point. They distributed the same questionnaire on relationship rules to men and women in Italy, Hong Kong, Japan and the UK. Each respondent was asked their opinion on how far thirty-three rules could be applied to a range of relationships, e.g. husband–wife, doctor–patient. Only four of the rules were rated important in all relationships in all cultures:

1 Respect the other person's privacy.
2 Look the other person in the eye during conversation.
3 Do not discuss that which is said in confidence with the other person.
4 Do not criticise the other person publicly.

Group differences

Different groups within one society or culture will endorse rules differently. Argyle found both sex and age differences in the endorsement of specific rules for virtually all the relationships studied:

- There were interesting sex differences in relation to rules of intimacy. Although in many relationships women feel it is more important to express and share emotions, they also endorse rules about privacy more than men. This was true for all four cultures.

- You would probably expect to find age differences in adherence to rules, given the rate of social change which has occurred over the last twenty to thirty years. This role of change has also affected our relationships, as current statistics and attitudes on marriage, divorce and living together will illustrate. Argyle found the greatest discrepancy between young and old subjects in the British sample. One fairly consistent difference across this culture concerned intimacy rules – younger subjects felt you should express emotions more generally.

The time factor – how relationships develop

As well as identifying how the various components of the social context can interrelate, we must not forget that these factors can change over time. Again, the study of our relationships can illustrate this point. Communication is an essential ingredient in all stages of a relationship and most investigators have suggested that any relationship is likely to pass through a series of stages.

We can see different aspects of communication at each of these different stages.[11] To explain the stages, we can look at some of the factors involved in making friends.

Becoming aware of others

Before you can establish a relationship with someone you obviously need to be aware of their existence. And you need to have developed an impression of them. Factors which I have already discussed under the heading of social perception are also relevant here. Particularly important is the influence of physical proximity, social similarity and physical attractiveness. If we are placed in close physical proximity with other people, as in the corridor of a student hall of residence or a workgroup in a department, then we are likely to develop friendships within that group of people.

We are also likely to notice others who seem to come from similar social backgrounds, and we shall be looking for verbal and non-verbal codes such as dress, mannerisms, accent, etc. Physical attractiveness is a further powerful influence. Of course, you may not judge physical attractiveness in the way that I do, but we may be strongly influenced by stereotypes. Psychologists have found that there is a clear and positive stereotype of 'physically attractive persons' which gives them a number of advantages over us lesser mortals – for example, they are usually seen as more competent and more intelligent.

Making contact

You are in your first morning of a new job. Your boss introduces you to a person who will be one of your main team members. You go to the coffee machine with him or her. What do you talk about? How do you get the relationship off to a good start? First meetings like this are likely to have a fairly predictable pattern of communication with the following characteristics:

- people exchange non-controversial information about themselves
- they talk about their background and tend to stick to facts rather than opinions
- the initial few minutes will involve fairly rapid turn-taking using question–answer sequences

This pattern is not very surprising: exchanging background information is a fairly interesting way of passing time and is not likely to lead to any conflict. More importantly it allows each person to gather information which will enable them to decide whether to develop the relationship. If I find from this initial encounter that you have a similar background to me then I may well decide to try to develop a close relationship. Or I may decide that you are a bit 'wet', perhaps because you seem to live up to one of my negative stereotypes.

There are some other interesting points about these initial exchanges:

- if one person in the conversation does not follow the typical pattern then confusion or conflict will develop
- we can be heavily influenced by stereotypes (and gender/sex stereotypes may be especially important as discussed in the next chapter)
- the context may well mean that we can safely assume that the other person has certain attitudes

If I happen to meet you dressed in your famous Captain Picard disguise or wearing your Vulcan ears or perhaps even a Ferengi skull cap in the lobby of a hotel where a 'trekkies' convention is being held, then I can start the conversation on a rather different basis than if we meet in the same attire in a dentist's waiting room.

Developing contact into friendship

This is the next stage in developing a relationship. There are a number of interesting aspects to this process:

- We need to self-disclose to each other so that we can deepen our understanding of each other. If I self-disclose to you then I will expect you to reciprocate. In fact you will probably feel obligated to respond. And I can use this to push the relationship along. If you do not want to push the relationship along at the same pace, you will have to 'slow me down'.
- We can use particular strategies to express our commitment to the other person, e.g. we develop mutual trust when I trust you with some information which I see as private and vice versa.
- We need to adapt to each other's styles of communication.
- Both verbal and non-verbal cues are important.
- We need to act in a way which is appropriate to the level of relationship we have reached.
- We need to achieve 'balance'. In order to make the relationship mutually satisfying, we need to agree on what each of us is going to put in to the relationship. This is probably never consciously discussed but problems will soon emerge if one of us feels the other is not 'playing fair'.

Conclusion

Perhaps the most important conclusion to emerge from this chapter is simply to reaffirm the importance of the social context. However, it is also important to try to consider the social context in more detail and identify the components which are influencing particular examples of communication. For example, several important principles were identified in the last discussion of how friendships develop. These principles are not absolute and will vary depending upon context. What is considered to be 'fair' or 'balanced' will depend upon a range of social rules, norms and perceptions. And this highlights my final point: the factors identified in this chapter are interdependent and so their impact in any given situation may well be the result of quite a complicated process.

Chapter 6

Social identity

In this chapter, I shall:

- identify the main components of our social identity
- explain how these components influence the way we communicate with other people

What is social identity?

Perhaps the best way of showing what I mean by social identity is by using an example. I have already discussed the conversation between Dr Pouissant and the police officer. If we look again at this in a little more detail and offer a possible analysis of the doctor's character and self-perception, I can demonstrate the various components of social identity at work.

In terms of personality, it is likely that Dr Pouissant was not a very aggressive or outspoken person. His colleagues and friends would describe his personality as polite, gentle and considerate.

This was the way he usually behaved to other people and he was not usually greeted in a hostile way. So he would be taken aback when he was attacked in such a way. He was not used to this treatment.

Dr Pouissant saw himself as respectable and law abiding. He was certainly proud of his status in the community and would have worked hard to maintain it. The police officer's behaviour had such an effect because of the picture which Dr Pouissant had of himself, his self-concept. Dr Pouissant was a qualified medical doctor. He was very aware that he was expected to behave in certain ways because of the position he occupied. Remember also that this was a time of considerable racial tension. He would also be very aware that some other members of the black community would regard him as a role model. And he would wish to live up to these expectations. This role also meant that he was usually accorded a fair degree of respect by other people. The police officer's attack deliberately broke the usual rules!

This analysis suggests that there are three components of social identity: personality, self-concept and role. In most situations, these are strongly related to another. For example, if you have a very outgoing personality then you will probably see yourself as socially confident and likeable and you will take on roles which complement this view of yourself, e.g. party organiser. This does *not* mean that our behaviour is totally or even primarily determined by our personality (I shall discuss this in more detail later). There is ample evidence which suggests that if people are thrust into particular roles then this can affect both their self-concept and their personality. I shall look at some of these processes in more detail by examining each component in them.

Personality

Most definitions of human personality reflect a number of general principles that seem to be borne out in everyday life:[1]

- each of us has a specific set of personal characteristics
- this set of characteristics is fairly stable over time
- these characteristics influence how we behave and communicate

In recent years, however, some psychologists have adopted a rather different perspective on human personality. They have decided that our personalities are not such a powerful influence on our behaviour after all. There have been several factors which have contributed to this change of mind, as follows.

The search for adequate theory

There are several psychological theories of human personality. There is no one theory which is universally accepted. All of the theories so far seem to have important imitations. For example, there are problems of measurement and prediction. Personality tests or measures do not seem to be very good at predicting how people actually will behave. There are several problems here, as follows.

Personality types

Many theories try to categorise people into types and then investigate the properties of each type. You have probably heard of the distinction between extravert and introvert personalities. Researchers have suggested a number of significant differences between the true extravert and the introvert:

- Extraverts can be described as 'tough-minded individuals who need strong and varied external stimulation'.[2] They are sociable, optimistic, impulsive, etc.
- Introverts are 'tender-minded people who experience strong emotions and who do not need the extravert's intensity of external stimuli'. They are quiet, introspective, pessimistic, etc.

Unfortunately for the researchers relatively few of us are 'ideal' types. Most of us possess a mixture of extravert and introvert characteristics, which makes predicting our behaviour more uncertain.

Consistency of behaviour

When you examine closely how people actually behave in different situations, you find that they are often not very consistent. A person who is usually quite quiet and shy may behave in a very extrovert manner in some situations. As a result of these factors psychologists have focused attention upon the interaction between individual personalities and the situations they find themselves in. I shall return to the influence of situations in Chapter 7.

My own view of human personality follows these developments:

- we do possess a range of personal character traits
- these traits do influence how we behave and communicate
- these traits are *only one* influence upon our behaviour

Following this line of argument, I suggest that your personality influences your communication in two main ways:

1 *Predispositions* Our personality characteristics predispose us to behave in certain ways.
2 *Limitations* Our personality characteristics establish very broad limits for our communication. This is like the way physical characteristics can limit what you do physically. For example, it is very difficult to be a good long-distance runner unless you have a particular sort of physique. Similarly with psychological characteristics, our personality establishes certain limitations. Of course, these are not absolute limitations – if you are aware of your limitations you may be able to devise strategies to overcome them. Consider the case of the person who would like to become a great stage comedian but who is hampered with problems – he can't remember jokes and his sense of timing is rotten. On the one hand, we could perhaps overcome his limitations by determined training. Who knows what several years' training could do for him? On the other hand, he could play on his 'weaknesses' and develop an act based upon his incompetence, perhaps borrowing from classic acts like those of Tommy Cooper, Jerry Lewis and Norman Wisdom or modern versions like Lee Evans.

To return to more serious issues, someone who scores very high or low on a particular personality scale such as introversion/extroversion may have real psychological problems in coping with everyday life. But an extreme may be an 'ambiguous gift'. Individuals who are aware of their own tendencies may be able to control them and use them to advantage. And this raises the question of self-awareness which is at the heart of any discussion of the self-concept.

Self-concept

One of the distinctive features of human beings as a species is that we can think about our own actions and reactions. Of course, we take this ability for granted. But consider the range of things it enables us to do. It allows us to reflect upon our past experiences and make plans for the future. It enables us to develop ideas about ourselves. It means that we can also develop opinions about how other people see us, and how we would like to be seen by other people.

This then is the essential idea behind the self-concept. A typical definition is that by Carl Rogers:[3]

> organised, fluid, but consistent conceptual pattern of perceptions of characteristics and relationships of the 'I' or the 'me', together with values attached to these concepts.

Rogers makes the distinction between 'I' and 'me'. This distinction was elaborated by George Herbert Mead as a way of representing how human beings come to develop a concept of themselves.[4] The 'I' represents the self as actor and the 'me' represents the self's reflections about itself. This may be clearer with some examples of how these ideas develop.

The 'I'

Very young babies do not seem to distinguish between their own bodies and their surroundings. They do not have a clear idea of themselves as actors who can control objects around them. For example, when a rattle is dropped out of view babies seem to believe it has disappeared and no longer exists. As they become older they realise that they can act independently of their surroundings and go looking for the rattle. As they become older still, they actively seek to become independent. Witness the determination with which young children attempt to do basic jobs like putting clothes on. The adult who attempts to intervene can receive a very hostile response even when the child is struggling against all odds. For example, Markova refers to some classic research film of young children which shows:[5]

> children's tremendous persistence…in trying to sit on a stone without realising that one must turn one's back to the stone if one wants to sit on it.

So these children have developed the 'I', what Markova refers to as 'the spontaneous and acting component of the self', but have not developed the ability to reflect on what they are doing – the 'me'.

The 'me'

The 'me' has been defined as the reflective and evaluative component of the self. In order to evaluate your own actions you need to be able to consider them 'from outside' – in other words, you must be able to observe your own behaviour as if you were another person. You must be able to understand how other people might react to your actions and understand their thoughts and feelings.

The self-concept as personal theory

Another way of understanding the self-concept is to see it as a theory which you (and I) use in our everyday life. It is a theory that you have constructed about yourself, sometimes consciously but sometimes unwittingly. And it is part of a broader theory which you hold about the entire range of your significant experience. Like theories used by scientists, your self-theory is a conceptual tool for accomplishing a purpose. The two basic functions which are important for my analysis are:

1 *Self-esteem* Your self-esteem is your estimation of your worth or value. Although we all seem to have a very basic motivation to develop positive self-esteem, there is plenty of evidence that many people do not achieve this – they develop low self-esteem and life can become a very miserable and dispiriting experience.
2 *Organising information* Your self-concept helps you to organise all the information you experience so you can cope with it effectively. We are surrounded by so much information which we could attend to everyday that we would be swamped if we tried to take it all in. The self-concept acts as a 'personal organiser' so we know what to do and do not have to think about the details of our actions all the time.

This proposition that the self-concept is a personal theory has much in common with an influential view that we, as we go about the business of attempting to solve the problems of everyday living, act like the scientist who is trying to solve more impersonal problems, as follows.[6]

We continuously make and test hypotheses

The scientist may develop a hypothesis about certain chemicals – the influence of CFCs on the ozone layer – and make observations and/or develop experiments to see if their hypothesis is valid. In the same way we develop hypotheses about the world around us and test them out. As I was huddled over the word processor battling with the very first draft of this chapter, my younger son (5 years old at the time) popped in to see me. He revealed that he 'cannot go to sleep because the dogs are barking and could he go to sleep in the bedroom on the other side of the house?' This was his latest and most creative variant on his regular bed-time theme of wanting to stay up a bit longer. He was checking me out to see if this story was any more successful than last night's version of 'I'm not all that sleepy'. After a few minutes of amiable conversation where I assured him that 'the dogs will go to sleep themselves in a minute', he trotted back to bed to reflect on the success of tonight's creativity. Like all children, he was continually generating ideas of new social behaviours and trying them out to see if they work. Adults also do this of course, although perhaps not so creatively.

We revise our concepts and hypotheses if they do not seem to work

If the scientific experiment does not work then the scientist develops a new hypothesis – a different way of explaining events. If my social actions do not work then I also have to revise my social concepts and perhaps become more sophisticated in my assessment of which actions will achieve the desired effect. As I finished typing that last sentence on the very first draft (working on the word processor in the upstairs spare room), our phone rang in the kitchen. By the time I had got downstairs my younger son had answered the phone: 'I heard it ringing and I thought I'd better answer it!' His early action of complaining about the dogs had earned a short 'stay of bed-time'. But he had hypothesised that a helpful action would be another very useful strategy for postponing the possibility of having to go to sleep. And he was right – as he had to know who had phoned and why, this took another ten minutes before he had to go to bed. Although he was generally very good at answering the phone, I did notice that he was not usually as quick during the hours of play!

We organise our observations into patterns (schemata) which then are organised into much broader schemata (which can be called theories)

The scientist takes a number of observations and extracts more fundamental principles. These principles are then developed into systematic theories which apply within certain limits. An apple falling on the head, along with many other observations and tests, can be developed into the theory of gravity. Likewise we may have observed our parents behave towards us and, consciously or subconsciously, developed our ideas of what acting like a parent involves. As a result we develop ways of reacting to our parents and we develop ideas of how we are going to behave when we become parents. If we sit down and think about it we can probably express what these theories contain – almost certainly they will include principles of reward and punishment, and concepts of discipline, responsibility and personal freedom.

If our experience were not arranged like this, then it would be impossible to behave effectively in a complex world with innumerable conflicting demands. Further, without such a system the individual would be overwhelmed by innumerable isolated details that would have to be recalled to guide any particular piece of behaviour.

There is one important difference between my approach and Kelly's: Kelly assigns little significance to emotion and his methods concentrated on thoughts and cognitions. I believe we must give emotion a position of central importance in discussing the self-concept. I shall say more on this later.

But how does the self-concept develop?

Mead proposed that the self-concept arises in social interaction as an outgrowth of the individual's concern about how others react to the individual. In order to anticipate other people's reactions so that you can behave accordingly, you learn to perceive the world as these other people do. By making estimates of how this 'generalised other' would respond to certain actions, you build up a source of internal regulation. This will guide and stabilise your behaviour in the absence of external pressures. Other social scientists have emphasised the interaction of the child with significant others, particularly the mother figure, rather than with society at large.

The role of communication

At this point we can emphasise the role of communication in developing the self-concept. Take the example of our knowledge of our own bodies, e.g. tall versus short. Both of these descriptions are obviously relative terms – taller/shorter than what? – but they have general connotations in our society. The 'hero' in fiction is usually represented as tall whereas comic characters are often represented as short people – so much so that at least one of the classic film stars of Hollywood, Alan Ladd, had to resort to tricks like standing on a box and being filmed from specific angles so as not to reveal to the watching millions that he was smaller than most of his leading ladies. So how do people acquire this item of self-description? There are two main ways:

1 Direct training – we're actually told directly.
2 Indirect training – we work it out from a variety of cues which indicate that we have characteristics in common with some other people, yet different from others. Children are usually fascinated by the discovery that they have hands and feet that look more like other people's than like those of the dog or cat that inhabit the same household. In the same way we learn that people differ in behavioural characteristics, such as friendliness, aggressiveness and helpfulness.

Both these methods rely on communication, and one important implication of this approach is the degree we can be affected by other people's impressions of us. This is why many psychologists have stressed the importance of the communications we receive from our parents or parent figures in developing our early ideas of ourselves. For example, some researchers distinguish three types of response we can make to each other in any interaction: confirmation, rejection or disconfirmation. These have very different implications for the self-concept of the person being communicated to.[7]

- *Confirmation* If I confirm you then I take account of what you say, I pay attention to you and I accept you have the right to express whatever you are saying.
- *Rejection* If I reject you then I do not accept what you say but I do implicitly accept that you have the right to express yourself in that way.
- *Disconfirmation* If I disconfirm you then not only do I reject what you say but also I reject your very presence as a person. I may ignore you, or treat what you say as irrelevant, or even deliberately misinterpret it.

Both confirmation and rejection implicitly recognise the other person's self-concept as valid. Disconfirmation threatens this validity. For a very simple example, take this mother–child interchange:[8]

Boy: Look, mom, I found a snail.
Mother: Go wash your hands.

The mother ignores the content of the boy's speech and delivers a very definite judgement of irrelevance which was probably reinforced by accompanying non-verbal signals of distaste. This one incident may not be deeply significant. But what if the process is repeated time and time again? And what if it occurs when the child is trying to say something which he or she considers important? For a more fundamental example consider an anecdote from a well-known female author.[9] As a child she felt her father had continually picked on her and dismissed her achievements. When she published her first novel and brought a copy home, her father greeted her with a very powerful disconfirming message. He looked at the book and commented: 'Costs £4.95…is it really worth it?' The one encouraging aspect of this anecdote is that the author had had sufficient strength to overcome the barrage of negative messages which she had received from her father over the years. And this shows that we can change the way we think about ourselves and behave differently.

One consequence of continual disconfirmation could be the development of very low self-esteem. And of course your level of self-esteem is reflected in your communication. A high degree of self-esteem is likely to lead to a confident, assertive communication style; a low degree to a tentative pessimistic style.

Social roles

The term 'role' originally came from the theatre. We talk about the various roles which the actors play when they give a performance. Some social scientists have been keen to develop this as an analogy with social life in general.[10] The notion is that we spend a good deal of everyday life 'performing', i.e. we play parts which are largely predetermined. I shall return to this analogy later but first I need to spell out the concept of role in more detail.

It was Ralph Linton, an American sociologist, who first popularised the concept of role in social science.[11] He was trying to develop a set of concepts which explained how human society was organised. He concluded that every society contained a variety of positions. For each position there was a status, which gave you your place in the pecking order of society, and a role, which prescribed the expected behaviour and attitudes.

People knew how to behave because of these roles. If you took up a position in society you would know how to behave because you knew what the role involved. This of course also meant that you knew how and what to communicate. Understanding society was a matter of outlining the roles for every position in that society. We can certainly look back to previous periods such as the late nineteenth and early twentieth century and note the concerns among the upper and middle classes about the 'proper way to behave' which generated a continuous stream of books and advice on etiquette to cover every possible situation. Nowadays, much of this advice sounds bizarre:[12]

> A public display of affection anywhere and at anytime is unrefined. Love is sacred, and its expressions should not be exposed to the rude comments of strangers.

Linton's approach to understanding roles became very influential, but some problems became apparent. It offers a rather 'static' view of society whereas we know that society does change over time. Roles do change. Also we can see that people do not necessarily agree on what a specific role involves. For example, there has recently been a lot of argument over the role of priests in the Anglican church:

- Should they be involved in political debates?
- Should women be allowed to occupy the role?

There are a number of ways of dealing with these questions. All of them have implications for communication.

Role set

No social role exists in isolation. Any given role is always related to other roles. You can hardly be a teacher unless there are pupils or students. In fact, for every given role (usually called the focal role), there are a number of other roles which are related to it. These other roles are called the role set. The most important thing about these roles in the role set is that each one makes demands upon the focal role. These demands are usually called the sent role. Figure 6.1 and an example should make this clearer.

Take the example of students as a focal role. Any student is likely to know their own ideas on how to behave as a student. They will find that other people in other roles expect them to behave in particular ways. This gives rise to another phenomenon which has very important implications for communication, as follows.

Role conflict

Role conflict occurs when there is some discrepancy between these different expectations. There are several varieties of role conflict. Perhaps the most significant in what is referred to as 'conflict-between-role-senders'. Going back to my student example, the student may find that lecturers expect them to devote virtually all their spare time to studying; other students may expect them to participate fully in union social activities. There may be other conflicting pressures which the student has to reconcile.

Role obligations

If different occupants of the same role seem to behave rather differently, perhaps this is because they have a slightly different idea of

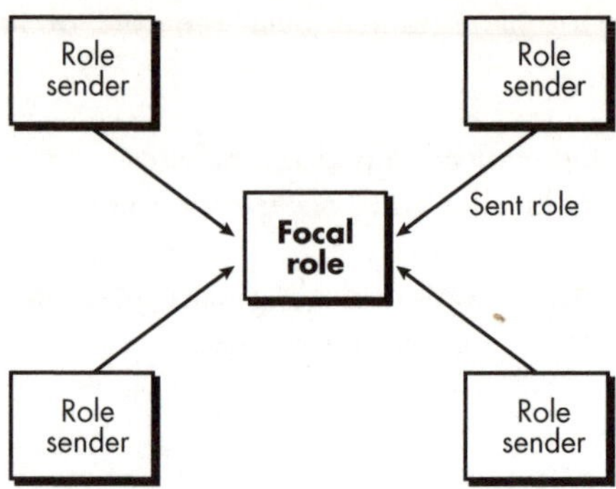

Figure 6.1 Role diagram

their role obligations. Any role is liable to have a wider range of obligations associated with it. To make things even more complicated, there is likely to be different types or levels of obligation. Dahrendorf talks of three levels of obligations associated with any given role:[13]

1 *MUST DO* These are activities which role occupants must do. If they do not, they will feel definite sanctions, probably legal ones.
2 *SHOULD DO* These are activities which role occupants should do but where the prospect of sanctions is not so strong if they fail.
3 *CAN DO* These are activities which are not 'required' but which the effective role player often includes.

Negotiated roles

Another approach which has emerged stresses that social roles are not totally laid down or predetermined. To return to the theatre analogy: in most plays, all the lines and stage directions are usually written down for the actors. However, the directors and actors can make an enormous difference to the play depending upon how they interpret the roles. They obviously know how to work together and have to plan how their roles will relate to one another. In other words, they have to negotiate roles with one another.

These processes of interpretation and negotiation also occur in everyday social life. For example, take a role which is fraught with problems – the role of parent. There are a number of ways in which husbands and wives can interpret their respective roles. Apart from the thorny question of what each partner should do, they have to negotiate how they do it and who does what. Problems arise when this negotiation does not take place. This does not mean that every married couple should necessarily sit down and discuss how they relate to one another, in the way that actors and directors discuss plays. Usually this negotiation in everyday life is a matter of gradual accommodation and change.

Another implication of this approach is the suggestion that successful social interaction and communication depends upon all the respective participants adopting complementary roles. This has been highlighted in recent studies of how people cope in embarrassing situations.

Conclusion

When we behave we decide upon our actions in terms of how those actions relate to the various components of our social identity. Of course, we do not necessarily do this consciously – many of our decisions are taken subconsciously. It is probably only when we experience conflict such as role conflict that we become aware of some of these processes. Perhaps we should think about these processes more often, as misunderstanding and conflict frequently arise from behaviour based on different interpretations of our social identity.

Another issue which this chapter has not resolved is the almost inevitable tension between these different components: how do we reconcile the different impressions of ourselves which we gain from everyday life? And this reflects what Richard Jenkins has called the 'internal external dialectic of identification' – the fact that 'identity must…be validated (or not) by those with whom we have dealings. *Social identity is never unilateral*.'[14] And this raises issues of social perception, which takes us to the next chapter.

Chapter 7

Social perception

In this chapter, I shall:

- define and illustrate the importance of social perception
- explain and examine a number of theoretical approaches which have been used to explain social perception
- discuss some important categories of information which we perceive and interpret in social events
- examine issues of accuracy and bias in our social perception

What is social perception?

By social perception, I mean those processes whereby an individual makes sense of and interprets the nature of the other people involved in the conversation, and the nature of the setting in which they find themselves. If that sounds rather a mouthful then I can easily illustrate the importance of social perception with a few examples, as follows.

The new lecturer example

In one very famous experiment, Harold Kelley gave a group of university students a short written description of a new visiting lecturer just before they received the lecture. Unbeknown to the students, two forms of the description were distributed at random. The only difference between the two forms was that the phrase 'very warm' was used to describe the lecturer on one version, and the phrase 'very cold' was used on the other. So each student read a description of Mr X something like this:

> Mr X is a graduate student in the Department of Economics and Social Science. He has had three semesters of teaching experience in psychology at another college. This is his first semester teaching this module. He is 26 years old and married. People who know him consider him to be a rather cold (or, 'very warm') person, industrious, critical, practical, and determined.

After the class (which included a discussion session lasting about twenty minutes), Kelley asked the students to rate the lecturer. There were marked differences in these ratings depending on which prior description the students had read. 'Warm' students saw the lecturer as successful, popular, happy, humorous, etc. 'Cold' students saw the lecturer as stingy, unsuccessful, unpopular and unhappy. There was also a marked difference in class participation: 56 per cent of the 'warm' students took part in the discussion; only 32 per cent of the 'cold' students did so.

This experiment suggests that there is some truth in the statement that we see what we expect to see. The students gained their initial impression from the written description and seemed to stick to it regardless of the evidence available to them. They also behaved in accordance with what they thought was true rather than actual events. This behaviour then reinforced their initial impression. If you participate in a discussion then you're liable to see the leader more positively than if you sit aloof, simply because you've received some reactions from him.[1]

This sort of process has been described as a 'self-fulfilling prophecy':

- someone is 'labelled' in a particular way

- this makes other people expect that person to behave in specific ways
- these other people then behave towards the labelled person on the basis of their expectations
- the person reacts and probably lives up to the expectations

An example may make this clearer. Suppose a new pupil arrives at a boys' school after a rumour that he is a 'trouble-maker'. The other pupils and teachers will expect him to live up to this reputation and may well greet him in a suspicious or hostile way. The newcomer reacts to what he see as a hostile welcome, possibly by retaliating in a hostile way, and the 'prophecy' has come true. Of course, labels can also be positive but the process will be the same.

There is some evidence that self-fulfilling prophecies can have long-term effects. Unfortunately Kelley's experiment only looked at a fairly short event. The class only lasted twenty minutes. What would have happened to the students' perceptions if the class had lasted longer, or if they had seen the lecturer again on a number of occasions?

The spectators' example

Another classic experiment within social psychology studied the perceptions of spectators after a particularly rough game of American football between Dartmouth and Princeton. The investigators asked spectators who was responsible for the rough play. If you have ever been involved in team sports you will probably not be surprised to learn that the supporters' perceptions were consistently different. For example, only 36 per cent of the Dartmouth students thought that their team had started the rough play, whereas 86 per cent of the Princeton students thought that the Dartmouth team had.

The social constructs example

Forgas studied how samples of Oxford students and middle-class married women perceived similar events.[2] He found that they had rather different sets of social constructs, and interpreted similar situations very differently. For example, the two groups had very different reactions to 'socialising with friends'. Students perceived events involving entertainment and socialising with friends with great self-confidence. While socialising with friends for students was a natural, self-selected entertainment, for the women it was a much more formal, organised affair. This meant they were very conscious of how they wanted to present themselves in these situations – they were concerned about 'making social mistakes' and the potential loss of face.

These differences reflected differences in the way the different groups saw the situation. They were not because of any systematic differences in personality characteristics. For example, the results do not mean that the students surveyed were all very self-confident. In fact, they reported frequent feelings of lacking self-confidence in other situations, e.g. situations where you have to become acquainted with strangers, such as parties.

So different groups can have very different subjective definitions of interactions, even though they involve nearly indistinguishable activities and 'objective' characteristics. This means that classifying social episodes in terms of 'objective' factors will almost certainly not tap the psychologically meaningful differences.

How can we explain social perception?

There has now been considerable research on the ways in which we perceive other people. Unfortunately there has been less attention paid to our perception of social situations. So I shall concentrate on the evidence that concerns person perception.

Person perception

The early work on person perception tended to focus on how people interpreted various personality traits.[3] Researchers looked at which traits seemed to be most important and which traits seemed to go together. Some interesting conclusions came from this work which was based on the notion of implicit personality theory, i.e. that we all have organised ideas of what personality traits usually go together. More recent developments have concentrated on how people develop their own ideas about other people (attribution theory) and on how these ideas are organised (personal construct theory). Unfortunately, all these researches developed from rather different backgrounds and so it is difficult to integrate them very smoothly into one explanation. However, I shall make some suggestions on this once I have examined each in turn.

Implicit personality theory

This notion is based upon a number of important findings, as follows.

Coherent perceptions

People do have a coherent picture of which personality traits tend to go together in other people. For example, if you hear someone described as warm then you are also liable to think that that person is popular, happy, successful, etc. Some of these associations seem to be very strong whereas others are relatively weak. For example, if you ask people to judge the intelligence of others based on a selection of photographs, then they will tend to choose people wearing glasses as more intelligent than those without. This also applies when you ask for first impressions of people who have only just met. However, after only a few minutes of conversation the effect disappears. There is no longer any consistent difference associated with wearing glasses. People are obviously using other cues from the conversation.

Organised perceptions

These impressions are organised so that some traits are much more important or central than others. For example, I have already described Kelley's 'warm/cold' experiment. These traits – warm and cold – do seem to be very influential. In a set of earlier experiments, Asch provided students with a list of seven traits which were characteristic of individual X.[4] The students then had to write a general description of X and also judge X on various dimensions. If X was described as warm or cold these adjectives coloured the whole descriptions which emerged along the lines that Kelley also found. Substituting other terms such as polite or blunt for warm or cold made much less of a difference.

Although this approach generated a great deal of interesting research it did not provide very convincing answers to a number of important questions, in particular:

- How are various traits organised?
- Why are certain traits central?

There has been more recent research designed to answer these questions but the general focus has moved on to the question of how people arrive at their own, often very unique, views on other people.

Personal construct theory

This theory was first developed by George Kelly who was concerned that theories such as implicit personality theory failed to recognise that all human beings are in some ways unique and that they develop their own very individual ways of making sense of the world. According to Kelly, we all have an internal set of mental categories which we use to organise our perceptions. He called these categories personal constructs and developed a technique to discover them – the repertory grid. This technique has been described as follows:

> the subject is asked for the names of ten to fifteen people in certain relationships, e.g. 'a friend of the same sex', 'a teacher you liked'. The names are written on cards and presented to him three at a time. The subject is asked which two of the three are most similar, and in what way the other one differs, thus eliciting one of his 'constructs'. When a number of constructs have been found, a 'grid' is made up in which all the target persons are rated on all the constructs. Statistical methods can be used to find the general dimensions which are most used by the subject.[5]

Personal construct theory was first developed for use in psychotherapy, for use with individuals. As a result it is not designed to establish broad generalisations about how people perceive one another. However, it has generated a great deal of research and can offer some interesting generalisations:

- men and women seem to use rather different constructs
- some people have very simple construct systems, other people fairly complex ones
- people with very simple construct systems will have a very distorted picture of other people; in extreme cases this can mean that they cannot behave very effectively in social situations

Attribution theory

Attribution theory is a more recent development which attempts to explain how people perceive one another. This theory is particularly interested in how people decide the *cause* of other people's actions. It can also be used to examine how we explain our own actions. One way of explaining this theory is to explain the model proposed by Jones and Davis.[6]

Imagine yourself observing another person, A, behaving. You would be able to observe two main things:

1 A' s actions
2 the effect of A's actions

For example, if A was shouting at X, you could observe this and see what effect this was having on the other person – are they paying attention, laughing, crying, or what? Let us assume that X is crying.

Attribution theory now tries to explain what sort of personal impression A makes on you. Do you decide that A is rude, angry and bullying? Or do you decide that A is doing what A is doing because of the situation rather than because of some aspect of A's own character? According to Jones and Davis, you make a series of judgements about A before you can finally decide on A's character. Firstly you decide upon:

- KNOWLEDGE: did A know that this behaviour would have the actual effect, i.e. make the other person cry?
- ABILITY: was A capable of producing this outcome intentionally? Or did A achieve that outcome by chance? For example, you do not decide that someone is a great golfer on the basis of one lucky shot even if it is a hole-in-one.

On the basis of these decisions you decide upon:

- A's INTENTIONS: what was A trying to achieve?

On the basis of this decision you then decide upon:

- A's DISPOSITION, i.e. A's personal characteristics

To return to our example, suppose you decided that A knew that shouting at X would make X cry, and that A is capable of deliberately shouting at someone to make them cry. You would then conclude that A intended to humiliate X and may well decide that A is cruel, nasty or whatever. If on the other hand you decided that A did not anticipate that shouting would make X cry, and that A is not normally capable of shouting aggressively at people, then you would look for other explanations. You would probably decide that A did not intend to humiliate X but that something else had caused A to shout and X in turn to cry.

This model can be used to explain how different people can arrive at different interpretations of the same incident. Take another mock example: imagine a large family party and focus on three characters – Arnold, an undergraduate student, his Uncle John and his Uncle Jack. The drinks are flowing freely and Arnold is observed drinking rather a lot of punch. Later on in the evening he becomes abusive and aggressive. He calls Uncle Jack 'a daft old git' and becomes even more colourful in his language to other family members. This upsets quite a few people and Arnold is politely shown the door. How did people interpret Arnold's behaviour? And how can we explain their interpretations, using the attribution theory model?

Arnold's explanation (the morning after)

> 'I am very sorry. I didn't know the punch was so alcoholic. Normally I'm not able to get drunk so easily. I didn't intend to upset people – it's just not my nature.'

Uncle Jack's version

> 'He knew exactly what he was doing. He's quite capable of pretending that it's the drink that's doing it. He intended to make a scene as he didn't want to come in the first place. He's a nasty, malicious young tearaway.'

Uncle John's version

> 'I'm sure Arnold didn't know he was getting drunk and nasty. He's not capable of doing a thing like that. He didn't intend to make a scene. He'll have to be careful what he drinks next time.'

Uncle Jack clearly sees Arnold's behaviour as evidence for his underlying, rather nasty disposition. Both Arnold and Uncle John suggest that Arnold's behaviour was caused by the situation – the accidental effect of an overpowerful punch. They do not use the event as evidence of Arnold' s underlying disposition.

Subsequent research has tended to alter some detailed characteristics of Jones and Davis' model but the basic principles remain. There has been considerable interest in the problem of deciding whether you attribute causes to the person (as Uncle Jack did) or to the situation (as Uncle John did). This seems to depend on a number of characteristics:

- *Distinctiveness* Is the behaviour distinctive in some way? The more distinctive the behaviour the more likely you are to attribute it to the person.
- *Consensus* If everybody agrees on your impression of X's behaviour then you will be more confident about attributing it to the person.
- *Consistency over time* If you see X as confident then you will stick to that judgement if your impression does not change with repeated observations.
- *Consistency over modality* If you see X as generous then you will stick to that judgement if X behaves generously in different situations.

The research has also shown that we are susceptible to a number of biases which I shall discuss later.

Reconciling the different approaches

As I said earlier the different approaches cannot simply be added together to provide a coherent model of person perception – they are based on rather different assumptions. However, they do point to a number of general conclusions which I can offer about person perception, as follows.

Organisation

Our perceptions of other people are organised. We do believe that certain characteristics go together in people even if there is no concrete evidence to support these associations.

Perception influences communication

Our perception of other people influences how we communicate with them. Kelley's 'cold' students tended not to take part in the class discussion.

Personal bias

Our perception of other people may be more of a reflection of our own beliefs about the world than of the other people's behaviour or actual personality. In an ingenious experiment, Dornbusch asked subjects to provide descriptions of other people. He then compared these various descriptions to see how much disagreement/agreement there was.[7] For example, he compared:

- A's description of person C
- A's description of person D
- B's description of person C

As persons C and D were different personalities you would expect A to describe them rather differently. And you would expect A and B to give similar descriptions of C. In fact, the study showed that subjects were viewing different other people by applying much the same constructs. There was usually more in common in A's description of different people than between A's and B's description of the same person.

Inferences

Our perception of other people may contain quite an elaborate set of inferences and decisions based upon a very wide range of evidence. This comes out very clearly from analyses of systematic biases discussed by attribution theorists, which I shall examine later.

Resistance to change

Our perception of people may be resistant to change, even in the face of contrary evidence. We may be 'taken in' by a self-fulfilling prophecy or we may simply choose to ignore contrary information. There is ample evidence for this in the research on stereotypes which I shall discuss later.

Perceiving the situation

As I said earlier, there has been much less research into the ways we perceive or interpret social situations. However, this is now changing.[8] Thus, there are a few useful points I can make, as follows.

Rules

People do recognise the rules which seem to be demanded by a particular situation, even though they may not be able to tell you the rules without a great deal of thought.

Constructs

In the same way that we have a construct system about people, we have constructs about situations. For example, in Forgas's study his sample of students used three major dimensions in judging the social situations they were involved in:

1 involvement/non-involvement
2 pleasant/unpleasant
3 know how to behave/do not know how to behave

People and situations

Our perception of other people is inextricably bound up with our perception of the situation we believe they are in.

How accurate are our perceptions of other people?

There is evidence that some people are much more accurate in their perceptions than others. It also appears that such skill is unrelated to age or experience. You cannot expect to become more accurate in your judgements of others simply by growing older. Unfortunately these generalisations disguise a number of quite complicated issues.[9] For example, what does being accurate involve? Suppose you are asked to predict the behaviour of Miss X, who is taking her dog for a walk in the evening when she sees a child falls off her bike in the road. Suppose you also know that X is an policewoman. If you happen to know a lot about police training and practices you would have a very good idea how the typical police officer would behave. The fact that X is technically off duty would probably make no difference. She would use all the expertise and experience from her training. So you could give a very accurate prediction of what X would do. But does this mean you are an accurate person perceiver? No – you would have displayed your expertise and understanding of police training, but you would not really have shown how accurately you can judge an individual's characteristics.

There are other problems which crop up in investigating this topic. For example, people's behaviour does change significantly across different situations. What is their 'true character'? Does it make sense to talk of someone's 'real character'? It has proved a lot easier to investigate errors or distortions in human perception and there is now considerable research on what those are and how they operate. I shall look at two of these sources of error in more detail – stereotypes and attribution biases.

Stereotypes

We are all familiar with a number of social stereotypes. A great deal of humour is based upon supposed 'facts' about specific social groups: the Scots are mean, the Irish are stupid, the Welsh can sing, etc. There is, of course, plenty of evidence to refute these categorisations but people may still believe them. And this brings us to a definition of a stereotype:

> A category is a stereotype when the members of a culture or a subculture unquestioningly believe that a particular concept characterizes all members of a group.[10]

Not all stereotypes are negative and the targets of stereotypes may agree with the judgement made of them. For example, both the English and the Americans see the Americans as easy going, casual, informal, etc. Some of the most important implications of stereotyping for the subject of this book are given below. Of course, stereotypes have much broader significance in social life because of their possible influences on an individual's sense of identity, and I shall try to bring out some of these influences by using gender stereotypes in the examples.

Stereotypes as 'overgeneral' beliefs

Surveys of gender stereotypes have found very clear stereotypes associated with the different sexes. The supposed male traits include competency, rationality and assertiveness – typical adjectives included active, adventurous, aggressive, dominant, strong, etc. The traits attributed to women tend to emphasise personal warmth and expressiveness – typical adjectives included affectionate, emotional, gentle, sensitive, submissive, etc. These differences are reported consistently in many different countries.[11]

An interesting illustration of the power of such beliefs comes from that well-known cultural phenomenon – *Star Trek*. In the pilot proposals for the original television series, producer Gene Rodenberry characterised the 'Number One' post as occupied by 'a glacierlike, efficient female who serves as Ship's Executive Officer'.[12] However, audience tests on the pilot episode ('The Cage') showed that audience reaction to the character 'ranged from resentment to disbelief'. Rodenberry agreed to drop the character and her personality traits were transplanted onto an alien, Mr Spock, who became Number One. Stereotypes won the day. Although *Star Trek* was a show about the twenty-third century, it was being viewed by an unenlightened twentieth-century audience – who resented the idea of a tough, strong-willed woman (too domineering!) as second-in-command. At least this suggests that some things have changed over the last few decades – witness the way Captain Janeway has been accepted at the helm of *Voyager* in the most recent *Star Trek* spin-off series.

On a more serious note it is important to remember that the beliefs which underpin stereotypes may be believed by both the target and the groups advocating the stereotype. For example, Brigham reports several studies where women seem to *expect* to perform more poorly on tasks than men, in ways that reinforce the traditional stereotypes.[11] Happily there is also evidence to show that these patterns may be changing.

Stereotypes as 'cues' to action

If you have a strong traditional sex-role stereotype then this will predispose you to act in certain ways. For example, consider the implications of the finding that:

> teachers…expect higher levels of intelligence, independence and logic from pupils described as possessing typically masculine characteristics.[13]

This expectation will undoubtedly be reflected in some aspects of these teachers' behaviour with consequent effect upon the pupils who have been categorised.

Attribution biases

Another area of possible bias and distortion in our social perception is the so-called attribution biases which came to light during the work on attribution theory mentioned earlier in this chapter. There is not space here to provide a comprehensive survey of these but I can mention a couple of the most 'dramatic' to highlight their significance.

Self-serving bias

Earlier in this chapter, I gave examples of errors due to faulty perception. This bias is due to motivation – usually the motivation to avoid blame. For example, teachers may claim responsibility for pupils' success while blaming lack of improvement on the pupils themselves.

'Just world' hypothesis

This is the tendency to believe that people are somehow to blame for any misfortunes that befall them. This is a most unfortunate bias to meet in a judge or magistrate, especially if you happen to be in the dock.

Conclusion

This chapter has tried to highlight some of the major processes underlying our social perception. Almost inevitably the discussion has focused on 'errors' and 'distortions' where perception can create misunderstandings and conflict. So perhaps the best way to conclude is simply by summarising major sources of error, using a list adapted from the work of Michael Argyle:[14]

- Assuming a person will behave in the same way in other situations. People can behave very differently in different situations, and it is important not to overlook situational causes of observed behaviour.
- Trying too hard to construct a consistent picture of the other. Of course, stereotypes can be important here, and there is also the danger of rigid attribution biases.
- Being influenced too much by first impressions. Physical appearance and accent may be especially significant, as may certain corresponding stereotypes.
- Making positive evaluations and giving favourable ratings to people from the same background.
- Being influenced too much by negative points.
- Making constant errors. This may be the consequence of an overgeneralised construct system, whereby everyone is regarded as second rate, aggressive, or whatever.
- Lack of attention. This can be a particular problem for people who are too wrapped up in their own dilemmas.

Chapter 8

Codes 1

Codes and language

In this chapter, I shall:

- explain why it is helpful to use the concept of codes when we analyse human communication
- introduce the range of different codes which are used in human communication
- explain important characteristics of human language
- analyse some important ways in which language works as a communication code
- introduce different approaches to the analysis of language in use (discourse analysis)

Why is the concept of 'codes' useful in the analysis of human communication?

Before I look at the implications of examining human communication as a set of different codes, I had better clarify what I mean by a code:

> A code is generally defined as a system into which signs are organised, governed by consent.[1]

An example may make this clearer: the Morse code. In this code, there is only a very limited set of signs – two taps of different lengths (long and short) are combined in various ways to represent letters. Only the two types of tap are used to avoid confusion. If you know the code then you can communicate with someone else who has the right equipment. If you do not obey the rules then your message will not be understood. Very experienced users are also able to do things that inexperienced users cannot. For example, a very experienced user of Morse code can often identify someone at the other end of the line simply from the way they tap, by using clues like the rhythm of the taps!

So important features of all codes are:

- the defined set of signs or symbols
- the rules for putting these signs together
- a group of users who recognise what these signs mean
- other groups who lack this knowledge
- different levels of expertise in interpreting the signs

All these considerations apply if we think about human language. And one reason for talking about codes is that any one human language, say English, is composed of a number of different codes depending upon who uses it and how they use it. Specific groups within society develop specific ways of using language which suit their own needs and which may not be readily understood by non-members. We shall return to this issue later, but for the moment we can use professional jargon as an obvious example. You may have attended a pop or rock concert and overheard the stage crew talking to one another using strange and wonderful terms – bins, eq, monitor, foldback. Some of these words do crop up in everyday speech but with a very different meaning, e.g. bin.

One obvious advantage of this special use of language is that it can make communication more economical or efficient. However, problems can occur if there is any scope for different interpretations in the language. Consider the pilot of the Boeing 747 who said 'We are now at take-off' to the air-traffic controller. He meant that the plane was *in the process of* taking off. The air-traffic controller interpreted this to mean that the plane was *waiting* at the take-off point. The resulting misunderstanding led to two planes colliding on the runway with a loss of nearly 600 lives.[2]

Problems are even more likely when a specialist has to communicate to a non-specialist. Unfortunately these problems can sometimes go unrecognised with tragic consequences. For example, there is evidence to suggest that the Pearl Harbour attack by the Japanese which brought the Americans into the Second World War could have been predicted if American officials had interpreted an earlier message from the Japanese correctly. Apparently, the American translators took the literal version of certain words rather than recognising the meaning which the Japanese intended and which Japanese natives would have recognised.[3]

On a more mundane level, consider the special language codes which are used by British doctors when communicating with patients. For example, if a doctor asks you 'Is your pain chronic?', what do you think this means? Some people interpret a chronic pain as a severe pain, others as a regular pain. This difference can mean a dramatic difference in how the doctor will interpret symptoms. The doctor is actually asking how regular the pain is, i.e. is it there all the time or not? Misinterpreting the code and giving the 'wrong' answer could lead to an incorrect diagnosis!

Another anecdote illustrates the potential tragedy which can arise from these sorts of misunderstanding. A patient had received tests for cancer. The doctor told him the tests were negative, i.e. no symptoms of cancer had shown up. The patient interpreted negative in an everyday sense of the term, i.e. bad, not positive, unfortunate, etc. He was so worried that he decided he could not face the illness and promptly committed suicide.

Just to make life more complicated, we have all the non-verbal signals available to us apart from those which are tied up in the language. A few examples here will show that we can also use the concept of code to cover non-verbal communication. For example, many gestures have meanings in one culture which are different or perhaps even the opposite in another. What do you think the following gestures mean and where could you use them?

(a) someone bends over to show their buttocks to you and slaps them in the centre

(b) someone raises their hand to you with the thumb and tip of the forefinger joined up to form a vertical ring

According to Desmond Morris, gesture (a) is an insult which would be regarded as obscene in many areas of Eastern Europe and the Middle East.[4] Visitors from that area to the UK may be taken aback to see an attractive young female use a very similar gesture in a supermarket advert on TV, to mean there is extra money in her pocket because of the supermarket's low prices. Gesture (b) means OK or good in North America and Europe but is probably best avoided in Arab countries where there are two very similar gestures which are either threatening or obscene.

These examples show that gestures can have systematic meanings in one culture which are very different in another. In some cases, they may mean the opposite. According to Morris, the 'head toss' where the head is 'tilted vigorously backwards' means 'yes' in Ethiopia and 'no' in Turkey.[5] This gesture also means 'no' in Italy, but only in those parts of Italy which were once under Greek control over 2,000 years ago. This suggests that some gestures can remain stable over very long periods of time even despite the increasing rates of social change and mobility.

What are the main characteristics of human language?

One of the most interesting features of human language is the fact that it appears to be unique to us. Although there have recently been some interesting experiments with monkeys and dolphins, no other species seems to have a verbal system quite like ours. Consider a few aspects of human language which we tend to take for granted:

- we can invent completely new words or phrases
- we can tell lies
- we can change the meaning of existing words, e.g. around twenty years ago, the term 'gay' simply meant frivolous or jolly

No animal species is able to do all these things with their communication. And this is largely attributable to the way in which human language works. We can start to appreciate some of the complexities of human language by looking at:

- how language is made up
- how language develops
- how we learn language
- how different types of language can be defined

How language is made up

The verbal system has understandably received most attention from researchers and theorists and we can fairly easily analyse the component parts. The explanations below show how you can look at language at various levels, each of which has its own rules and characteristics:

Level of analysis	*Definition*
Phoneme	Basic unit of sound used in speech

Every human language has a fairly small number of basic sounds (usually around thirty). These are combined in various ways to create words. Some languages have sounds which do not exist in others, e.g. the Scottish pronunciation of 'ch' in loch comes from the Gaelic and does not exist in Standard English.

Level of analysis	*Definition*
Morpheme	Smallest meaningful unit of language

This is a word or part of a word. For example, bed contains one morpheme, bedside contains two, and bedridden contains three.

Here we need to look at the meaning of words. And this is where we notice a major difference between human and animal language. For humans, any given word can have different meanings depending on the context in which it is used, e.g. give. We also develop our own unique associations for words, e.g. for me, the mention of raisins always brings back memories of school dinners for reasons too painful to describe.

Level of analysis	*Definition*
Utterance	That combination of words which expresses an idea

Written language is expected to conform to the rules of English grammar, e.g. every sentence must have a verb. As we see later in this chapter, just to make matters more complicated, spoken language often breaks these rules and yet is perfectly acceptable and understandable.

I could continue this analysis into several more levels but this disguises some important complications. This is a 'bottom-up' analysis of the language code, i.e. starting from the smallest units and working up the scale. When we listen to and interpret what other people are saying we also seem to use 'top-down' analysis. In other words, because of our tendency to perceive in organised patterns we look for overall structure and interpret the detail in the light of this overall 'map'.

How language develops

One of the most fascinating areas of language study is the investigation of the ways children develop their language skills, and the way these build up over the first few years of life. Table 8.1 illustrates the main early stages.[6]

From this brief summary, we can see some of the complexities of the language system starting to emerge – for example, the importance of the social context in determining exactly what someone means. By this two-word stage, children are able to have quite extended exchanges with the adults around them although this often depends on the adults doing quite a lot of 'translation' work. And this raises issues of how children learn to develop their language.

How we learn language

One feature of early child/adult talk is the way adults encourage and reinforce the child's speech by asking questions, by expanding what the child says, and by inviting the child to say more. The child is doing much more than simply imitating the speech of those around him or her, and we still have large and embarrassing gaps in our knowledge of how these processes work.

Table 8.1 Early language development

Stage	*Characteristics*
Crying	Small babies have at least three different types of cry which parents learn to recognise: hunger, pain and a third to indicate some combination of bored/tired/uncomfortable. These cries have different pitches and rhythms. Before long, parents and carers will notice a fourth type of cry emerge which is simply designed to capture adult attention. The baby has made the first move into social interaction through communication.
Cooing and babbling	Sometimes these sounds do sound conversational; sometimes babies seem to be just trying out their vocal chords.
Early expression	Recognisable expressions seem to emerge around nine months. These are often used to communicate specific thoughts. For example, one of my children used 'gogum' to mean 'I want some more'. As these recognisable words grow, cooing and babbling dies away. Also the expressions are used in a variety of ways. The child will now start to use recognisable words (like 'dada' for daddy) and will use them for different purposes (with different intonation dada can mean 'hello daddy', 'that is daddy', or 'where is daddy?').
Two-word utterances	The child starts to put two words together ('dada help') and starts to develop a command of syntax. As with the single words, the same two-word sequence can be used in different contexts to mean different things.

We do know that some codes are more complicated or difficult to interpret than others. For example, children often fail to recognise sarcasm. A sarcastic remark is often distinguished from a sincere remark by the pattern of intonation and it seems that this is quite a complex code to interpret, as we shall also see about other non-verbal codes in the next chapter.

Another important feature of language learning is that children pick up the dialect and accent from the speech community in which they live and this will have very important interpersonal consequences. If you have a specific accent then you will pronounce words in the same way as other members of the specific social group or people from the same region. For example, in the UK compare how Liverpudlians, Geordies and Highlanders would pronounce 'book'.

Your dialect includes your pronunciation plus all the other language differences which characterise your area or social group. For example, different dialects use different words and different sentence structures. For example, when I first came to Sheffield I was baffled by the local use of the word 'while' as in the sentence 'I'll not see you while 10 o'clock.' It was only when I realised that this was a local version of 'until' that I could interpret it.

One of the most important differences between accents is their different status. In the UK, the accent which is regarded as the most prestigious is what is known as received pronunciation (RP). Originally from a dialect of the south-eastern parts of England, this accent became associated with powerful economic and government centres, as well as being used in the major public schools and in universities like Oxford and Cambridge. It became the standard form of English used by the BBC and has been described as 'the most widely understood and spoken of all the accents within the British Isles'.[7] In a series of experiments looking at how we respond to accents, Howard Giles found that RP was rated highest for status while the lowest ratings went to inner-city accents like Cockney and the Birmingham accent.[8] Other studies have suggested that RP speakers are often rated more highly than speakers with regional accents in terms of characteristics like intelligence and ambition. On the other hand, people with regional accents are seen as more talkative, friendly and with a better sense of humour. There also seems to be a clear pecking order in the regional accents. These differences in our response to accents will also colour our responses to what people say.

More recent research has suggested that there are significant differences in the way we react to different strengths of accents. Giles found that people could accurately distinguish between different strengths of a particular accent, and that this led to different judgements – the broader the accent, the more negative the evaluation. There are other possible more alarming findings. For example:

- British doctors may be influenced in their diagnosis by the patient's accent. They may be more likely to diagnose psychosomatic illness in someone with a strong rural accent than in someone with an RP accent. The implication here is that people perceived as higher in social status are also seen as less likely to suffer mental difficulties.

- Teachers' judgements of their pupils' abilities can be affected by the pupils' accent or dialect. Again the RP or higher-status accent is seen as more intelligent.

Of course, all of these generalisations about accent are subject to change as society develops. BBC television and radio now boast a wide variety of regional accents in contrast to the very standardised conditions which existed up until the 1960s. As society becomes more 'accepting' of regional accents, perhaps the last outpost of RP on the BBC will be the national news programmes.

Although many regional dialects in the UK have virtually died out, there are still very strong differences across the country in terms of vocabulary and sentence structure: for example, if you want to order a sandwich in some parts of Scotland you need to ask for a 'roll'; while in Yorkshire you have to understand the subtlety of 'breadcakes'. Examples of regional differences in sentence structure would include the Welsh expression 'go to the pub is it?' to mean 'shall we go to the pub?'

Of course, some speakers retain their dialect to represent an important aspect of their social identity. An examples here would be the use of Creole by Jamaican speakers. Another example would be the slang which may be adopted by a particular subgroup within society.

Different styles of language

One way of investigating the way language is used in different contexts is to use the linguistic concept of register, as originally defined by Halliday in the 1960s.[9] He argued that language varies as its function varies, and so it differs in different situations. He used the concept of register to describe a variety of language which can be distinguished according to its use. Register can then be subdivided into three basic headings: field, tenor and mode.

Field means the activity, setting or topic in which the communication takes place. For example, when I discuss the joys of computing with my colleagues I am liable to use expressions such as software, floppy disks, CD-ROMs, bugs, etc., which would not crop up in a conversation about different topics. This is not just a matter of scientific or technical vocabulary as you can recognise very distinctive uses of language in a wide range of activities, from fashion to property advertising. One of the problems we have in new situations is choosing which register to use.

Tenor refers to the type of relationship which is implied in the language. This would include aspects of politeness, formality and status. An example of different uses of language would be the different forms of address which we saw used to such a powerful effect between Dr P and the police officer in Chapter 1.

Mode means the channel of communication. For example, we know that there are marked differences between written and spoken speech. Some of the important features of spoken speech are:

- Pauses
  Of course we can use punctuation to indicate pauses in written speech but these only give partial indication of how long pauses are expected to last.
- Fillers
  Expressions such as ‘ah’, ‘er’ and ‘um’ are very common in speech.
- Repetitions
- False starts and corrections
- Back channel behaviour
  This is the term that linguists use to describe the non-vocal reactions of the non-speaking members of the conversation. These are expressions like ‘um’, ‘hmm’ and ‘yea’ which help to keep the conversation moving along.
- Markers of sympathetic circularity
  This is another linguistic description which rolls off the tongue and which refers to parts of the speech which encourage the listener to go along with the speaker’s point of view, i.e. expressions like ‘like’, ‘you know’, ‘know what I mean’.

Language as a set of communication codes

The examples and illustrations used so far in this chapter should have suggested one of my main points: that it is misleading to think of language as ‘one thing’. It is a set of codes which different individuals and groups use in very different ways. The following few examples will illustrate this complexity.

Rules of address

These are the rules we use in a particular context to signal the 'correct' relationship with the other person. The conversation with Dr Pouissant which I used back in Chapter 1 shows how such rules can be manipulated. Some languages have very clear expressions which are used to signal different relationships. For example, the French use *tu* to mean 'you' in an intimate, close encounter whereas *vous* means 'you' in a more formal, distant encounter. We English have to signal that difference in other ways: by using pet names with someone very close; by using first names with friends; and by using titles (Mr, Dr, Sir) or last names in formal situations.

An example from the English Midlands also shows some of the values which we attach to our language identity. In this area, people use 'love' as a friendly address to others of all ages and both genders. After a complaint from a member of the public that bus conductors were being 'too familiar' by using this form of address, the local bus company suggested that their staff should avoid it. This attempt at 'language control' was then roundly condemned in both the local and national press as an attack on local cultural traditions!

Language as an intercultural barrier

The complexities of language codes are often highlighted in communication across cultural boundaries. Jandt suggests that there are five main barriers to surmount.[10] As well as problems because the different cultures might not have equivalent experiences or concepts, there are the following specific language problems:

- The lack of equivalent words.
- The lack of an equivalent idiom, as in the difficulties some other languages have with such 'obvious' English expressions as 'he kicked the bucket' or 'break a leg'.
- The lack of equivalent grammar or syntax. In English, the same word can work as noun or verb or adjective as in 'lift a thumb' or 'thumb a lift'. This does not work in other languages.

These language problems can often explain some of the language 'howlers' which can crop up when English is translated too literally:

- In a Swiss restaurant menu: 'Our wines leave you nothing to hope for.'

- Or the Moscow hotel sign: 'If this is your first visit to the USSR, you are welcome to it.'

The importance of social and cultural variables

Having introduced various linguistic concepts and tools, it is important to re-emphasise that language is always used in a social and cultural context. Linguistic concepts on their own can never provide a full explanation of the meanings which we attach to communication. Two examples will illustrate this point and provide a backdrop to the survey of non-verbal codes which starts the next chapter:

1 The nature of metacommunication.
2 The importance of strategies and expectations.

Metacommunication

In Chapter 2, I introduced the concepts of representation and presentation: the notions that we always communicate both content – information about the world – and information about the relationship that we are in (or want to be in). This is an example of the longstanding notion that communication always contains some sort of 'commentary' on itself at a different level which can be interpreted by the person 'receiving the message'. Various authors have proposed this 'second-level communication' but have not always defined it or used a consistent definition.[11] Leaving aside these theoretical difficulties for the moment, consider the practical difficulties of interpretation in the following example:

> You are in school, aged 15 years old and I am your Mathematics teacher. I start off today's lesson by saying 'I am giving you a test tomorrow'. Which of the following 'metamessages' are you likely to perceive in my message? How would you decide which one or which ones to believe?

- I am in authority and I want to make sure you know it.
- This section of the course is really important and I want to make sure you know it.
- I feel tired and disillusioned and I need a bit of a break tomorrow.

- I know you have not been working hard lately and this will prove it or change it.

Strategies and expectations

Consider the following example and decide your strategy:

> After working as a bank clerk for five years, you have been charged and convicted in a court of law for fraud (you did do it, by the way). The judge will sentence you after he hears your final statement. What should you say in this statement? Which of the following things do you think the judge would like to hear?

- You say that you admit you are guilty.
- You say you are responsible – it is nobody else's fault.
- You say you are sorry for what you have done.
- You explain why you did it (you needed the money for…).

Based on studies of real cases involving white-collar offenders, the answer is: you should include all four![12] The more convincingly you explain all four, the lighter the sentence! In other words, the more your statement conforms to the judge's ideal of the 'right explanation' the more lenient he will be towards you. So the language you use is being 'measured' against a very specific set of expectations.

This idea that we interpret language against what we expect people to say in the specific context can have very dramatic consequences in situations like the courtroom (in the next chapter, we shall see corresponding arguments about non-verbal behaviour), and this principle also affects everyday interactions. For example, if you've overslept and crawled in late for work or college, which of the following excuses would you be more likely to use?

(a) 'I needed the extra sleep this morning to get ready for this afternoon's workshop' or 'there was a power cut and the alarm did not go off'.
(b) 'My car ran out of petrol' or 'I decided to take a new shortcut and I got lost'.
(c) 'The traffic was really bad as usual' or 'The circus lorry accident meant tigers were running up the motorway'.
(d) 'I did not really want to come this morning' or 'My car got hit and I had to wait for the rescue services'.

These excuses differ on four dimensions:

1 Intention (from 'I did mean to' to 'I did not mean to').
2 Controllability (from 'the situation was under my control' to 'the situation was completely out of my control').
3 Stability (from 'the conditions were as usual' to 'the conditions were completely unexpected and unusual').
4 Locus of control (from 'I was in control of what I did' to 'I was not in control of the situation').

Research suggests that 'good' excuses – which make the other person less angry – are made up of reasons which include external, unstable, uncontrollable, and unintentional causes. Again what people say is being interpreted against a social template of what *should* be said in this sort of occasion.

Different approaches to discourse analysis

Although we can offer some generalisations (like the one which ended the last section) which may help in practical crises, the fact is that we do not really have enough evidence to capture the rich variety of the daily accounts we offer others to explain our everyday actions. We need to understand the cultural variables as well as look at the style and content of the language. And we also must consider the non-verbal accompaniment – which takes us to the next chapter.

One encouraging development over the last twenty years has been the increase in research on everyday talk. In fact, discourse analysis has been one of the fastest growing areas of research in linguistics and in the social sciences. Anyone researching in this field has to grapple with fundamental questions which have already been highlighted in this chapter, such as:

- What is the relationship between what we say and the social context we are in?
- How does the structure of language relate to how we use it?
- How is what we say converted into meaning by the listener?

In one of the most useful overviews of this area, Deborah Schiffrin suggests that there are six main approaches to discourse analysis.[13] Each approach comes from different theorists, using different methods and theoretical assumptions. To illustrate some of these differences, I have taken examples from three perspectives which most strongly relate to issues covered in this book, as follows.

The speech act approach

This uses what is known as speech act theory. This theory suggests that we use language not just to describe the world but to cover a variety of acts. For example, we say what we are going to do and we also try to persuade others to do things, in direct or indirect ways. If I say 'I promise to ring you tomorrow' then I have not just described something – I have 'performed the act' of promising.

When I say something I can perform more than one act. For example, suppose we meet at a formal dinner and I say 'Can you pass the salt?' This can be understood as both a question and a request. How would you respond? How would you expect me to act if you simply said 'yes' and did nothing else? You have responded as if it was simply a question. I suspect that I would see you as odd or even rude, unless you were able to convince me that it was some kind of joke. So the theoretical problem for speech act theory is to work out how people decide what sort of speech act they have just heard and how they need to respond to it.

To take a more complicated example, consider the phrase 'Y'want a piece of candy?' Schiffrin analyses this example as a question, as a request and as an offer, and finally decides that it can only be understood as a combination of all three.[14]

Interactional sociolinguistics

This concentrates on the way language is used in and reflects the social context. Consider the situation where a black student approaches his instructor immediately after an informal seminar at a major American university and says:

> 'Could I talk to you for a minute? I'm gonna apply for a fellowship and I was wondering if I could get a recommendation?'

The instructor says that this is 'OK' and suggests that the student comes along to the office to talk about it. As the instructor walks off, the black student turns and says to other students: 'Ahma git me a gig!' This can be roughly translated as 'I am going to get some support'.

The detailed analysis of this conversation shows how the black student changes his speech style to suit the different social contexts – contrast the style when he makes a polite formal request to the instructor as opposed to explaining his actions to his friends and his peers.[15]

The ethnography of communication

This approach often uses participant observation to examine our everyday interaction. The perspective uses both anthropological and linguistic ideas and was largely developed by Dell Hymes.[16] Hymes was also responsible for developing the 'speaking grid'. This uses SPEAKING to suggest that we can examine a conversation by analysing each of the components:

- S stands for scene and setting
- P stands for participants
- E stands for ends (the purposes and goals which people have and the outcomes of the conversation)
- A stands for act sequence (which looks at the form and content of the message)
- K stands for key (which means the tone or the manner of the conversation)
- I stands for instrumentalities (which consider the channel – including verbal and non-verbal – and which look at the forms of speech used)
- N stands for the norms (which cover both the norms of interaction and the norms we use to interpret the interaction)
- G stands for genre (which covers the textual categories used in a conversation)

Common themes

Although these approaches offer different ways of examining a specific conversation, they share common concerns which have very practical implications, such as:

- How do we come to understand the shared rules which allow us to understand one another?
- How do we shift our language styles in different situations?

They also share a number of important principles.[17] One of the most important for the theme of this book is that we cannot understand language in conversation simply by looking at the linguistic concepts. We also need to consider how the language forms relate to broader cultural forms and meanings. A few final everyday examples will emphasise this point and reflect the creativity and depth of human communication.

And the action is?

You are Andy. Consider the following conversation and decide what you have been asked to do before you read on:

Doris: Uhoh!
Andy: Okay.

You need a clue? Doris is looking in the refrigerator as she speaks. Now decide what you have been asked to do before you read on.

Doris's speech act can be expanded to include *at least* the following points:

- We're out of milk.
- I can't get any today.
- You could stop off at the shop on the way home.
- Can you do that?

You can probably find examples in your own home of conversations which also rely on a substantial 'unsaid' mix of assumptions and shared knowledge. Other less mysterious examples include the way we rely on indirect observations to make requests. Or in the following case, a very definite command:

> Were you born in a field?

In our house and in many UK households this means 'shut the door'. The urgency of the command is expressed through volume and intonation and perhaps the occasional extra word. And this takes us back to the importance of the non-verbal accompaniments which are the focus of the next chapter.

Chapter 9

Using codes 2

Incorporating the non-verbals

In this chapter, I shall:

- analyse how we can describe and categorise the non-verbal codes which are used in human communication
- review major studies on the nature of these non-verbal codes
- investigate the power of non-verbal codes and show how verbal and non-verbal codes work together in human communication
- re-emphasise the importance of cultural differences in human communication codes

What is non-verbal communication (NVC)?

Back in Chapter 3, I introduced the idea of NVC and suggested that a number of different signals were involved, which included the following:

- facial expression
- gaze
- gestures
- posture
- bodily contact
- spatial behaviour
- clothes and appearance
- non-verbal vocalisations
- smell

But how do these signals really work? After all, as I showed in the previous chapter, we have various systematic ways of subdividing language into its component parts. Can we apply similar concepts to our NVC? Simply presenting a list like the one above does seem to beg some important questions:

- Do all these signals work the same way?
- Can they all convey equivalent meanings?
- Are they equally important in terms of their impact?

Before reading on you might like to consider which non-verbal (and verbal) signals you pay most attention to in the following situations:

- when you want to know whether the other person likes you
- when you want to know whether the other person is lying to you
- when you want to know whether the other person is miserable or depressed

Classifying NVC

There have been two main ways of subdividing and classifying different types of NVC: one is to try to classify the different verbal and non-verbal codes into different communication systems; the other is to try to classify the functions of these different codes.

Communication systems

One popular example of this approach comes from Fraser.[1] He suggests four communication systems as follows.

Verbal

This is all the words we use, and the ways in which we organise them.

Intonation

This includes all those variations in pitch and stress which accompany the words in speech. If we make systematic variations in the emphasis we put on different words then we change the meaning of what we are saying. Consider the different interpretations of the following sentence if you place a heavy emphasis on different words in it:

> 'I don't think you know what you're doing'
> Could be '**I** don't think you know what you're doing'
> Or 'I don't think **you** know what you're doing'
> Or 'I don't think you know what you're **doing**'

Changing the emphasis changes the emotional tone.

Paralinguistics

This is all those vocal sounds which accompany speech but which are not the actual words we use. This category includes such phenomena as 'ums', 'ahs', splutters, giggles, pauses, silence, hesitation, etc. Some of these signals seem to have very clear meanings, e.g. 'Um' is usually a sign of agreement and can be a very useful reinforcer (see Chapter 3). Other signals seem to have much more ambiguous meanings, e.g. hesitation.

Kinesics

This includes body and facial movements. Many body and facial movements seem to have a very clear meaning although this meaning can vary from culture to culture. For example, one signal that has been extensively studied is eye gaze, and I shall review some of the major studies later in this chapter.

This model is useful in highlighting the variety of codes available and putting them into a more coherent framework than a simple list. But does it really tell us how the different codes work?

Identifying the functions – what do the codes do?

At first sight this question may seem nonsensical. Obviously, we use the codes to communicate. But *what* are we communicating? In fact it is useful to analyse three uses for the codes we have described, two of which we introduced in Chapter 2.

Representation (information)

We communicate in particular ways in order to give the other person information; in other words, to pass on our representation of how we see things.

Presentation (relationship)

We communicate in particular ways in order to present ourselves as the type of person we are (or would like to be). I can elaborate this definition of presentation by subdividing it into three subcategories and relating them to the following example. If we are strangers standing at a bus stop and I turn to you and say 'nice weather today', I have probably communicated far more to you than just a simple piece of meteorological information. I may well have communicated some aspects of the following:

- *Social/personal identity* You will have decided various things about me from my use of words, tone of voice, etc. If I wanted to create a particular impression then I could use the different codes accordingly.
- *Current attitudes and feelings* You will have probably decided from my tone of voice and posture whether I am feeling happy or sad and whether I really do want to have a conversation or am just being polite.
- *Social relationships* I could have established a particular relationship at the bus stop if I had included some form of personal address, i.e. some version of your name or title. We have already seen how powerful rules of address can be. They are also a very important part of everyday encounters. Consider how you react if a stranger addresses you by your first name. And are there more subtle rules at work, e.g. would it make a difference if I said 'good morning' or 'hello' or 'hi'?

Interaction regulation

When we have a conversation, we are not normally aware of all the signals we use and all the rules we obey in order to regulate the interaction, i.e. to make the conversation orderly and coherent. In most conversations, people obey a set of simple rules – everybody takes turns to speak, only one person talks at a time, etc. If these rules are ignored the conversation breaks down. As the conversation proceeds, the participants have to use specific codes, e.g. they may use eye gaze to signal when they are ready to speak or when they want to finish speaking. The following extract from Fraser suggests the typical way in which British speakers seem to use eye contact when they speak.[1] As you read this account, ask yourself the following questions:

- Does this pattern reflect how people use eye contact where you live?
- Can you observe this sort of pattern in every type of situation?
- How does this pattern differ from other cultures?
- How far can differences create misunderstanding or conflict, e.g. when a British person tries to talk to someone from a different cultural background without recognising that there may be different rules in operation?

> The conversation may be initiated by mutual eye-contact, indicating that the participants are ready and willing to interact. Once the conversation has started, each person looks at the other intermittently. These looks or glances are directed around the other's eyes, last between 1 and 10 seconds each or between 25 and 75 per cent of each person's total time. The amount of time that each spends gazing at the other is considerably more than that spent in mutual eye contact.
>
> The listener is likely to spend more time looking at the speaker than the speaker at the listener. When the speaker, while in full flow, does look at the listener the latter is likely to nod or give an encouraging vocalization. The speaker, when he starts, probably looks away. When he comes to clear grammatical breaks in what he has to say, the speaker is likely to glance briefly at the listener. When he approaches the end of his contribution he will look longer at the listener. If, however, the speaker hesitates

or pauses because he is stuck for a word, or an idea, he is not likely to look at the listener.

But how general are these patterns? How far can we apply these general results to specific interactions? In order to suggest some answers to these questions, I shall review some important lines of research into NVC below.

Patterson offers a more elaborate view of the functions of communication. He identifies seven:[2]

1 Providing information. For example, we can express how we feel through our facial expression.
2 Regulating interaction, as explained above.
3 Expressing intimacy. For example, when we gaze into another's eyes or move closer to express our feelings.
4 Expressing social control. For example, we can also use non-verbal signals to emphasise status or power.
5 Presentation. This is *not* the same as Danziger's use of the term. Patterson talks here of using non-verbal signals to create or enhance an image, as in the 'showbiz couple' who exaggerate their shows of affection in public to prove to the surrounding media gaggle that they really are 'still together', despite those rumours of flying cutlery in their hotel room.
6 Managing affect. This is where we use non-verbal signals to demonstrate the strength of our feelings.
7 Helping to achieve goals. This is where we use non-verbal means to help achieve tasks and the signals are interpreted in this way. An example would be a doctor giving a patient a detailed physical examination and using space/gaze/contact for professional purposes rather than suggesting intimacy.

Patterson's approach highlights some less obvious aspects of NVC and also emphasises the way non-verbal signals work together to create meaning, another issue we return to later in this chapter.

Another way of categorising the functions of NVC comes from Ekman and Friesen who suggest that non-verbal signals serve as:[3]

- emblems, where a non-verbal sign has a direct verbal meaning, like a wave of the hand to mean 'hello'
- illustrators, which are gestures and movements which illustrate what we are saying

- regulators, as in the descriptions of interaction regulation above
- adaptors, where we manipulate an object or part of our body and where we seem to be trying to handle the emotion in the situation, as when we clasp our hands before the penalty kick is taken (I pray that this penalty will go in!)
- affect displays, where we simply display our emotions, as in facial expressions

One way Ekman has used this system is to analyse the way we express emotions and the way we can distinguish between genuine expression and deception. For example, is there a 'genuine smile' which we find difficult to fake and which reliably demonstrates happiness?[4]

Looking at some classic studies

One way of demonstrating very carefully the importance and the difficulties of analysing NVC is to look at some of the classic studies of non-verbal signals. Rather than try to say just a few words on all the signals, I will concentrate on a few areas which highlight important problems:

- the meaning and use of eye gaze
- social distance and cultural norms
- non-verbal cues to deception

From gaze to eye contact to intimacy and equilibrium

One of the classic studies which influenced successive generations of researchers was the study of eye gaze published by Adam Kendon in 1967.[5] He recruited pairs of students who did not know one another and recorded their conversations in the laboratory. He then did a very detailed and painstaking analysis of how the students looked at each other when they were talking and listening. His findings have often been quoted since as the standard pattern of eye contact, at least in Western cultures, and you can find them summarised above in the quotes from Fraser. His other important contribution from this early work was to propose that eye gaze had three very important jobs: to express our emotions, to monitor the actions of the other person, and to regulate how the conversation flowed.

We can start by reviewing some of his findings (again you might like to compare this account with Fraser's). He found that individuals looked at their partners for about 50 per cent of the time. This was the *average* result and there was a wide range of individual differences, ranging from less than 30 per cent up to 70 per cent. Individuals looked more while they were listening than when they were speaking. He also studied the amount of eye contact which went on. Again there was a range of scores and most eye contact occurred in very short bursts, usually only lasting about 1 second. It appeared to Kendon that each pair of students reached some sort of unspoken 'agreement' or understanding which governed how long they looked at one another.

There were other interesting findings which influenced later researchers:

- When the speaker came to the end of what they wanted to say they would tend to look at the other person.
- If someone hesitated when they were speaking they would tend to look away. People seemed to be glancing away in order to avoid distraction while they gathered their thoughts so they could continue to speak fluently.

The overall conclusion which had a major impact on subsequent studies was that looking was very closely synchronised with the pattern of speaking. So Kendon suggested that gaze was an important signal which regulated how conversation flowed.

This sort of account of this research has appeared regularly in much more recent texts. But they often fail to mention the several subsequent studies which paint a more complicated picture. For example, in the late 1970s, Geoff Beattie carried out a very similar experiment on tutorials at the University of Cambridge.[6] He found a very different pattern of gaze. Kendon's conclusion that a look would signal the other person to start talking did *not* seem to happen. This study suggested that people were using other cues to decide when and where not to speak.

A series of experiments by Derrick Rutter also failed to support all of Kendon's original findings. The idea that we use gaze to give the next speaker their turn does seem to depend on the kind of interaction that we are involved in. This was acknowledged by Kendon himself in 1978 when he suggested that: 'what can serve to cue the next speaker to his turn is quite variable'. He also suggested that

> the participants' understanding of each other's current communicational intentions plays a central role.[7]

Another very important early study of eye gaze was by Michael Argyle.[8] He suggested that eye contact was an important signal of the degree of intimacy which existed between two people. The more eye contact there was, the closer the relationship between the two people. As a result, if someone tries to establish more eye contact with you than you think your relationship deserves then this will make you feel anxious. You will try to compensate for this by decreasing the amount of eye contact and restoring the balance, or what Argyle calls the 'equilibrium'. It is not just eye gaze which is involved here. Intimacy is also signalled by distance, the intimacy of the topic, smiling, and other non-verbal signals. A practical example of how this equilibrium theory works would be the way people behave in a crowded lift or on a crowded tube train. Here people are squashed together. They are very close to one another, which is one of the signals of intimacy. In order to make sure that none of the other passengers get some misleading ideas, everybody works very hard to avoid eye contact and avoid any other signals such as touch.

This suggests some very important conclusions which are often neglected in the more popular accounts of NVC:

- Specific non-verbal signals may not work in the same way in different situations. Although there may be general cultural patterns, they will vary in different situations within that culture.
- We usually look for meaning in the combination of non-verbal signals rather than just focusing on one.

Social space

Among the studies most quoted in the general books on body language are studies of personal space and territory. For example, consider the six people who are sat round a table in a coffee house in the positions shown in Figure 9.1: which pairs of people are most likely to talk to one another?

According to work by Robert and Barbara Somner, the most likely conversation is between F and A.[9] There are other likely patterns:

Figure 9.1 Positions round a coffee house table

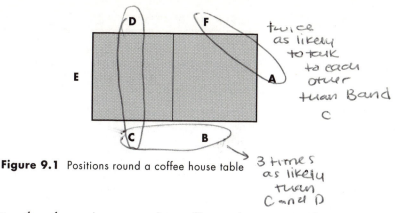

- the other main conversations will occur between people in positions B and C, and C and D
- F and A are twice as likely to talk to each other as B and C
- B and C are three times more likely to talk than C and D

This shows that our position suggests how likely we are to talk. Other research suggests that our position affects the *type* of talk we are likely to engage in. The right tangled position across the end of the table is much more 'friendly' than the confrontational position where people sit face to face across the table. Again many of the 'NVC guide books' will suggest that you should change your seating position depending on what kind of conversation you intend to have with the other person. Of course, remember that the *combination* of other signals will influence how all this non-verbal behaviour is interpreted.

Another study of space which received considerable publicity was the work by Edward T. Hall on how we think of and use the space around us (often called proxemics).[10] He suggested that there were four basic distances which we would use when talking to people in different relationships. These four distances and the measurements for American culture are explained in Table 9.1.

Two obvious questions arise from this analysis:

1 Do different cultures share the same measurements?
2 What happens when somebody breaks the rules?

The answer to this first question is obviously 'no'. Different cultures have very different senses of the social distance. Compare

Table 9.1 Hall's model of personal distance

Space	*Distance*	*Use*
Intimate	Either bodily contact or between 6 and 18 inches (15 to 45 cm)	Very close intimate relationships
Personal	From 18 inches up to 48 inches (45 to 120 cm)	Close friends
Social	From 4 to 12 feet (120 to 360 cm)	During formal introductions or in general public situations
Public		Public or theatrical occasions

the English notion of personal space (which is broadly similar to the American) with the use of space in Arab culture. This last example shows why courses on non-verbal customs can be very useful to people who intend to travel to a very different culture. The answer to the second question is: 'depends'. How people respond will depend on the situation and their interpretation of why the person broke the rule.

Another of Hall's interests which has been less widely reported was his concern with time. He has written about the possibilities of misunderstanding and miscommunication which arise from different senses of time. For example, what does 'a while' mean in our everyday speech, as in 'I'll come to see you in a while'? How do you respond to punctuality, or the lack of it? If someone is waiting for you and you are late for the appointment, how long does it take for them to start feeling insulted? The answers to all these questions differ markedly across different cultures.

Non-verbal behaviour and deception

Obviously there are many forms of deception. For example, Steve Duck suggests that most deception between partners in a relationship involves withholding thoughts or feelings rather than saying something which is deliberately untrue.[11] For this section I shall focus on the non-verbal signs that might accompany direct lies.

According to a recent British daily newspaper, the following body language and gestures are 'tell-tale signs' that somebody is lying in a job interview:[12]

- grasping the chair too tightly
- scratching their nose
- smiling, without raising their eyebrows

Another gesture which is highlighted is any 'increase in hand shrugging'. The article claims that this means that the person is trying to disclaim responsibility for whatever they're talking about. These claims are based upon a presentation to a national recruitment and selection conference by the well-known British psychologist, Professor Adrian Furnham. He is quoted as saying that very few interviewers can spot the crucial signs of lying even though a very high percentage of interviewees will lie at some point. Whether Furnham's speech was quite as dogmatic as the article implies is a question for media analysts. For our purposes, this article raises the following very important questions: Can we be absolutely sure that a specific non-verbal signal proves that the other person is lying? How can we distinguish between a gesture which indicates that someone is trying to deceive and a similar or identical gesture which might mean nerves or anxiety?

Several studies have shown that we may not be as good at spotting lies as we think we are. For example, consider the studies which show that:

- When we try to judge whether someone whom we do not know is lying, we rely upon rather stereotyped cues, such as any awkward gestures or less than fluent language. Unfortunately, these stereotyped gestures are just as likely to be caused by nerves.
- The accuracy with which people can spot lies in controlled experiments is usually no more than 60 per cent. We could achieve 50 per cent accuracy by chance.

As a result, Friedman and Tucker have proposed a model of deception which is much more complicated than just spotting specific signals.[13] They suggest that we need to consider four major factors:

1 Input factors. These are individual and situational factors which might influence a person to deceive. For example, these would include the deceiver's personality, their past history with the other person, their communication skills, their motivation to lie, and their emotions.
2 Behaviours which *have* been shown to accompany people's attempts to deceive. These include hesitation and other errors in speech, and body language like the dilation of eye pupils.
3 Behaviours which people often *feel* are clues to deception but which are often caused by other reasons. For example, these include gaze patterns, facial expression and the rate of speech.
4 Detection factors. These are factors which affect the success of the person trying to spot the deception and include attention, sensitivity to the non-verbal cues, knowledge and past history of the other person, and personal stereotypes.

The main argument is that *all* these factors influence how we spot and respond to deception. As a result, what they call the search for 'the single true indicator of deception' is a hopeless ambition. Although we can develop skills which make us more likely to detect when other people are deceiving us, Friedman and Tucker conclude that 'some people can deceive most of the people most of the time'.

How powerful is NVC?

Before looking at overall issues of power and impact, I need to return to the issues of specific gestures.

Although I have emphasised that we usually judge other people's non-verbal behaviour by looking at the *combination* of non-verbal signals, there are situations where one type of signal may be especially important. To start with a personal example, some years ago I was training students for future job interviews using our TV studio. We would record an interview (with me playing the role of interviewer) and then play it back to see how the students responded to questions and to see whether they could improve their performance. One thing I noticed during the interviews was that candidates often changed direction in what they were talking about, sometimes almost in mid-sentence. When we reviewed the tapes, I noticed that these changes usually followed one of my gestures – they came immediately after I leaned back slightly in my chair and stroked my beard. I did not see this gesture as significant and it was certainly not connected with my impressions of what the candidate was saying. Unfortunately, the candidates did not see it that way. They saw this gesture as part of my judgement of their behaviour. They took it to mean that I had disagreed or objected to what they had just said and immediately changed their line of conversation to try to rescue the situation. I reviewed my non-verbal behaviour after this session and was very careful to avoid that gesture in future.

In the introduction I mentioned that there is supposedly a piece of body language which will enable you to control which part of your message is best remembered by the other person or your audience. This gesture is taken from the book by David Lewis.[14] He recommends the following actions when you get to the part of the message which you really want to emphasise. Assuming that you are right-handed (left-handers should reverse the hand and eye) then what you do is:

- raise your right hand towards your right eye as you reach the important part of the message
- once your hand has reached your eye, repeat the key message which you want to get across

The logic behind this gesture is that the other person will follow the movement of your hand and this forces them to make eye contact with you. Once you have achieved this eye contact, repeating the message will emphasise it and ensure that it is memorised.

As far as I know, there have been no systematic studies of the effects of this 'power lift' and this illustrates one of the main problems in responding to advice on NVC. Is this a tried and tested method which has been shown to work with a variety of audiences from different cultural backgrounds? Or a tactic which seems to work with some of the people some of the time? Or just an interesting idea? Lewis does not really say. You may like to experiment for yourself. If you come up with any interesting results, please let me know.

What happens when the signals are ambiguous?

Most of the time, we use the different codes to support and complement one another. For example, a few words of praise can be accompanied by a pat on the back and a smile. However, in many situations the relationship between the codes can be ambiguous or even contradictory. In these cases, the person on the receiving end has to decide what is the 'real' meaning.

Why do people send ambiguous messages?

Have you ever talked to someone who is doing something else at the same time? An example could be a boss talking to a subordinate while he (the boss) is checking through his mail. If you were the subordinate and started speaking, how would you feel if the boss did not look at you and gave no signals to convince you that he was listening? You may come to a stop fairly abruptly. And then if the boss says 'carry on, I'm listening', what would you do? When I have been in this position, I have sometimes tended to carry on speaking as requested but not put any real effort into it. In other words, I believed the non-verbal signals of lack of attention and disinterest and I ignored the verbal reassurance.

One reason why someone (like this hypothetical boss) should behave like he did is that he is unaware of what he is doing. People are not necessarily aware of all the non-verbal signals which they are giving out. This means that you may be giving a misleading impression. Perhaps the boss really was listening!

What happens when signals contradict each other?

It can be difficult to disguise what you really feel. Ekman and Friesen coined the term 'leakage' to describe situations where specific non-verbal messages were sent by an individual who was trying to display a different impression.[15] An example was the psychiatric patient who was trying to persuade hospital staff that he was no longer highly anxious. He managed to produce a relaxed facial expression and talk in a confident manner but he gave himself away by sitting in a very tense awkward position.

The example of the paper-shuffling boss and the concept of leakage both imply that NVC can be much more important or powerful than the words used in a conversation. This is the impression given in the quotes I used back in the Introduction which you may like to reconsider before reading the next section (see page 10).

Firstly let's explore the general implication that NVC is responsible for the 'social meaning' which is expressed in a conversation. In other words, I look to see how you behave towards me in order to decide things such as whether you like or admire me and I may ignore what you say. There is certainly some evidence to suggest that NVC can be very powerful, but researchers have begun to question some of the generalisations which came out of the early research, as in the following example.

In the 1970s Michael Argyle and colleagues had suggested that:

> the NV (nonverbal) channel is used for negotiating interpersonal attitudes while the verbal channel is used primarily for conveying information.[16]

This claim was backed up by the results from a series of experiments where subjects were confronted by an experimenter who used a planned combination of verbal and non-verbal messages. The experimenter had been trained to deliver three verbal messages which suggested different attitudes (hostile, neutral and friendly) in each of three non-verbal styles (again being hostile, neutral and friendly). After the experiment, subjects were asked to rate the communication they received from the experimenter and it was discovered that the non-verbal message had the most effect. For example, if a friendly verbal message was presented with a hostile non-verbal style then the subject interpreted this as a hostile communication. The conclusions of this study are quoted almost verbatim in very recent texts.

However, Ellis and Beattie have criticised these experiments on three counts:[17]

1 The verbal and non-verbal styles used could have seemed 'exaggerated' and not typical of everyday life.
2 Only one female experimenter was used – described by Argyle as 'an attractive, female student aged 23' – which raises the issue of how subjects might have reacted to different encoders.
3 The subjects were 'compelled to attend to the communication' in a way which is perhaps not typical of everyday encounters.

When Beattie repeated the experiment using both a male and female encoder, he found a more complex pattern of results. Looking at the hostile–friendly dimension, he found that the typical patterns discovered by Argyle *only* occurred with the female encoder. In other words, with a female encoder, the non-verbal message of hostility or friendliness would be believed if the verbal message was different.

With the male encoder, the non-verbal component did not outweigh the verbal and this was true for both male and female subjects. Could the 'power' of the NVC in the Argyle experiment be attributed to other factors? For example, do we attend more to the NVC of attractive people? Is there a different perception of male and female experimenters in the university context which means that the different NVC is judged differently? There is both anecdotal and research evidence that women face significant barriers to achieving high-status positions in organisations like universities. Could this study also be reflecting some of the social stereotypes of the time about male/female differences?

But if this study can be questioned in terms of methods and outcomes, what do we make of the precise statistics in the quotes I listed earlier?[18] Certainly, the impact of NVC has been studied and quantified by some researchers. But these researchers were usually looking at the general emotional tone of non-verbal compared with verbal messages under very specific conditions. It is stretching the point to claim that these statistics represent universal truths which apply equally to every situation.

And finally – returning to cultural issues

Fernando Poyatos has coined the term 'cultural fluency' to describe someone who cannot only converse in a foreign language but also act and interact in a way which is recognised as appropriate by native speakers of the language.[19] He illustrates some of the potential problems caused by a lack of fluency with the anecdote of an American friend visiting him in Madrid. While his speech and language were more than adequate, he caused much consternation at the dinner table by a sequence of very un-Spanish eating habits:

- criss-crossing his fork from one hand to another
- keeping his left-hand on his lap
- biting from a bread stick rather than breaking a piece off
- pushing some food with his thumb
- licking his fingers rather than using his napkin

At first sight this may seem just a trivial example of minor embarrassment. What if his behaviour had been interpreted as *deliberately* rude or provocative? And what if the situation had been more important than an informal meal? Specific body signs are associated with specific groups or cultures. There is the reportedly true anecdote of the American spy operating in German-occupied territory in the Second World War who first aroused suspicion because of a few incidental non-European habits like the way he crossed his legs on sitting down. Crossing legs over at the knee is the standard British and European leg-cross whereas putting one foot on top of the opposite knee is a more typical American style. Desmond Morris suggests that it is:

> A predominantly male form of leg-crossing…[which] originated as a cowboy posture, related to their lifestyle and clothing.[20]

In contrast to its acceptance in the USA, this form of leg-cross should be used very carefully in some areas of the Middle East where showing someone the sole of your foot is regarded as an insult. This reinforces the idea that gestures may hark back to previous and perhaps long-forgotten life-styles – after all we only shake hands with people to prove we are not carrying a sword (which explains why left-handed knights were regarded with some suspicion in the days of King Arthur).

But are some of these examples really good illustrations of a message in code? We do not normally cross our legs in order to send a message! On the other hand we could do. One way of gaining acceptance in another culture is to adopt those mannerisms which are acceptable in that culture. Even more important is the need to avoid mannerisms which may cause offence. On some occasions in some cultures, crossing your legs, even in an accepted style, would be seen as very rude, i.e. you would be seen as behaving too casually and informally. Many a foreign explorer may have lived (or not!) to regret certain casual gestures which unfortunately were part of the code of insults or antagonism as far as the local natives were concerned. Luckily for today's travellers, we now have several guides to non-verbal differences across the world although they may not take account of all the regional and subcultural variations.[21]

Conclusion

Perhaps the most important conclusion to draw from this and the previous chapter is to emphasise the variety and complexity of the codes which human beings use to communicate with one another. As well as having to contend with the general ambiguities which are inherent in such a flexible system as human language, we must also recognise that specific groups in society have developed specialised code books for specific purposes.

The identification of non-verbal codes adds further levels of complexity and has particular significance when we examine interactions between people from different cultures or ethnic backgrounds. We should be cautious in deciding how the different codes operate and how they relate to one another. The simple distinction between verbal and non-verbal communication is far too 'crude' – there is a much more complex set of systems at work which deserve more sophisticated analysis. We still have much to learn about the nature and interaction of the various codes and researchers have begun to question some of the very dramatic and clear-cut propositions which emerged from the early research.

Section C

Issues and controversies in interpersonal communication

Chapter 10

How useful are 'popular' models of interpersonal communication?

In this chapter, I shall:

- explain what I mean by popular models and why it is important to analyse them
- describe and evaluate the main concepts from two popular models: transactional analysis and neurolinguistic programming
- raise some general issues about the 'popular understanding' of how we communicate

What do I mean by 'popular models' and why is it important to analyse them?

A couple of personal examples will illustrate both what I mean by popular models and why it is important to analyse them. A few years ago I decided to buy a new car. After working out exactly what I wanted, I approached the showroom, owned by a major company distributing one of the leading brands in the UK at that time. The sales assistant immediately launched into his sales patter, an obviously well-practised routine which was designed to make me feel relaxed and inspire confidence in his knowledge and integrity. As I knew exactly what I wanted, I did not need to be persuaded by any routine. But it took me at least ten minutes to persuade the sales assistant that I really did know exactly what I wanted and did not need any sales pitch. Once he knew that he would make the sale, he visibly relaxed and we started talking while the paperwork was processed. When he discovered from the forms that I was a university lecturer, he said that I would probably be interested in his training manual as it was 'all about communication'. As I leafed through the pages, I noticed that virtually all the concepts were taken from transactional analysis (TA). He assured me that all the ideas in the manual were 'absolutely true' and that he relied upon the techniques in every sales opportunity. I asked him if he knew where the ideas came from and he did not have any idea.

So this salesman had been taught (and was very definitely using) ideas from a system which as far as he was concerned was the 'established truth' on how people communicate and which he accepted more or less uncritically. He did not know where the ideas came from but was happy to use them. He also felt that his colleagues in the showroom shared his faith in the manual.

My second example comes from a friend who recently got the opportunity to do some survey work for a large public organisation. Before he started the work, he was paid to attend a one-day seminar in communication, which was part of the training for everyone doing the survey. As he had a degree in communication, he was looking forward to the day. He came back from the day less than happy. The content of the seminar was presented with what he described as 'almost evangelical zeal', but he found that many of the ideas were far too simplistic. He also found that some of the claims were at odds with the research he had studied on his degree course. When he asked questions or challenged any of the ideas, the trainer seemed to take this as a personal attack – reacting very negatively and defensively, and being very firm that all the principles were based on years of experience which 'always worked'.

In conversation over lunch, my friend enquired about the trainer's background. He discovered that the trainer was a former computer worker who had been converted to this system after attending a training course himself. He had been so convinced by the ideas that he had set himself up as an independent trainer. Apart from that training, he had virtually no background in social science, and had certainly never been involved in any systematic study of human psychology. I looked through the manual which my friend brought back from the seminar and soon discovered that all the ideas were taken from neurolinguistic programming (NLP).

I'll look at the main ideas behind TA and NLP below, and briefly describe how they were developed. But even without questioning the validity of these ideas, these two examples highlight several aspects which I find worrying, including:

- the unquestioning acceptance of the ideas, in both examples
- the assurance that specific techniques 'always work' regardless of the social or cultural context, again in both examples
- the very limited experience (coupled with almost evangelical commitment) of the trainer in the second example

In both examples, I am *not* questioning the sincerity or honesty of the individuals concerned. I *am* questioning whether it is really right to adopt any one specific system with such an uncritical attitude. So one way of looking at popular analyses is to turn my concerns above into questions:

- What are the ideas based upon? (Do they come from therapeutic experience or research or what?)
- Are the ideas critically examined? (Is there any self-criticism or any recognised limitations to the ideas?)
- Are they applied in a way which recognises the specific social context? (Is any account taken of social and cultural differences?)
- Who are the gurus or advocates? (And what is their expertise based upon in terms of experience, training, etc.?)

I shall come back to these questions after examining the origins and basic concepts of TA and NLP in more detail.

What is TA and how does it work?

Your alarm clock has not gone off at the set time. You wake and realise that you and your partner have only ten minutes to get up, feed the cats, have breakfast, wash, and leave the house. In the ensuing mayhem you cannot find your watch. As you charge around the kitchen, you ask your partner: 'Have you seen my watch?' How would you feel if you received one of the following responses? For each alternative, imagine how your partner is feeling and thinking, and how you would react:

(a) 'I told you last night not to leave it lying around.'
(b) 'It's on the kitchen table.'
(c) 'This can-opener never works properly for me.'

We shall return to this domestic drama after investigating the origins and basic concepts of TA.

How did TA come about?

It is ironic that a man who went on to become one of the most widely read psychotherapists of all time was turned down for membership of his local psychoanalytic institute. This man was Eric Berne.[1] Although he had been in training and practice for over fifteen years, he was told by the institute to apply again – but not until he had done a few more years of further training and personal analysis. This rejection by the psychoanalytic establishment in 1956 spurred him to develop his own ideas further. He had already started this by publishing articles which criticised aspects of conventional psychoanalysis and developing alternative approaches. This probably did not help his application to the institute!

Berne developed his alternative theory, transactional analysis (TA), and his first book on TA in psychotherapy appeared in 1961.[2] It was widely read by other therapists across the USA. Among his many innovations, he decided to use colloquial names for psychological concepts on the grounds that his clients would not have to learn elaborate psychological jargon to understand what he was telling them.

In 1964, he published the book that turned many of his concepts into household names – *Games People Play*.[3] Although he originally wrote this book for a professional audience, it very soon achieved best-seller status and was translated into many languages. The title was even borrowed for a best-selling pop song of the day and Berne's concepts and ideas were regularly repeated in the media. Not only were people reading about his ideas but also they were applying them to their everyday lives.

Berne defines a game as a set of behaviours which follow a regular and predictable sequence. These behaviours lead to an equally predictable and unpleasant psychological outcome for the individuals involved. The problem is that people play games without being consciously aware of them, which led him to conclude that:

> most human relationships (at least 51 per cent) are based on trickery and subterfuges, some lively and amusing and others vicious and sinister.[4]

However, people *can* reflect on their behaviour: they can *become* aware of the games and change what they do in order to develop more open and honest relationships. Across the USA, couples read the book and analysed their relationship in terms of psychological games. We shall come back to these ideas and their impact later.

Berne continued to write during the 1960s and produced the most comprehensive summary of the ideas shortly before his death of a heart attack in 1970.[5] Since then, his ideas have been further developed and publicised by organisations such as the International Transactional Analysis Association (ITAA). There are now several variants of TA but this chapter focuses on the so-called 'classical' school of TA, which is the most widely quoted version and which is closest to Eric Berne's original philosophy.[6]

The ITAA controls a system of training and examination for students who wish to gain professional accreditation in TA. This involves three levels: the basic entry course; practitioner training and examination; and further training and examination for those who wish to teach and supervise. Training up to practitioner status can take from four to five years.

There is obviously not space here to provide a full summary of TA concepts. However, I can discuss some of the key ideas, such as: the way the personality is expressed through ego states; the analysis of interactions; and the way that we express ourselves at different levels.

Ego states

The notion of the ego is a fundamental idea in traditional psychoanalysis. When Freud developed his theory of the structure of the human personality, he talked about the ego as that part which dealt with external reality. But he used the ego as an abstract concept. He did not believe that you could directly experience your ego and he did not suggest any particular behaviour associated with this part of the human personality. But later psychoanalytic writers did suggest that the ego could be available to human experience.[7]

Eric Berne developed this idea and decided that ego states could be experienced from the inside. In other words, you can be aware of your own ego state. Ego states can also be observed from the outside as they are associated with specific behaviours. If I know what to look for, I can observe your behaviour and decide which ego state you are in. His definition of an ego state was:

> A consistent pattern of feeling and experience directly related to a corresponding consistent pattern of behaviour.[8]

After observing the behaviours of his patients, he decided that there were three distinct categories of ego state which he called Parent, Adult, and Child:

> each individual is three different persons, all pulling in different directions.

> these (ego states) represent the three people that everyone carries around in his or her head.[9]

You will find other texts where the ego states are described very concisely:

> Broadly speaking, the Parent believes, the Adult thinks, and the Child feels.[10]

But this definition must be expanded: the Parent ego state is where you adopt feelings and behaviours which you learnt from the parent figures who cared for you when you were a child. In the Adult ego state, you feel and behave in a logical and rational way in order to cope with whatever is happening in the world around you. In the Child ego state, you feel and behave in ways which are emotional and playful and which can be described as 'relics' of your own child. But are these distinctions as straightforward as this account implies?

Some TA practitioners are very critical of what they call the oversimplified model expressed in the quote above, which suggests that the Child is 'all about feelings', leaving all thinking to the Adult and all the value judgements to the Parent. For example, Stewart and Joines are very critical of what they call the 'watered down' and 'trivialised' version of TA.[11] They emphasis that *all* three ego states can involve thinking *and* feeling *and* making value judgements. They also highlight another possible oversimplification. Berne talked of each ego state as a category – you do not have just one set of behaviours and feelings to represent, say, your Parent. There are a variety of ways in which Parent can express itself.

When I have explained this system in courses and seminars and asked my listeners to apply it to their own behaviour, most of them can. You might like to try it yourself. Think of the way you have behaved over the last few days: can you remember an occasion when you behaved, thought and felt as you did when you were a child? Perhaps this was an occasion where you felt strong emotion. Applying it to myself, I can immediately think of a work situation the other day where I felt excluded and 'left out' – those feelings of hurt and unhappiness took me right back to painful emotions from childhood experiences. In other words, I slipped into my Child ego state.

I can also think of situations in the last few days where I have been encouraging and offered help (from my Parent) and where I have been solving problems and responding to the here and now (Adult). Berne suggested that we experience one of these ego states at any one time and that we will shift from one ego state to another as the situation changes. Again I have found it useful to think about my own experience by analysing these shifts. For example, going back to my problem at work the other day, my immediate reaction came from my Child. But I did not stay in this for long as my Adult took over to try to find out whether the other parties really did mean to exclude me. I chose not to go into my 'sulky child' pattern which my family have occasionally brought to my attention!

Berne and other TA theorists went on to develop a more complicated analysis by subdividing the Parent and Child. For example, most TA analysts suggest that there are two divisions to the Parent:[12]

1 The Controlling Parent copies the controlling behaviour of your parent figures, as in 'go to bed', 'behave yourself', 'tidy that bedroom' etc.
2 The Nurturing Parent copies the caring or 'looking after' behaviour of your parent figures, as in the cuddles, bandages

and other comforts which are applied to the child who has just fallen off a bike.

When you become a parent yourself, you can find that this sort of analysis shows just how much of your behaviour is modelled on your own early experience.

There are also ways of subdividing the Child:

- The Adapted Child reflects the way you felt and behaved as a child as you adapted to the demands and constraints from your parent figures.
- The Free Child reflects the way you felt and behaved as a child when you were not responding to parental demands.

I shall ignore the further subdivisions which have been suggested, as we need to move on to the most powerful application of this system – when we look at how we interact with other people. We can analyse interactions in terms of the ego states which people adopt – Berne's notion of transactions.

Transactions

Berne called a transaction the 'basic unit' of social interaction. The simplest transaction is a single communication from me and the response from you, as in:

'Hello' – 'Hi'
'Good morning' – 'morning'

This can be represented as a diagram (Figure 10.1) reflecting the three ego states of each person, as in the transaction:

'Where is John?' – 'He's in the restaurant.'

The diagram shows my Adult addressing your Adult and receiving a response from your Adult. This is what Berne called a complementary transaction where you receive a response from the ego state which you addressed. You can have complementary transactions involving the other ego states, P–P, P–C, C–C and so on.

But what if our conversation above had gone differently?

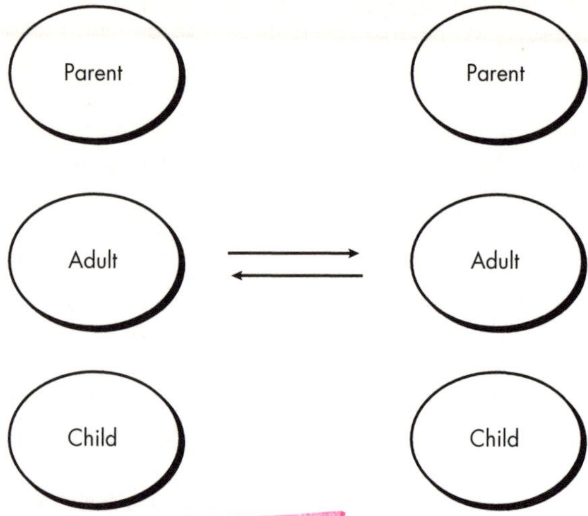

Figure 10.1 Complementary transaction

'Where is John?' – 'Go find him yourself.'

This looks more like the diagram in Figure 10.2.

An A–A stimulus has met a P–C response! This is an example of a crossed transaction where we will have to adjust our ego states if we do not want this conversation to develop into a row. Perhaps the row has already started!

The final main type of transaction is what Berne called the ulterior transaction which you need to analyse at two levels:

1 The social level – what seems to be happening on the surface, usually Adult to Adult.
2 The psychological level – the covert or hidden message which reflects how the people really feel.

To return to my personal example, even though I had convinced the salesman that I was going to buy the car, he could not resist the temptation to try to hook me with one ulterior transaction: 'There is a special offer on the additional components pack at the moment but that will push it beyond your budget.' Superficially, this looks Adult to Adult but of course he had never actually established my budget. The 'real' message is Parent to Child: 'I can show you this

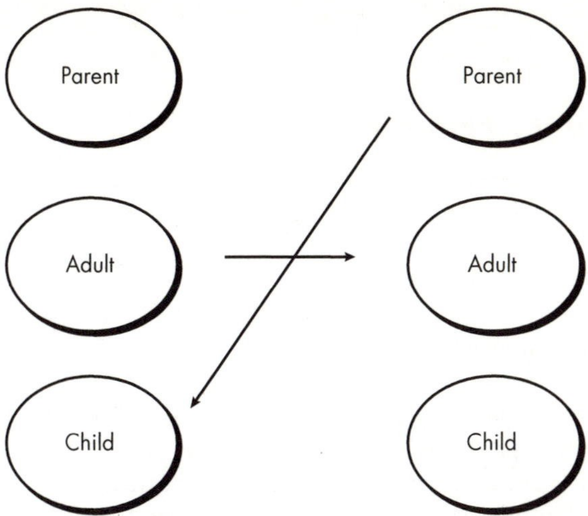

Figure 10.2 Crossed transaction

shiny new toy but you can't have it.' As my Child screams 'I want it! I want it', I either give in or go into my Adult and put my credit card away.

Using these distinctions, let's return to the domestic melodrama which started this section. 'Have you seen my watch?' sounds like Adult to Adult if it is presented as a straight question with no non-verbal overtones. By changing the intonation, it could be Child to Parent ('please help me; I'll never be able to find it for myself'). Or it could even be Parent to Child ('you're always moving my stuff around – what have you done with it this time?'). Assuming it is A–A, how would you describe the following responses?

(a) 'I told you last night not to leave it lying around.'
This sounds like P–C even without expanding on the non-verbal signals.
(b) 'It's on the kitchen table.'
Adult to Adult?
(c) 'This can-opener never works properly for me.'
This sounds like it could be Adult to Adult. But why not answer the question? Is there an ulterior motive involved? Depending

on the non-verbal signals, this sounds more like Child to Parent.

Spotting the ego states

All of this analysis depends upon being able to diagnose effectively your own and the other person's ego state. How easy is this?

> In every-day life most people can readily and quickly acquire the facility for recognizing their own and others' ego states with a minimum margin of error.[13]

Most TA texts will give you a checklist of likely verbal and non-verbal indicators to go with each ego state, along the lines of Table 10.1.

But recognising the ego states may not always be so straightforward. Berne himself suggested that you need to examine four different viewpoints before you can be absolutely confident that you have correctly identified my ego state:

1 My behaviours, using indicators like Table 10.1.
2 How my behaviours make you feel – if I have made you feel you want to take care of me, then it is likely I have been operating as Child to Parent.
3 *My own* assessment of what I am doing and feeling.
4 Historical analysis, where you look at what I have done in the past and had similar reactions.

Table 10.1 Characteristics of the ego states

Ego state	*Verbal indicators*	*Non-verbal indicators*
Parent	Using evaluative, critical or moralistic words. Discussing right and wrong.	Concerned, comforting or critical tone of voice. Caring or controlling gestures.
Adult	Practical focus on the task or problem at hand.	Even, calm voice.
Child	Emotional expression – jokes, talks about hopes and feelings.	Spontaneous and energetic gestures.

As Berne concluded: 'the more of these standards that can be met, the sounder the diagnosis.'[14] This emphasises both the importance of detailed analysis and the collaborative nature of TA as he practised it. You need to recognise how I think and feel and vice versa if we want to understand our interactions.

Games

A chain of transactions can be a game if it includes the following:

- a repeated sequence of behaviours
- the players are not aware of how they are manipulating the other person or being manipulated
- there is an exchange of ulterior transactions
- both players end up with negative feelings
- there is a moment of surprise or confusion near the end of the game where the players seem to have switched roles

Berne used slang for his concepts and he described the six stages of a game as:

Con + gimmick = Response – Switch – Crossup – Payoff

Consider the following conversation between tutor (T) and student (S) and the game analysis:

The conversation	*Game analysis*
S: 'I want to do a individual project next semester but I do not have a topic yet.'	Superficially, this looks like a straightforward Adult to Adult exchange. But psychologically it is Child to Parent. The Con is that S does not 'really' want to be helped as we see later.

T: 'Why don't you look at the list of suggested titles from last year?'

T's gimmick is the way they always feel they have to help someone by taking control and offering advice. This response shows they have been hooked.

S: 'Yes but I want to do something that I am really interested in.'

T: 'Why don't you talk to the students who have already chosen their titles?'

Another few rounds of 'why don't you' and 'yes but' until…

S: 'Well, thanks anyway for trying to help.' (Gets up and leaves.)

The game continues until S pulls the Switch here and ends the conversation. This leads to a moment of confusion (the Crossup) where T is taken by surprise. Both parties have their Payoff of negative feelings:

T: 'em…no problem.'

S walks out feeling annoyed that T 'wasn't much help, as I expected'. S is also depressed that they will 'never be able to sort out this project' which reinforces the negative feelings which the game is designed to support. T feels annoyed that the student was so unwilling and this may reinforce their belief that they are 'no good at helping students'.

Berne and subsequent authors provided detailed analysis of a large number of games along with strategies for defeating or avoiding them.[15] For example, in this case, what if T had responded differently from the start and refused to offer advice: 'I see, but first we'd better work out what you're interested in. Why do you want to do a project?'

If you want to experiment with these ideas on your own behaviour then it is worth doing a bit more preparation: read some more detailed accounts of game analysis; remember to apply a detailed analysis of ego states; and discuss your ideas with others.

Remember that TA was *not* designed to be a manipulative tool to be used on other people.

Neurolinguistic programming: origins and philosophy

Neurolinguistic programming (NLP) was founded in the 1970s by two Americans – Richard Bandler and John Grinder. Bandler was a student of mathematics and computer science who switched to psychology after becoming interested in therapy. He studied some well-known therapists and identified the behaviours which seemed to make them successful in their work with clients. He then tried to repeat these successful behaviours for himself and found that they also 'worked'. He developed this notion of modelling successful behaviour and it went on to become one of the fundamental ideas in NLP. He then met Grinder who was an associate professor of linguistics with a special interest in grammar. They decided to cooperate and work together, teaching and giving seminars on how to enable people to change and to behave more effectively.

Their seminars attracted increasing interest and an edited transcript became their first major book, *Frogs into Princes*, first published in 1979.[16] In the same year, *Psychology Today* published an article which summarised their ideas and NLP started to reach a wider audience. *Frogs into Princes* went on to become a best-seller, and was the first of many books which have promoted NLP to a general market. In the last twenty years, NLP ideas have also crept into a number of best-selling management and communication texts, as well as being widely used in training.[17]

NLP is often described as a 'revolutionary' approach to human communication. The aim is to change *how* you think. This will then change what you think so that you have a better chance of achieving the goals you set yourself. NLP texts usually place considerable emphasis on defining your goals. They then go on to provide techniques for building relationships and achieving rapport with others, using both verbal and non-verbal techniques. Perhaps the simplest expression of the philosophy is from the initial book by Bandler and Grinder. They claim that anyone only needs three things 'to be an absolutely exquisite communicator'.[18] These are:

1 A clear idea of the outcome you want.
2 Flexible behaviour. You need to be able to behave in a variety of ways so that you can find the behaviour which will work in the specific situation.
3 The ability to recognise the responses you are getting from other people. If you can do this, then you will be able to 'home in' on the behaviour which achieves the response you want from the other person.

Again, I cannot offer a complete summary of NLP within these few pages but I can highlight some fundamental ideas and principles, as follows.

The emphasis upon NVC

This is illustrated in the following quotes from Bandler and Grinder:

> the verbal component is the least interesting and least influential part of communication

> When you make a statement or ask a human being a question they will always give you the answer non-verbally, whether or not they are able to consciously express what it is[19]

They are also keen to recommend strategies and techniques which we have come across earlier:

> Non-verbal mirroring is a powerful unconscious mechanism that every human being uses to communicate effectively.[20]

However, they are also critical of some conventional views of NVC. They reject the notion that each body language signal has a clear and specific meaning. Rather, they talk about body language as providing 'information about process'. Body language can indicate how a person is responding rather than giving you specific signs or meanings.

Representational systems

One of the most fundamental ideas of NLP is that we think using three main representational systems. Consider how you think and what goes on inside your head when you think about different things. The three systems are:

1. Visual, where you see visual images as you think.
2. Auditory, where you hear sounds inside your head.
3. Kinaesthetic, where you think in terms of feelings.

For example, if I was talking to you at the moment and asked 'are you comfortable?', what would go on inside your head as you respond? Assuming you are comfortable, would you experience visual images, or restful sounds, or would you experience some bodily sensations of relaxation?

NLP claims not only that we think using these systems but that we also *express* ourselves in terms of these systems. It also suggests that we have a favourite or most-often-chosen system. For example, if you are primarily a visual person then you'll tend to use language which corresponds with that representational system. You will say things such as 'I see what you mean' or 'that looks fine to me'. And this leads to one of the most important practical implications of NLP – the idea that we can easily build a relationship with someone by *matching* their representational system.

Of course, to use this technique you have to be confident about which representational system the other person is using. And that leads to another important idea – that there is one reliable way with which you can recognise somebody's representational system: you can monitor their eye movements. You may like to try this out with friends or relatives to see if the generalisations offered by Bandler and Grinder reflect your experience. They claim that the most characteristic eye movements associated with the three systems include the ones given in Figure 10.3.

It is worth emphasising that Bandler and Grinder say that there are other ways of recognising someone's representational system, such as from tone of voice, but that eye movements are the easiest to learn. They also say that 'All generalisations are lies'.[21] They accept that some people may have different patterns but still maintain that everyone will have a consistent pattern within themselves. Other authors (and the training seminar I described at the

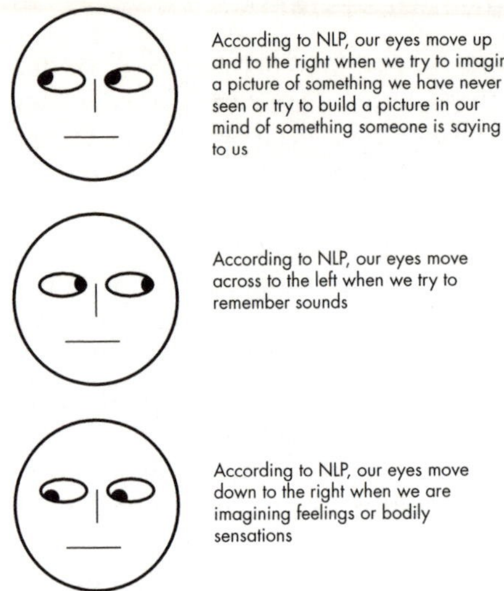

According to NLP, our eyes move up and to the right when we try to imagine a picture of something we have never seen or try to build a picture in our mind of something someone is saying to us
According to NLP, our eyes move across to the left when we try to remember sounds
According to NLP, our eyes move down to the right when we are imagining feelings or bodily sensations

Figure 10.3 Typical eye positions (for right-handed people) according to NLP

Source: Based upon O'Connor and Seymour (1990)

beginning of this chapter) simply offer the standard pattern. The snag with this analysis is that it has not been supported by systematic research.

The metamodel

NLP also offers tools for interpreting and improving the way we communicate through language. Again this focuses on the form of language and suggests ways of helping you understand what people are 'really saying'. To borrow a phrase from one well-known introduction: 'it reconnects language with experience'.[22] This is based on the idea that, when we translate our thoughts into language, we never give a complete account of what we are thinking. We are affected by three processes:

1 We only say some of the information and leave other things out.
2 We simplify what we say.
3 We generalise and do not spell out all the conditions in what we are thinking about.

The metamodel offers a series of questions to reverse these processes and arrive at the full and detailed communication. For example, suppose someone says 'the kid has had a fall'. This sentence contains what NLP calls unspecified nouns – both 'kid' and 'fall' are generalised descriptions which could mean a number of alternatives. To clarify the thought, you need to ask questions to extract detailed information.

What implications does this chapter have for the rest of this book?

There are some interesting comparisons and parallels between NLP and TA:

- both started within therapy and have been generalised to a range of other situations
- both have been popularised and widely publicised
- both offer strategies for 'improving your life' which rely upon communication analysis and strategies
- both have been developed and changed in ways which might not live up to their originators' ideals (I doubt if Eric Berne would been too happy with my salesman's use of ulterior transactions)
- both are often rejected or ignored by 'traditional' textbooks on communication

Both also contain ideas which I think are interesting and useful. But both systems may be the victim of an unfortunate combination: 'popularisation' and mass acceptance on the one hand, and 'non-acceptance by conventional social science' on the other. Advocates of the systems have also expressed concerns about 'popularity'. For example, one of Berne's closest collaborators, Claude Steiner, expressed concern for the future of TA back in 1974. He felt that its popularity could lead to it being:

> homogenized, reinterpreted, and thus destroyed by the mass market which is using it so as to make the largest amount of profit without regard for its scientific integrity.[23]

The downside of popularisation is that ideas are often oversimplified, as in my discussion of ego states and TA above. Also, many texts (including this one!) introduce the analysis of ego states, transactions and games and leave it at that. They do not continue into the deeper analysis of life scripts and life positions which often start TA texts.[24] TA theorists see these long-term scripts as the more fundamental mechanisms which drive us to behave in particular ways. Is it worth me analysing my games if I do not have an overall picture of how these games reflect my long-term goals for myself?

Another worrying aspect of popularisation is that ideas may be 'oversold', as in: 'This book will change your life' or 'you can use the principles and techniques…to make fundamental and lasting changes in your behaviour'. Of course, these claims may be true but the danger is that readers will not recognise difficulties and possible barriers when they are putting the ideas into practice. And there is also the possibility that 'trainers' may not be fully expert. The 1990 British edition of *Frogs Into Princes* ends by urging readers 'to attend only those seminars, workshops and training programmes that have been officially designed and certified by Richard Bandler and John Grinder'.

This issue of professional credibility leads me to my final point – the way these systems have been largely ignored by conventional social science. Before I wrote this paragraph, I checked the three textbooks which I recommend to students as summaries of current social psychology. Although they all have at least one chapter on interpersonal communication, none has any mention of TA or NLP or any of their main theorists. And this reflects the balance of research into these areas. While there has been some attempt to study some of the claims of NLP re NVC and research on how it works in training, this is a relatively small amount. Compare the number of research studies against the number of 'guide books' which have been sold and you have a very uneven balance.

Society is very careful (most of the time) when it comes to checking the physical medicine or vitamin tablets we can consume. Consider the extent of the research, development and the elaborate safety tests which apply to the preparations we can buy from the chemist. Yet, social scientists do not seem very interested in the 'psychological medicine' or the self-help preparations which are widely available. They have largely ignored many of the ideas which we ordinary mortals are reading about and acting upon. And that is the last thing my Parent has to say!

Chapter 11

Do men and women communicate differently?

In this chapter, I shall:

- highlight the most difficult and controversial aspects of this topic
- review the argument that language is inherently sexist, and briefly look at how language does represent the world in terms of gender
- examine evidence and research which suggests that men and women do behave differently when they communicate
- examine contrasting theories to explain possible differences, with particular emphasis on current popular theories
- identify the major implications of current popular views

Why is this topic so controversial?

One of the problems in researching this topic is that the views and attitudes we have about gender differences are often felt very strongly. This is not surprising when you review the very real discrimination which women had to endure in the past. Consider the following advice from a 1941 etiquette book:

> Once during an evening is enough for a woman to state a definite and unqualified opinion.

This example was quoted by a newspaper feature which interviewed women who studied at Cambridge University during the 'days of discrimination'.[1] It is worth remembering just how badly women were treated in comparison with their male counterparts – and this is only fifty or sixty years ago! The feature contained many examples of blatant discrimination, including:

- the Head of English who would shout 'I spy strangers' if he saw women students in his lectures and who would refuse to continue till they left
- the student who remembered that 'men never had to make their own beds or do their own chores, as we did'
- the fact that, before 1948, female students who graduated were *not* allowed to attend a graduation ceremony

Of course, the social context has changed, but the debate over male and female characteristics still generates strong opinions. As I was doing the final editing on this chapter, the British press reported an 'explosive piece of research' which suggests that 'successful female bosses...are no different in performance or style from their male counterparts'.[2] This is contrasted with the alternative view that women bosses have specific advantages over their male counterparts in modern organisations: 'they are relationship-oriented, not interested in traditional bureaucracy, able to juggle several tasks and good at sharing power'. I cannot resolve this debate within this chapter but I can highlight the very strong and contrasting opinions expressed in this article, which range from strong support to equally strong disbelief. There is also an interpretation which suggests that this research has ulterior motivation, i.e. it shows that 'men are getting frightened' by female progress in the workplace.

Because of these divided opinions and strong feelings, we need to be very careful when we review the research evidence. Research studies have suggested a number of differences between males and females in their communication. This has included areas such as

NVC, use of power and influence, strategies, and conversational style. And there are also reported differences which relate to perceptions and expectations. The way males and females report how they communicate, and the way males and females are perceived by others to communicate, can also differ.[3] However, you should approach these studies with extreme caution for at least two fundamental reasons, both of which will crop up again later in this chapter:

1 *Stereotyping* Discussions of male/female differences often seem to rely on social stereotypes rather than direct observations. This is especially unfortunate at a time when traditional sex roles and stereotypes seem to be in a greater state of flux or change than has been the case for some time.
2 *Methodology* Many of the often-quoted studies in this area are very limited in terms of their procedures and choice of subjects.

Is language inherently sexist?

This view has been very powerfully expressed by authors like Dale Spender.[4] There are three main parts to her argument:

1 The language we use determines our world-view.
2 Meanings are invented and controlled by men.
3 Language is usually used 'oppressively', as when 'he' is used to cover both genders.

The idea that our language can determine our world-view is one perspective on the relationship between language and culture. If we look at how language reflects our culture, then we can certainly find quite a large proportion of our everyday vocabulary which is, in some way, culture specific. For example, Hudson lists several English words which are difficult if not impossible to translate directly into French, including brown, chair and carpet.[5] But does this mean that French speakers have no conception of a carpet or do they just use different expressions? Hudson also comments on the surprising differences you can find between dialects. For example, he compares Irish English with mainland English. The common mainland expression 'I have known' has no direct equivalent in the Irish dialect. To say 'I have known his family all my life', the Irish dialect uses a different form – 'I know his family all me life'. But do these differences reflect different thought processes? We can find even more dramatic differences when we compare languages from very different cultures. However, we can also find very different uses of language which refer to much the same concept in different cultures.

The claim that language *determines* thought is often referred to as the Sapir–Whorf hypothesis, after the two anthropologists whose early research tended to support this claim. Edward Sapir and his student Benjamin Lee Whorf researched American Indian languages and concluded that the grammar of a language had a very powerful effect upon how the people thought, that it was '*the* shaper of ideas'.[6] For example, if you ask a Navaho Indian to hand you something then you use a different Navaho word depending on whether the object is long and flexible like string, long and rigid like a stick, or flat and flexible like paper or cloth. This means that the Navaho language forces its users to pay attention to the shapes of objects in ways which are completely ignored by the English verb 'hand'. Studies of the consequences of this language difference do suggest that it makes some difference to the way people think – Navaho-speaking children are much more sensitive to shape than their English-speaking counterparts. However, current researchers view language and grammar as *only one* of many influences upon our thought processes.

Close study of the rather stereotyped and sexist language often used in dictionaries (usually if not exclusively written by males) supports the notion that meanings have been invented and controlled by men. There is a recent example which suggests things may be changing. The French Academy is the body in France which has tried to 'protect' the French language from 'pollution' by the adoption of foreign terms and expressions such as Americanisms. They have protested loudly over the decision by female government ministers to call themselves 'la' minister (as opposed to 'le'). The problem for language purists is that French nouns are classed as male or female, and minister is normally a male noun. The Academy has called upon the ministers concerned to revert back to the male form of the noun – but I suspect that this is one battle which they will not win.

This also relates to the further part of Spender's argument, that language is consistently used in an oppressive way. Hudson identifies two general tendencies which can reinforce prejudice and bias against women.[4] The first covers all those words which apply to one gender or the other and where the female version has a less positive or negative meaning. For example, compare 'master' and 'mistress'. The male meaning is positive and good while the female meaning is bad or derogatory. For another related example, how many English words can you think of to describe a sexually promiscuous woman? Now think of how many words there are to describe a sexually promiscuous man. You will be able to construct two lists – the female one will be much longer, possibly up to ten times longer! The other tendency is where we use a word which is supposed to apply equally to both genders but is often qualified to show that the female form is somehow unusual. For example, why do we talk of a woman doctor but *never* a man doctor?

Although this analysis does support the idea that there are some consistent biases expressed in language, this does not mean that language is the problem. Consider the following brief reports from two British national newspapers:

> A man who suffered head injuries when attacked by two men who broke into his home in Beckenham, Kent, early yesterday, was pinned down on the bed by intruders who took it in turn to rape his wife.
>
> (*Daily Telegraph*)

> A terrified 19-stone husband was forced to lie next to his wife as two men raped her yesterday.
>
> (*Sun*)

Both these examples are used by Deborah Cameron to suggest that it is not necessarily language in itself which is at fault.[7] Compare the very different representations of the husband and wife in both these accounts. The focus in both is on the male and his feelings and injuries. The fact that his wife suffered much more serious injury and trauma is presented almost as an afterthought. The way that the language is used – the sentence structure, the use of adjectives, the ordering of the events — supports a male-oriented interpretation of this event. The language is used to reflect the perception rather than driving it. In other words, if people have a prejudiced or biased view of the world then they will use language to support these views. We need to consider broader issues of representation, the influence of the social context, how values and attitudes are expressed, and how assumptions are expressed.

So can we 'reform' language to avoid such bias? There have certainly been concerted attempts to revise words or introduce new expressions to shift the balance. Examples would be the use of new terms like 'Ms' or supposedly neutral terms like 'chairperson' or 'chair' to replace terms like chairman which seem to reflect male dominance. However, we can find that these strategies are often only used when there is a woman involved – chairman means male and chair or chairperson means female – rather than being used to refer equally to males. This suggests that equality still has a long way to go.

Do men and women behave differently when they communicate?

Many texts provide detailed lists of differences. These are often based on the work of Robin Lakoff who suggested that women use language differently in the following ways:[8]

- Women make much less use of specialised vocabularies.
  They use fewer technical expressions.
- Women use expletives differently.
  They use far fewer obscenities and swear words.
- Women use different patterns of intonation.
  They speak in a softer and less 'dramatic' way.
- Women are much more likely to be 'superpolite'?
  They tend to be 'overcorrect' in following social rules.
- Women use what is known as 'hedges' more often.
  They are much more likely to embellish what they say with hedges such as 'well', 'kinda', 'y'know'.
- Women use jokes and humour differently.
  They are much less likely than men to tell jokes.
- Women use more tags.

Tags are an interesting example which is worth discussing in more detail. Examples of tags are 'he's been drinking again, *hasn't he?*'; 'the way prices are rising is horrendous, *isn't it?*'; 'you were missing last week, *weren't you?*'; and 'open the door for me, *could you?*'. Not only are women supposed to use more tags but other research suggests they usually use them differently. According to Janet Holmes, men use more 'modal' tags.[9] These tags are used to encourage the other speaker to supply further information, as in the 'hasn't he' and 'isn't it' examples above. On the other hand, women seem to use more affective tags, which express feelings of togetherness and belonging.

This sort of research is usually used to justify the claim that women have a 'weak, hesitant and powerless' style of speech. But have we enough evidence to decide? There are several reasons why we need to be suspicious of the existing research and the typical conclusions, as follows.

We do not have enough 'everyday' research?

There are different interpretations of the research, e.g. on tags. For instance, the results may reflect gender-role expectations – women may feel obliged to act that way to conform to the common female stereotype. The results may reflect the conversational role which the women took on, e.g. the women acted as 'carers' in the group and their language reflects this role. The results may simply be the result of actual power relations in the situation.

Other limitations in some of the existing research are that it often fails to take account of participants' goals and strategies. It also often fails to recognise that the same feature might mean something different in different situations.

A couple of other lines of research, as follows, will illustrate that this topic is by no means as cut and dried as some introductory texts suggest.

The sex prestige pattern

I have already talked about status differences in language, as in the difference between RP and regional dialects in English. In many other societies, there is an important status distinction between the standard form of the language and the non-standard forms. Several studies have shown that, where there are these two forms of the language, then women will tend to use the high-status form much more than men. This generalisation seems to hold true for all social classes. In societies where it does not seem to happen then there may well be other forces at work. For example, in some countries women have far less access to education. As a result they will have far less opportunity to learn the standard form of the language through their education. But how do we explain such a pattern? Is it because women are behaving atypically, or do we need an explanation which looks at male behaviour? Does this simply reflect a male tendency to use more non-standard forms?

What do interruptions really mean?

One very influential study by West and Zimmerman suggested that men interrupt women in conversation more than expected.[10] They concluded that men were responsible for 96 per cent of interruptions in conversation between men and women. This finding can of course be interpreted as evidence of domination and social power: those with power and status talk more and interrupt more. It is worth looking at this study in some detail as it illustrates some of the difficulties of investigating this topic.

Ellis and Beattie question how far we can generalise the results from this study on a number of grounds:[11]

- The limited sample of subjects – all were middle class, under 35 and white.
- The limited nature of the conversations – all were two-person settings and only consisted of 'everyday chit-chat'.
- The reporting of results.
  Only the total number of interruptions were used to develop the conclusions. This implies that all the males act in much the same way and this disguises the fact that the male subjects differed dramatically in their behaviour. In fact, one of the eleven males did contribute nearly one-quarter of the interruptions.
- Results from other studies.
  They report a number of conflicting studies. For example, Beattie himself found no differences in the volume of interruptions in a study of mixed-sex university tutorial groups.

So Ellis and Beattie draw the conclusion that:

> the question of male and female dominance in conversation through the medium of interruption is far from conclusively answered. The data are still somewhat contradictory, and the interpretation of the data still not certain.

There is another problem: can we be sure that every interruption actually means the same thing?

These studies normally define interruption as an expression of power. As the more powerful members are likely to dominate the conversation, they will tend to talk more and they will also interrupt others in order to gain the floor. But this analysis may be misleading. If you look more closely at how and why people interrupt, a different picture may emerge. Some studies have suggested that women interrupt in order to show support and agreement with the original speaker. Men will interrupt both to agree and to disagree. There are also cultural differences to take into account – consider conversations in Japan where interruption is very rare and where allocating the turn to the next speaker is a very important cooperative process.

How can possible differences in communication be explained?

Early theorists (who were male) had a very clear view: women's speech style was 'different and inferior'. This is usually described as deficit theory. We can thankfully dismiss the claims of previous generations that this is a direct result of 'women's intellectual inferiority'. But there is a second possible explanation that is more worthy of consideration: the notion that women are socialised to behave in a less powerful way and so adopt the language style which suits this status. And deficit theory does suggest an obvious 'remedy' for powerless speech – women need to change.[12] But given the major changes to society, the dominant current explanation offers a very different picture.

Two cultures

Maltz and Borker provide an interesting account which suggests how gender differences in communication can develop.[13] They start with the observation that boys and girls spend most of their play in single-sex groups. Following the patterns established in the culture at large, these groups have different forms of social organisation. Girls will cooperate and share power. This develops their skills in responding to relationships and situations. The typical boys' group on the other hand is a hierarchy where issues of status and identity are much more prominent. As a result, boys sharpen their competitive tendencies and are more concerned with status. Once established, these differences carry forward into adulthood where men become more inclined to argue and compete for status and where women concentrate on cooperation and building on other people's contributions. One interesting development is that this academic analysis has now become an item on the best-seller lists.

The so-called two-cultures theory suggests that men and women have two different styles of communication which reflect their different goals and strategies, and which are equally valid. According to this approach, the solution or remedy to gender misunderstanding is mutual understanding and acceptance. Men and women must learn each other's ways and respond appropriately (although there is still the question of who has the major responsibility for this job of reinterpreting). Two examples of this approach are worth exploring as they have *both* achieved international best-seller status: the work of Deborah Tannen and John Gray.

The work of Deborah Tannen

She suggests that men and women have different rules for interaction.[14] For example, what does 'uh-uh' mean? She suggests two possible interpretations: 'continue, I'm listening', or 'I agree, I follow you'. The first is the typical female reaction which emphasises social support and encouragement; the second is the male message for agreement. Of course, these differences can very easily lead to miscommunication. If you (male) suggest a trip to the theatre as the way to spend the evening, and receive an 'uh-uh' response from the female in your life, then you assume that this means agreement. What happens when you rush in with the tickets and find her curled up in front of the TV for the night: 'But I didn't agree'?

The work of John Gray

According to John Gray, 'men and women are supposed to be different'.[15] The most crucial aspect of this difference for the way we communicate is in our 'sense of self'. For men this sense of self is defined: 'through *his* ability to achieve results'. For women this sense of self is defined: 'through *her* feelings and the quality of her relationships'.

Gray argues that men and women behave differently because of this fundamental difference in personal identity. For example, when confronted by a stressful situation, an upset man 'stops talking' and 'goes into his cave'. In other words, a man will retreat into solitude and try to work things out for himself. In a similar situation, a woman will seek out the company of friends and openly discuss her concerns and feelings.

Gray also suggests that men and women use language differently to express requests: compare the male 'would you empty the bin?' with the female 'could you empty the bin?' The difficulty here is that the male interprets the female request as a 'put-down' which implicitly challenges his competence or his commitment ('of course, I *could* empty it').

A final example from Gray is his claim that women use poetic licence to express their feelings, as in 'nothing is working' or 'we never go out'. The difficulty here is that men interpret these remarks literally and tend to respond with information rather than the required social support ('we went out to the theatre two weeks ago'). This factual response is seen by the woman as tactless and uncaring and a spiral of misunderstanding starts to grow.

Conclusion

So do we now have a clear answer to both the what and why of gender differences in communication? Are these theories adequate? Admittedly, I have only given a very sketchy overview of both Gray and Tannen, so perhaps I have not given their work a fair hearing. Tannen's work is based on many linguistic studies and she has written many books for the academic community.[16] And she does provide a very reasoned response to her critics.[17] On the other hand, Gray does not quote research studies. His justification is the 'thousands of couples' who have been able to 'transform their relationships' by attending one of his workshops. But is this because of the opportunity to talk openly with each other rather than the power of Gray's philosophy? Can we be sure that 'remembering that we are supposed to be different will help you to be more loving'?[18]

Even after these considerations, I am left with three fundamental reservations about the two-cultures theory as expressed by these authors:

1 The theories still seem to ignore or play down differences within and between women (and men).
  All women and all men are treated in much the same way – the differences are described as clear cut and universal. (This is

especially true of Gray; Tannen is much more concerned to emphasise that she is dealing with generalisations based on observation and that 'of course there will be exceptions to the patterns observed'. She also emphasises that 'To say that women and men tend to speak in different ways in this culture and in this time does not mean that they must go on speaking that way, or that biology is destiny'.)17

2 The theories do not pay sufficient attention to issues of power and values.
This is perhaps the most fundamental problem. For example, as a typical male, do I now have permission from John Gray to retire to my 'cave' every time I feel upset? Am I free to exclude my partner from any discussion of my feelings? Surely that is OK if that is the natural behaviour? If my partner objects to this exclusion, am I right to ignore her?

3 The theories make implicit assumptions about 'good' communication.
In the same way that I questioned some of the assumptions implicit in popular models of communication in earlier chapters, I would question some of the assumptions, especially in the books by Gray.

And finally – the practical issues?

There are also some very clear practical issues which emerge from reading this literature on male/female communication:

- What is your style of communication (and what impact does it have) when you talk to members of your own and other genders?
- How do you respond to others of the same and other gender?
- Will reading this chapter (and hopefully doing some further research for yourself) change *your* behaviour?

Chapter 12

Does assertiveness work?

In this chapter, I shall:

- explain why assertiveness is such an important topic in interpersonal communication
- define what we mean by assertiveness
- compare assertive, aggressive and submissive behaviour
- explain some of the techniques which are used in assertive communication
- discuss whether assertiveness really does 'work'

Why is assertiveness important?

There are at least three reasons why assertiveness is an important topic within interpersonal communication.

Firstly, it appears that 'assertion training has become one of the most popular, if not *the* most popular, way of developing social skills'.[1] This popularity is not just confined to formal training courses and workshops. Many popular self-help books use assertiveness principles even if they do not use the term. And some of these popular texts offer glittering prospects:

> When I discovered assertive communication, my life changed. I saw that there was a way to be direct, open, and honest without being obnoxious. I realised I could express myself clearly and concisely without resorting to manipulation or intimidation.[2]

And this highlights my second reason: as with other popular theories, there is a danger that assertiveness will be accepted too uncritically. One of my student groups recently did a project investigating the success of assertiveness training. They contacted all the training providers they could find in the area and asked the direct question: 'What evidence do you have that your training is successful?' None of the trainers were either able or willing to provide evidence over and above the 'happy sheets' used to record the participants' immediate impressions of the course. This is perhaps not surprising as none of the trainers had been invited (or paid) by the organisations they worked for to carry out follow-up studies. But what does this training really do for the participants? And do the effects last?

My third reason for looking at assertiveness in a bit more detail is the way it claims to build an explicit relationship between values, attitudes and behaviour. This raises issues of ethical behaviour and morality which are often left implicit in other methods. Some of these general issues have already been raised in Chapters 10 and 11 so this chapter is shorter to avoid repetition.

How did ideas on assertiveness develop?

The history of assertiveness training goes back several decades to the 1950s when a number of therapists started to devise ways of helping individual patients who had serious problems in expressing themselves and standing up for their rights. It was recognised that giving these individuals more self-confidence, along with specific skills and techniques, would help them to cope more effectively with everyday life. In the 1960s, these ideas spread to a much wider audience. There was a dramatic growth in personal development courses and social skills training of all different types. Many trainers recognised that assertiveness was not simply valuable for people with very serious difficulties. Many professionals and people in their everyday lives decided they could benefit by communicating more assertively.

From 1970 on, books on assertiveness started to appear which were aimed at the general public.[3] Initially, most of these were aimed at women as assertion was seen as 'one way for women to deal with sexism and oppression by men'.[4] Since then we have seen assertiveness training programmes used by many professions and in many different organisational settings. Numerous guide books have appeared and there has also been considerable research on the skills and value of assertiveness training.[5]

What do we mean by assertive communication?

A typical definition of assertiveness, taken from one of the well-established texts, is:

> Assertion involves standing up for personal rights and expressing thoughts, feelings and beliefs in direct, honest and appropriate ways which respect the rights of other people.[6]

This definition brings out some of the key features of assertiveness:

- recognising that you have basic human rights which should be respected by others
- recognising that these rights include being able to express your feelings and needs
- communication which is direct, honest and open
- expressing mutual respect for other people and their rights

When we talk about personal rights, these are usually expressed in a list which includes the following:[7]

> 'I have the right to express my thoughts and opinions, even though they may be different from those of others.'
> 'I have the right to express my feelings and to take responsibility for them.'
> 'I have the rights to say "No" without feeling guilty.'
> 'I have the right to be listened to and taken seriously.'

What are the different styles of behaviour?

All the books on assertive behaviour define three styles of behaviour: assertion, aggression and submission (or non-assertion). These are often expressed as a continuum with assertion in the middle:

Aggression ——— Assertion ——— Submission

But perhaps a better way of comparing styles of behaviour is to look at the two underlying dimensions:[8]

1 From indirect expression through to direct expression.
2 From coercive behaviour through to non-coercive behaviour.

This gives the diagram shown in Figure 12.1, which suggests four styles of behaviour. The fourth style is where you express aggression in an indirect way without direct confrontation.

For this chapter, we shall concentrate on the three main styles, as follows.

Aggressive behaviour

This includes some form of threat which undermines the rights of the other person. It is about winning, regardless of the other person's feelings. The verbal and non-verbal accompaniments to aggressive behaviour include loud and abusive talk, interruptions,

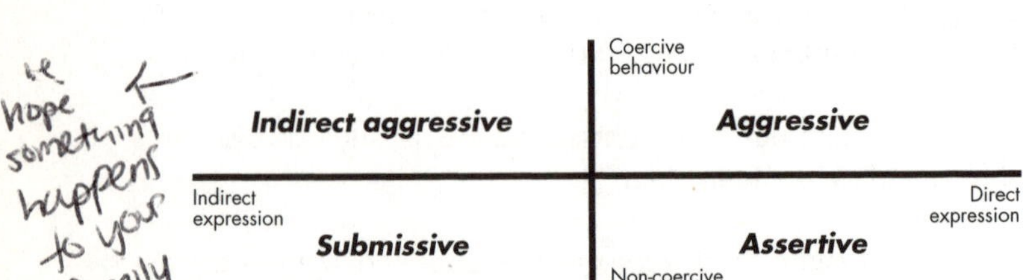

Figure 12.1 Styles of behaviour

Source: Hargie, O., Saunders, C. and Dickson, D. (1994) *Social Skills in Interpersonal Communication*, 3rd edn, London: Routledge, page 273

and glaring or staring eye contact. Individuals who regularly use aggressive behaviour may well 'win' in the short term but will usually be disliked. They also run the risk of inviting an even more aggressive response.

Submissive behaviour

This behaviour gives in to the demands of others by avoiding conflict and accepting being put upon. Verbal and non-verbal accompaniments include apologetic and hesitant speech, soft speech, nervous gestures and a reluctance to express opinions. Submissive individuals will be seen as weak and easily manipulated. They will certainly not inspire confidence in others.

The verbal and non-verbal behaviours associated with these styles have been demonstrated quite clearly in research studies as well as from observation of everyday life.

Assertive behaviour

The characteristics are open and clear expression, firm and fluent conversation, and quick spontaneous answers. The non-verbal components include medium levels of eye contact; appropriate facial expressions; smooth gestures; relaxed but upright body posture; and appropriate paralinguistics. There is more good news in the research evidence: as well as inspiring confidence in others, assertive individuals will tend to 'feel more in control of their lives, derive more satisfaction from the relationship and achieve their goals more often'.[9]

Different types of assertive behaviour

There are various ways of categorising assertive behaviour. Ken and Kate Back define six main types of assertive behaviour which can be divided into two levels.[10] The practical implication of this is that you should normally start by using a low-level assertion. If this is not successful then you try a high-level assertion. The three types at the lower level are:

1 *Basic assertion* This is where you simply give the straightforward statement of what you need, want, believe or feel. For example, 'I bought this radio here yesterday and it will not pick up any signals on FM. I need to have it replaced.'

2 *Responsive assertion* This is where you check the other person's needs or feelings. For example, 'what do you think we should do?'
3 *Empathetic assertion* This is where you state your needs and wants but also explicitly recognise the other person's point of view or feelings. For example, 'I understand that you feel uncertain about this new way of doing things, but I need to do this in the new way this afternoon'.

The three high-level types are:

1 *Consequence* This is the strongest form of assertion – where you tell the other person what will happen to them if they do not change their behaviour. It should not be phrased as a threat and should offer the other person the chance to change before there are any consequences. Because it can be so easily interpreted as a threat, this is probably the most difficult form of assertion to use.
2 *Discrepancy assertion* This is where you point out the discrepancy between what you have agreed previously on what seems to be happening or is about to happen. This also usually means repeating what you want in the situation. For example, 'last week you said you would give me the opportunity to work on the Frankenstein project straight away. You have not contacted me and I would like to start this week.'
3 *Negative feelings assertion* This is where you point out the effect that the other person's behaviour is having upon you. This usually contains four components:

   - description of how the other person has behaved (expressed as objectively and as descriptively as you can)
   - statement of how the other person's behaviour affects you
   - description of how you feel
   - description of what you want or would prefer

   For example, using these four components in the same order:

   'When you hand in your part of the project at this time on the Friday.'
   'It means I have to work over the weekend.'

'I feel annoyed when this happens.'
'So I would like to collect stuff from you on Friday lunchtime in the future.'

The best way of considering the value of these techniques is to examine a practical situation of your own. Think of a situation where you wish to improve your communication with another person – this could be telling your partner about some annoying habit of theirs or telling your boss about some difficulty you are having with his or her management style. Consider what you have done so far, if anything. Why has it not worked? Does the other person know about your feelings at all? Which of the above techniques might help you to get your message across? How would the different techniques be received by the other person? Would they respond better to, say, basic or empathetic assertion? Before you actually try any, read the last part of this chapter.

So does assertiveness always work?

The account of assertiveness which I have offered above suggests that it is an extremely effective form of behaviour from which everyone can benefit. My own view is that virtually everyone can benefit from *considering* both the values and techniques of assertiveness. And there is also significant independent evidence to show that training people in assertiveness can change their behaviour in positive ways. However, there are a number of issues and factors which can complicate what happens when people use assertive techniques, and which are sometimes ignored by the more enthusiastic advocates.[11]

Assertive behaviour may be 'misread'

If you construct an assertive message using the techniques listed above, can we guarantee that the message will be seen as assertive by the person on the receiving end? Unfortunately, the answer is no. People adopting assertive behaviour can be seen as less likeable and less friendly. Their behaviour may also be seen as 'inappropriate'. In particular, assertive behaviour may be *seen* as aggressive, especially when the person is behaving differently from the way they have acted in the past. As a result, assertive behaviour is potentially 'risky', especially as it is often used in situations where there is some emotional tension.

Assertive behaviour may be defined differently

There is research evidence that there are different definitions of assertiveness which will have powerful practical implications. For example, the professional literature emphasises the way that people can 'express their own rights'; untrained women stress the importance of consideration for others; whereas untrained men seem to see assertiveness in terms of power and influence. A training programme which fails to recognise and deal with these differences in values and perceptions may simply fail or even be counter-productive.

Gender roles

Given the focus on people's rights, it is not surprising that women's groups have been especially keen to incorporate assertiveness training in order to combat some of the prejudice and discrimination they can face at work and in the home. But the research suggests that male assertion and female assertion can have different consequences and so reliance on the same techniques may actually work out differently. This raises issues of gender roles which relate to the previous chapter, and issues of personal choice. If you are female and choose to use assertive techniques, how will you react if males see this as aggressive? Is this your problem or theirs? Should we simply accept the status quo? There is the uncomfortable finding that 'Women appear to make a conscious decision not to assert their rights by direct confrontation and thus not to challenge the traditional feminine sex role'.[12]

Situational factors

Certain types of assertiveness may well work better in some situations than others. This raises the issue of which type of assertive message to use (and how to make that decision).

Cultural background

The typical guide book on assertive behaviour proposes values which are culturally acceptable in North America and Western Europe, although there are some important differences both within and between these continents. Other cultures place very different values upon humility and submission. In these cultures, assertive behaviour may be regarded as inappropriate or even offensive in some situations.

Conclusion

As with many of the topics we have covered in this book, one conclusion is that we need more practical research on some aspects of assertiveness. For example, how should it work in multicultural organisations?

Perhaps the most appropriate general conclusion is that assertive behaviour is one style of behaviour which can be used in social situations, and which is worth considering if you feel that you are having difficulty in expressing yourself directly. But the complexity of communication which I tried to get across in Section B means that it *cannot* be considered a magic wand which will always work. The impact of assertive messages will depend upon a range of social and cultural factors.

Section D

Going beyond interpersonal communication

Chapter 13

Communication and groups

In this chapter, I shall:

- outline the most important features which distinguish one-to-one, face-to-face communication from communication in groups
- define a psychological group
- discuss the relationship between group membership and communication
- introduce the particular problems of communicating across group boundaries (intergroup communication)

What makes communication in groups any different from interpersonal communication between two people?

For the moment I shall concentrate upon communication within one small group (some textbooks call it intragroup communication).

All the components of interpersonal communication are relevant, but additional factors need to be taken into account. For example, think of a group in which you participate. Would you say you were a member of that group? If you do, how important is that membership to you? People do feel and act in certain ways as a result of being members of certain groups. But does it make sense to talk of membership of a pair of people? I would say not, although I am not disputing the fact that pairs of people can have very special relationships, as in marriage.

Social groups are another level of social behaviour which needs to be considered in its own terms. Some early writers took this point of view to an extreme position and argued that there was a 'group mind', i.e. that groups could have consciousness or emotions almost independent of their members.[1] Versions of this view are still prominent in some branches of psychoanalysis. I follow a more 'moderate' line which is nicely represented in the following quote from Muzafer Sherif, although you will have to ignore the rather sexist implications and recognise that both men and women can be members of groups![2]

> We cannot do justice to events by extrapolating uncritically from man's feelings, attitudes and behaviour when he is in a state of isolation to his behaviour when acting as a member of a group. Being a member of a group and behaving as a member of a group have psychological consequences. There are consequences even when the other members are not immediately present.

Becoming a psychological group

When does a collection of people become a group? A collection of people is not necessarily a group, in the sense of being a psychological group. When I talk of groups I wish to talk of psychological groups, i.e. where the individuals involved recognise that they are members of the group and where that membership has some psychological significance for the members. For example, imagine the average bus queue standing waiting for a bus, probably in the rain if British weather is on typical form. Here we have a collection of people. But are they a group? Probably not. They are more likely to see themselves as a collection of individuals who simply happen to be in the same place at the same time. They do not normally exhibit any of the characteristics we usually associate with a psychological group, as follows.

- *Interaction* Members of a group act and react towards one another, and these interactions are liable to develop in particular ways over time so that a regular pattern or structure emerges.
- *Perception* Members of a group will see the group as 'real' and will define themselves as members. They will also develop a group boundary, i.e. they have a shared definition of who is in the group and who is outside the group.
- *Norms* I have discussed norms before and I have also commented on the 'power' of group norms in everyday life, particularly when we observe very 'public' expressions of group membership such as clothing.
- *Roles* We have also encountered the concept of role on a number of occasions. At a group level you can think of fairly formal norms associated with certain positions such as the chair, or more informal roles which can develop in a group, e.g. the 'joker' who is 'expected' to keep the other members cheerful.
- *Emotional relationships* Group members develop affective or emotional relationships with one another over time. They are unlikely to be neutral or indifferent to one another. And of course relationships between members of a group can be very 'powerful' and long lasting.
- *Goals* A group will develop shared goals, purposes or objectives.

You can use these characteristics to describe a two-person relationship but they do not apply in quite the same way. For example, group norms are often agreed and enforced by the majority of members who then 'police' any minority who try to step out of line. The notions of majority and minority do not make sense when there are only two people involved and where we have to look at how each individual uses power.

This set of six characteristics is not the only way to define a psychological group but it does suggest the most basic features.[3] There are a couple of points to bear in mind though:

- *Dimensions* It is important to consider each of these characteristics as dimensions which vary along a continuum. You can represent a group in terms of where it would stand on each of the six dimensions. You can expect any particular group to change in these dimensions over time. For example, different groups will have different degrees of interaction, ranging from groups which only meet occasionally to groups which are in almost permanent contact.

- *Importance and boundary* This list of characteristics does not suggest which is the most important. This may be different in different situations. For example, a number of studies suggest that as long as people perceive themselves as a group then they will act accordingly regardless of how much or little contact they have. The most important characteristic then is the group boundary – the distinction between who is in and out of the group.

Types of groups

There are different types of groups. And different types of group exhibit different characteristics. But what different types do exist? Tajfel and Fraser offer the following list:[3]

- family groups
- friendship groups
- workgroups

These are easily recognisable in everyday life and they do operate somewhat differently. Tajfel and Fraser also suggest that social scientists have 'created' two other types of group with distinctive characteristics:

- laboratory groups
- experiential groups

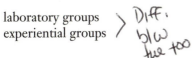

Laboratory groups

Laboratory groups are those groups of students (mainly American) who are brought together for a fairly short period of time to carry out social psychological research on group interaction. The problem is that, as the groups only last for a short time, they almost certainly do not develop any important goals, roles or norms as you would expect in 'real' groups. Some critics have christened these groups 'nonsense groups' because they have so few of the characteristics we associate with everyday social groups. This criticism does mean we must be careful in applying the results of such studies to real groups. It also raises the broader issue of whether we can generalise from laboratory experimental studies. I would argue that it is possible to make useful generalisations provided you are aware of the limitations of the studies in question.[4]

Experiential groups

In the last twenty years there has been an upsurge of interest in groups which meet in order to understand their own interpersonal processes and develop their members' social skills, i.e. their understanding of themselves and others. To understand the point of experiential groups, you need to understand an important distinction in small-group research – the distinction between TASK and PROCESS:

> TASK: This is what the group does, i.e. the job or task it is established to carry out.
>
> PROCESS: This is how the group operates, i.e. how members relate to one another and influence one another.

For example, a workgroup is likely to have fairly well-defined tasks – the group will have certain jobs to do and there will be sanctions if they do not do these jobs properly. The process of the group includes the various ways in which the members get on with one another. There may be a very cordial atmosphere with a great deal of cooperation or there could be a struggle for leadership with a lot of antagonism. Often these process issues are not discussed openly and any tensions are likely to build up over time until there is an inevitable explosion. For example, the following process problems often characterise ineffective groups:[5]

- *Battle fatigue* This group cannot agree on common goals. Meetings are running battles where different members try to push their view forward and blame others for poor performance to date. Morale is low and the real cooperation only emerges when a common enemy is identified.
- *Father knows best* This group has a boss with very clear ideas on how the work should be done, who expects loyalty and obedi-

ence from members and gives rewards on that basis. As a result criticism of the boss's ideas rarely happens, if at all. Creativity may well be stifled – the individual who has bright ideas which do not fit in with the boss's master plan may well be 'shut out'.

In everyday groups there is an emphasis on completing the task, but in experiential groups the main focus is understanding the process as it happens. Of course this process contains a number of different elements, including group members' feelings and reactions to each other, the general atmosphere in the group, and role and leadership issues. As a result it is not surprising to find many different types of experiential groups with different emphases.[6] For example, T-groups aim to develop participants' skills in interpersonal and group processes whereas encounter groups usually concentrate on individuals' self-understanding. It is very difficult to provide a brief description of experiential groups which can be readily understood by someone who does not have direct personal experience of them. They are very different from most everyday groups but can provide very significant insights into how 'normal' groups operate. Unfortunately they have become rather controversial and it is difficult to find a balanced discussion of their virtues and failings. Many general textbooks provide a rather distorted picture. In particular, they emphasise one aspect of one study which suggests that these groups can harm a significant number of participants. Unfortunately this study has a number of significant weaknesses and limitations, and more recent research suggests that the general conclusion is unwarranted. On the other hand there is evidence to suggest that different types of experiential groups benefit different people and that it is important to have an experienced and responsible group leader. Given the appropriate circumstances, these groups can achieve learning which other methods cannot reach![7]

Do groups develop over time?

One fairly common finding is that a small group passes through certain stages of development. These are briefly summarised as follows:

Forming

- The group tries to work out what the task involves.
- Members are rather wary and try to test out the atmosphere.

Storming

- Members may respond emotionally to the demands of the task. There is dispute over what needs to be done.
- There is a lot of conflict and argument between group members and usually a struggle for leadership.

Norming

- There is an open exchange of opinions and interpretations and the task is agreed upon.
- A friendly atmosphere develops and members take on fairly definite roles.

Performing

- Solutions to the task emerge.
- People carry out their roles in relation to one another.

This theory of group development appears in most introductory texts in communication.[8] Unfortunately the research evidence does not totally support it. A few alternative positions have emerged:

- Other stage theories have been proposed which have some evidence to back them up.
- Some researchers have suggested that groups alternate between different phases rather than go through a definite series of stages. For example, some problem-solving groups alternate between a phase where they concentrate on the task and a phase where they concentrate on their personal relationships.[9]

Some studies have suggested that groups do not follow the stages described above in exactly this order. For example, there does not always have to be a stage of conflict, i.e. storming. At the moment it is difficult to decide between these alternative models of group development because there is not enough research evidence which looks at natural everyday groups. To summarise the main evidence at the moment, I would say that:

- you can assume that a group is likely to go through certain stages
- the exact nature and sequence of these stages will depend on a number of factors such as the leadership of a group

How does group membership influence communication?

Membership of a group influences communication in a number of ways. Here I only have space to examine two, almost contradictory, influences. On the one hand a group can develop norms which restrict its members' behaviour and communication; on the other hand a group can provide support and understanding for its members and allow them to express themselves in ways which they otherwise would not have done.

Conformity pressures in groups

Conformity can be defined as a change in a person's behaviour or opinions as a result of real or imagined pressure from a person or group of people. This definition is fairly typical but does have its limitations.[10] It fails to distinguish between pressures from a group, which we shall concentrate on in this section, and pressures from an individual. This latter pressure often gives rise to obedience which is a rather different psychological experience.[11]

The most widely reported experiment on conformity to group pressure is the classic study by Asch which is vividly described by Aronson from the subject's point of view:[12]

> You have volunteered to participate in an experiment on perceptual judgment. You enter a room with four other participants. The experimenter shows all of you a straight line (line X). Simultaneously, he shows you three other lines for comparison (lines A, B and C). He asks you to choose which of the three lines is closest in length to line X. The judgment strikes you as being a very easy one. It is perfectly clear to you that line B is the correct answer, and when your turn comes, you will clearly say that B is the one. But it's not your turn to respond. The person whose turn it is looks carefully at the lines and says 'Line A'. Your mouth drops open and you look at him quizically. 'How can he believe it's A when any fool can see that it's B?' you ask yourself. 'He must be either blind or crazy.' Now it's the second person's turn to respond. He also chooses line A. You begin to feel like Alice in Wonderland. 'How can it be?' you ask yourself. 'Are both of these people blind or crazy?' But then the next person responds, and he also says 'Line A'. You

> take another look at those lines. 'Maybe I'm the only one who's losing his mind,' you mutter inaudibly. Now it's the fourth person's turn, and he also judges the correct line to be line A. You break out in a cold sweat. Finally, it's your turn. 'Why, it's line A, of course,' you declare. 'I knew it all the time.'

This dramatic description represents the kind of conflict that Asch's college students went through. Certainly they did become anxious and embarrassed. But how did they respond? It is important to be clear about the pattern of Asch's results. For example, do some people give in all of the time? Or do most people give in some of the time? These two patterns of results lead to very different conclusions on the 'power' of group pressure.

Unfortunately, many textbook accounts of Asch give a rather vague description of his results and present an almost overwhelming 'victory' for conformity pressure over individual judgement. Asch was certainly surprised by the number of subjects who conformed, but it is important to remember two points:

1 It is a very unusual situation – we expect people to differ in their opinions but not in a straightforward and unambiguous judgement. This very unexpected element certainly put extra pressure on the subjects.
2 Most subjects gave in some of the time – only a few gave in all of the time.

This experiment has been repeated on a number of occasions with similar results. It is usually considered as the classic demonstration of the power of a group to influence its members. This is rather ironic as Asch originally wished to investigate factors which could decrease conformity behaviour, which he subsequently did with variations on his original experiment. However, explaining these results is not so easy – we can still argue over why Asch's subjects behaved in the way they did. One reason for this is that there are at least two different forms of pressure which a group can exert over its members:

1 *Normative pressure* Members follow the norms of the group because they wish to be accepted and liked by other members. In other words, people wish to be accepted and liked by other members.

2 *Informational pressure* Members pay attention to other responses as this gives them information which helps to clarify the situation. In other words, people wish to be correct and use other people's responses to help them arrive at the right answer. This may be particularly important in ambiguous or anxious circumstances.

Although Asch's experiment is typically regarded as an example of normative pressure, some subjects clearly felt informational pressures. For example, some suggested afterwards that the stooges' responses meant that they must have misinterpreted the experimenter's instructions. Asch's experiment was taken for granted for many years. In the 1980s, his results were challenged by two British psychologists, Perrin and Spencer.[13] They repeated his experiment with undergraduate subjects in a British university and found no conformity at all! They then repeated the experiment with other groups and found results broadly similar to Asch's with groups who placed more importance on their group cohesion, e.g. with young unemployed West Indian boys.

They conclude that their experiments illustrate the importance of the broader historical and social context in which investigations are conducted. They suggest that Asch's subjects (American college students in the 1950s) were a generally conformist group because of the time they lived in, i.e. the infamous McCarthy period in the USA. British undergraduates in the 1980s were a more independent non-conformist group. Asch himself agreed that these considerations must be taken into account.[13]

Thus, I can conclude that groups do exert pressure on individuals to toe the line in particular ways. How far these pressures will influence individuals depends on a number of factors, including:

- the social context
- the membership of the group
- the group norms
- the nature of the task

So far I have been talking about conformity as it might crop up in typical everyday groups. Given special circumstances, these can be much more powerful. Janis coined the term 'groupthink' to describe:

> a way of thinking in which a cohesive group's need for unanimity overwhelms the members' realistic appraisal of alternative courses of action.[14]

In a very cohesive group, where there is a strong pressure for consensus, groupthink may occur and give rise to mistaken group decisions. Janis was particularly interested in classic blunders made by powerful groups, such as the Bay of Pigs incident which nearly triggered the Third World War back in the 1960s. This abortive invasion of Cuba was masterminded by a small group of advisers in the US government. No one in the group doubted their decisions although these were obviously suspect to outside observers. Janis proposes several factors necessary for a group to develop groupthink, including the presence in the group of powerful individuals who enforce the party line. Another example may have been the group surrounding Hitler in the Second World War. Thus, Janis does *not* propose that cohesion must give rise to inferior decisions, which is an impression sometimes given by textbook accounts.

One interesting implication here is that a group can consciously adopt ways of communicating which eliminate the risk of groupthink. Janis has made a number of recommendations along these lines. For example, at each meeting, one member of the group is given the role of 'devil's advocate' whose job is to spot potential problems or pitfalls in the group's decisions.

Another frightening example of group influence concerns the term 'deindividuation'. Philip Zimbardo coined this term to describe the situation where individual members of a group 'lose' their sense of individuality and fulfil their roles even at the expense of their own moral values. The classic experiment which illustrates the phenomenon was Zimbardo's prison experiment which I described in Chapter 6.

The important point about these examples of group influence is that they all depend upon certain patterns and styles of group communication. If the members are aware of these pressures then they can choose to communicate in a different way with different end results. And this brings me to my next section.

Group membership as a liberating influence

Discussions of conformity in groups often portray conformity as a negative phenomenon which has unfortunate consequences as in the Asch or Zimbardo experiments. However, conformity is a necessary part of social life. Without some acceptance of common standards or values, social life would simply disintegrate. It is also true to say that groups can develop norms which help people to develop more freedom in their actions rather than less. At first sight this may seem a contradiction in terms. A few practical illustrations will help to clarify this, as follows.

Therapy groups

In the last thirty years, the work of Carl Rogers has been enormously influential in psychotherapy, the treatment of people who are suffering from some form of mental disturbance. Originally, Rogers worked with individual patients or clients. He developed very pronounced views on how a therapist should behave in a one-to-one situation. For example, he suggested that the therapist should display warmth and caring for the client and this should not depend on the client behaving in a particular way (unconditional positive regard). He also urged therapists to act openly and honestly but *not* to give advice. He argues that the role of the therapist is to help clients work through their own problems and arrive at *their own* solutions.

One way of interpreting these recommendations is to say that Rogers has provided a specific set of communication rules for therapists. He also hopes that members of the group will adopt the same rules by following the leader's example. Thus, the norms of the group incorporate trust, acceptance and innovation. When you feel that you can trust others, and that they accept and value your personality, then you will not be wary of trying out new behaviour and learning from others. In other words, your communication will become more 'open' – you will feel less restricted or embarrassed in discussing personal problems or anxieties. You will develop skills in self-disclosure (see Chapter 3).

Although many psychotherapy groups do not follow Rogers' theoretical approach, they usually do claim some if not all of the benefit of group work which he outlined – the development of trust and mutual help. And Rogers' ideas have also been influential in more widespread applications of group work.

Experiential groups

Rogers felt so strongly about the 'liberating' effect of therapeutic group experience that he went on to develop a particular type of experiential group – the basic encounter group. This is designed not as a therapeutic experience but as a way of enabling 'normal' people to gain insight into their own behaviour. The role of the leader and the overall process is much the same as described above. Again, Rogers is enthusiastic about the likely outcomes (and women can participate as well!):

> Thus, in such a group the individual comes to know himself and each of the others more completely than is possible in the usual social or working relationships. Hence he relates better to others, both in the group and later in the everyday life situation.[15]

There is evidence to suggest that encounter groups can provide these results although they are perhaps not as 'powerful' as Rogers first suggested. What is much less clear is what exactly happens in these groups, and how this creates these effects. Systematic research on these questions has recently emerged but has not yet provided very clear answers. I can conclude, though, that these groups do develop a structure and atmosphere which enable members to experiment and change.[16] And it is important to stress the role of communication in these groups.

Self-help groups

In the last thirty years, there has been an enormous growth in the numbers and membership of self-help groups and organisations, such as Alcoholics Anonymous, Gamblers Anonymous, SHARE, CARE, etc. Although there is a tremendous variety of such organisations, they do share common characteristics:

- mutual care and support
- the emphasis on sharing of experience
- the philosophy that helping others can also benefit yourself
- putting people together with a common problem or circumstances

Unfortunately there has been relatively little systematic research on these groups. As a result, I can only repeat the point that small groups can offer an environment in which people can develop new and innovative behaviour. And the role of communication is crucial. A group can become a vehicle for social support and individual development if it develops the appropriate norms and patterns, e.g. if members are able to self-disclose and trust each other. Where communication is allowed to develop a dogmatic and authoritarian pattern then the damaging effects of conformity pressures will emerge.

Intergroup communication

Intergroup communication is communication between two or more different social groups which may be small face-to-face groups of the sort I discussed in the last section or more general social groups such as different social classes or ethnic groups. It is important to distinguish between interpersonal, intragroup and intergroup communication. These are different levels of communication and different processes operate at each level.

Most of the research on intergroup relations has examined situations where two groups are in competition or in conflict. In these circumstances, communication is liable to be both important and difficult. There is a fairly consistent set of behaviours which crop up in these circumstances, including the following:

- Members develop biased perceptions within each group. They will exaggerate the value of their own efforts and be quite certain that they know the other group's position even when they do not.
- Each group will become very close-knit and conformist. It will concentrate very hard on the task in hand (usually beating the other group!).
- Each group will choose leaders who are liable to be authoritarian and strongly focused on the task.
- The groups will actually discriminate against one another at every available opportunity.

The implications for communication are fairly self-evident. Exchanges between the groups are liable to be unfriendly or hostile.

Messages will be misinterpreted or misunderstood and there is liable to be a progressive escalation of conflict.[17]

The classic illustration of these phenomena was Muzafer Sherif's summer camp experiments. Sherif and his colleagues 'took over' an American summer camp on three separate occasions, in 1949, 1953 and 1954, and dutifully observed and investigated the activities of the participants who were unaware that they were, in fact, experimental subjects. Of the three experiments, the most widely reported is the last one, usually known as the Robber's Cave Experiment, after the name of the summer camp. There are numerous graphic accounts of the conflict which followed. There were fights (which everyone agreed had been started by the other group); insults were exchanged; the groups destroyed each other's property; and, in each experiment:

> the conflict mushroomed to an almost intolerable level. The staff was extremely hard-pressed in trying to prevent an outbreak of serious disorder.[18]

Having created this high level of conflict, the Sherifs took several steps to reduce it, including attempts to increase friendly social contact, and a collaborative game against another camp. The only approach that did reduce the conflict was what they called 'superordinate goals'. In Carolyn Sherif's own words:

> the contact between equals, in order to cause change, had to involve interdependence of a kind that required the resources and energies of all the members of both groups. There had to be some goal to be achieved in the environment that they couldn't ignore, but that everyone was needed to do.[18]

So why do groups have such difficulty in establishing harmonious relationships with one another?

Having established that groups can have great difficulty in communicating with one another on friendly terms, we need to ask why this should be the case. Must competition inevitably lead to destructive and unnecessary conflict? Early attempts to answer these questions suggested that we should look at individual processes. For example, it was suggested that discrimination against out-groups was initiated by individuals with particular personality characteristics or by individuals who were very frustrated. It had been believed for some time that frustration leads to aggression towards a convenient scapegoat. But this sort of explanation cannot explain many examples of conflict such as the Sherif experiments.

Following the Sherifs' work, researchers turned to explanations which discussed the social groups as groups rather than as collections of individuals. The Sherifs concluded that, where there was a 'realistic conflict of interests', the competition led to a strong identification with the in-group. This then led to the discrimination against the out-group.

A different line of explanation was established by British and European researchers. They concluded that a more fundamental process of social identification led to the discrimination and conflict. In other words, you place yourself (or are placed) in a particular social category and this becomes part of your social identity. For this to be meaningful, you have to compare your group (category) with other categories. When you make this comparison, you look for something distinctive or positive. Thus, your group is seen as better than the group you have compared yourself with. This satisfies your motivation to be a person of some value, i.e. to have high self-esteem.

This book is not the place to offer a detailed comparison of the different approaches.[19] Both these perspectives have interesting implications for communication, and some important weaknesses. For example, discrimination between groups does not necessarily follow as a result of relevant social comparison – group membership means different things to different people in different situations, and this needs more investigation. Furthermore, psychological explanation must be seen alongside consideration of social and historical factors. For example, the Sherifs' summer camp groups were equally powerful. What would have happened if one group had been more powerful than the other? In many real-life situations, we are only too aware that the other group is more or less powerful than we are.

Can communication resolve these intergroup difficulties?

In previous sections we have concentrated on intergroup conflict which is obviously where communication is most important. But can groups communicate with one another so as to avoid unnecessary conflict and discrimination? They can do, but only if they take into account the following points:

- Group members should be aware of typical intergroup phenomena so that they can be cautious in their assumptions and opinions regarding the other group. They should not jump to conclusions and develop 'us–them' attitudes. In other words, they should try to avoid the typical perceptual biases.
- Group representatives should try to avoid win–lose situations and attempt to clarify their group's role and position in any negotiations with the other group.

Communication is obviously very important as it underpins both these points. But it is even more important that the groups actually want to solve any differences they may have. Both the above points depend on members and leaders actually wanting to come to terms with one another, despite their differences. In many situations the differences between groups are so emotionally charged that such willingness will not exist. Without the willingness, it is difficult to imagine strategies which will resolve the conflict, although many authors have tried to propose them. Alternatively, communication can make matters worse by creating an 'us–them' attitude which is not what the participants really want. A casual remark may be interpreted as condescending and the spiral of discrimination starts!

Chapter 14

Final thoughts

Is computer-mediated communication (CMC) a new form of interpersonal communication?

In this chapter, I shall:

- discuss the issue of mediated communication – how the channel of communication can affect the meaning of communication
- analyse the differences between computer-mediated communication (CMC) and interpersonal communication
- suggest ways in which you can evaluate, further develop and extend the material in this book

How can the channel affect communication?

In Chapter 2, I was rather critical of the linear model of communication. However, it is useful in some respects. It does make it clear that all messages are conveyed through particular channels of communication. This is not surprising, as the two men who first developed the model (Shannon and Weaver) were particularly interested in one channel of communication – the telephone. So far in this book I have concentrated on situations which involve two people communicating face to face. Of course you can argue that this involves a number of different channels, e.g. visual, auditory, kinaesthetic, etc. These channels may not always be fully used even in a face-to-face conversation, but what happens when some of these signals cannot be used? What happens in situations where communication is mediated by some artificial means, e.g. by some electronic medium like the telephone? I shall look at some general ideas on this before focusing on research which has tried to explain how people communicate through computer channels.

Different channels may have very different implications for communication. For example:

- a specific channel will affect the form of information which passes through it
- different channels have different impacts
- different channels have different social meanings attached to them
- particular sorts of messages may be seen as more appropriate for specific channels

In any practical situation, whatever happens will be related to a specific combination of all these implications. They are difficult to separate in practice. A few examples and case studies will illustrate some of the complexities.

The low-fi phone

Modern telephone technology uses some very advanced electronic devices but the actual telephone handset into which you speak is relatively cheap and crude. In each handset there is a small microphone and loudspeaker. Both of these are fairly simple devices which cannot reproduce high-fidelity sound. As a result, the tone of voices which you hear is not a very accurate reflection of the tone you would hear if that other person was present. This does not affect us when we are talking to someone we know as we can rely on subconscious processes to supply the 'missing' information. But it can lead to misunderstandings when we talk to strangers. You can gain a very inaccurate impression of the other person's personality because of the way their tone of voice has been misshapen by the low fidelity of the telephone.

Another illustration of a similar effect is the way we can be disappointed when we see radio personalities like disc jockeys in the flesh. Sometimes, they do not 'live up to their voice'. This may be partly because they use deliberate effects on radio, such as echo machines which add drama and richness to the tone of voice. A historical example would be the number of stars of the silent cinema who were unable to cope with the demands of the new talking picture. The film *Singin' in the Rain* is a very clever parody of this era, if you need an excuse to watch it for purely academic reasons!

English as it is spoke

Another example is the differences between spoken and written language, which was highlighted in Chapter 8. You may have suffered from a teacher or lecturer who has written out his or her notes and simply reads them out. Writing good spoken English is a useful skill which does need thought and attention as any television newsreader or scriptwriter will tell you.

What has happened to the videophone?

A videophone is a telephone which has a television screen attached so that the callers can see one another while they are talking. At first impression, this seems like a very useful idea. When they were first marketed, many writers accepted this at face value without recognising the more subtle implications of different channels of communication. For example, Eyre concluded that it was an 'obvious aid to communication'.[1]

Unfortunately for the manufacturers of videophones, this may not be the case. People use different channels of communication for different purposes, and this applies to the ordinary telephone. People in business typically use the telephone to send short urgent messages. Seeing the other person could actually be a disadvantage here because of the tendency to fill out the conversation with social chat. When you meet somebody face to face you do expect to exchange some social greetings but you do not expect to do the same in a telephone call unless you know the person very well. So, manufacturers of videophones who aimed their product at the business market did not initially establish their product despite quite intensive marketing and advertising. This is obviously affected by economic and technical considerations but perhaps it is also true that manufacturers failed to appreciate a basic principle of communication – that the channel of communication does matter to people.

The technology which made the videophone a practical possibility has now been developed in other ways which seem to be more successful. Teleconferencing has become quite common in many organisations – where people in different parts of the country can conduct a meeting without travelling to meet one another. They are connected by a video or audio link. In a video link, the individuals concerned sit in a small television studio and talk to their colleagues in other television studios in other parts of the country. By looking at television sets in the studio, each individual can see all the other individuals involved, usually through a split-screen presentation like the ones used by television quiz shows such as *University Challenge*.

The main advantage of teleconferencing is the savings in costs which are possible. People do not have to travel great distances with the possibility of an overnight stay and hotel costs. But will teleconferencing replace face-to-face meetings? Will people accept that the television channel is equivalent to face-to-face meetings? Users often emphasise the need for training and practice to make best use of the system and that face-to-face contact is still the best way of having the 'first meeting'.

If teleconferencing has become accepted for a range of meetings, what are the practical limits of this technology? For example, in recent experiments in the USA, prisoners are not brought to court but stand in front of television cameras in a small studio in the prison. There is a television link to the courtroom as with teleconferenced meetings. The television system has some advantages – it saves transport time and costs and appears to speed up the trials. Many lawyers are unhappy with it, though. As one prosecuting counsel put it: 'When I question someone I want to see what their whole body is doing. I want to see how they're shuffling their feet' (also see the discussion of leakage in Chapter 9). For these reasons, teleconferencing may not be widely adopted for meetings where there are powerful interpersonal issues involved, e.g. disciplinary tribunals.

New forms of communication lead to new forms of social gathering: they do not necessarily replace the old forms. In fact the old forms may actually be used more. For example, although cinema attendance declined dramatically with the advent of television, this did not mean that fewer films were seen. Television could not survive without a regular supply of feature films, which can also attract some of the largest audiences.

Explaining CMC

Two years ago, I used to walk into my office each morning, check the answerphone (which was often full of messages) and look through the pile of memos and notes which would be sitting in my in-tray. Today, I walk in and find at most a couple of messages on the answerphone and probably no written memos. Email is now the dominant channel for messages across my organisation and can vary from literally a couple of words to several screens of text. Email is also increasingly replacing written mail from outside. As well as daily work messages, there are the newsgroup messages – one I check every day always has messages from strangers with exotic names whose identity is a mystery to me. But why have they taken on these different personas? I have not contributed to that newsgroup to date – is my 'lurking' because I have not found anything useful to contribute, or is this electronic shyness? And this raises one of the critical questions: is this a new form of social communication with different rules and constraints to the interpersonal? Can we believe recent newspaper reports which claim that abuse and harassment through electronic communication means are more common than the face-to-face variety – the notion of 'flaming'? There is also the increasing use of the Internet to publish information and to research and support personal interests.

This brief anecdote highlights four major issues which have been explored and which relate to major themes in this book:[2]

1 The lack of non-verbal cues in electronic communication.
2 The language of CMC exchanges.
3 The way that participants express (or conceal) their identity.
4 The possible formation of community through CMC.

Missing signals

There is a considerable body of research into situations where the usual range of non-verbal cues can only play a limited part – such as making a phone call. For example, Derek Rutter developed a theory of 'cuelessness'.[3] He suggests that we are influenced by the aggregate number of usable cues or signals we can perceive from the other person. We use these cues to form an impression of 'psychological distance' which he defines as the feeling that the other person 'is "there" or "not there"'. This feeling then influences the content, style and outcome of the interaction. Using this model you would expect that phone conversations would create more of an impression of psychological distance and would lead to more impersonal conversations.

This is not simply a matter of theoretical interest – it has important everyday implications. For example, if you know you have to negotiate with another person, do you choose to meet face to face or would it be to your advantage to use the phone? If you have the stronger case on paper then it may help to use a more impersonal medium and avoid developing a more personal relationship with the other person.[4]

The language of CMC

Although you are typing into a computer and therefore writing messages in CMC, this does not mean that the messages are like other writing: 'exchanges are often rapid and informal, and hence more like spoken language'.[5] As a result, researchers have tried to investigate the special linguistic characteristics of CMC, as well as special features which writers have used, like emoticons such as :-), to insert emotional comments.

Identity in CMC

This notion that CMC is more impersonal has led to predictions that CMC will encourage people to behave in less 'orderly' ways. Because of the anonymity and impersonality, people will be much more inclined to be rude, abusive and antisocial. As with most global generalisations about human behaviour, we can find evidence both ways: some studies show more antisocial tendencies; some studies do not. This has led to theorists exploring the nature of the on-screen interactions and showing that how the person views their social identity within the interaction is a deciding factor.[6]

Community in CMC

In CMC, we can create identities for ourselves which mean that we are not automatically judged in terms of all the usual social cues such as race, gender, class, etc. Some commentators have argued that this gives an opportunity for more 'democratic' communication across existing social boundaries. On-line communities have certainly been created and we can observe how they have developed norms for interaction (so-called 'netiquette') and handled conflict between members with more or less success. But these communities may simply reflect inequalities we find in face-to-face interaction, especially where gender is revealed.

Whatever the final outcome of this line of research, it is obviously going to become increasingly important as CMC becomes more widespread. Perhaps some future edition of this book will have to reflect the fact that face-to-face communication and CMC are *both* major forms of social interaction for the majority of people, and the relationship between the two will be a critical issue for us all. And this leads to the final section of this book.

Going beyond the story so far

The main purpose of this final section is to suggest ways you can *develop and expand* upon the material in this book. So I am not going to repeat all the major issues and concepts I have used. Rather I want to make a few predictions and highlight some basic assumptions which are worth further exploration. In doing this I shall also highlight potential criticisms of the approach I have adopted. This is an introductory text, so I have had to save space by simplifying some of the arguments. Have I made it look too simple and straightforward?

The future of interpersonal theory and practice

I am not alone in thinking that interpersonal communication

> is a rapidly developing field of study and, as knowledge increases, further skills and dimensions will be identified, and awareness of interpersonal communication expanded accordingly.[7]

So one very safe prediction is that research interest in interpersonal communication will continue to grow. I also predict that research will concentrate on the following general issues.

The interdependence of concepts, processes and social context

Having suggested that there are a number of fundamental components to interpersonal communication, I also emphasised that these components are interdependent. The components interact and depend upon one another. This interaction depends upon the context and that means we must view global generalisations with some caution (such as the power of NVC discussed in Chapter 9).

What I have not explored in any real depth is how these factors interact and how they influence each other. Specific situations may need much more detailed explanations. For example, I mentioned the equilibrium theory of NVC back in Chapter 8, which suggests that we try to achieve the right balance of non-verbal intimacy signals when we talk to others. There are now at least three well-known refinements of this theory which offer different perspectives on the relationship between the signals, our feelings and our responses.

The influence of social and cultural variables

I have repeatedly argued that social and cultural variables are important. But have I made this point strongly enough? And at what point do interpersonal factors become outweighed by cultural variables? And at what point do economic and historical factors need to be taken into account?

These issues are significant if we try to analyse very complex events from an interpersonal viewpoint. For example, one analysis of the Gulf War suggested that a critical factor was the very different use of language codes by George Bush and Saddam Hussein.[8] According to this analysis: 'Arabic allows lengthy rhetoric, raw emotion, blatant exaggerations, demands, even threats (not necessarily to be carried out)'. This was very far from the quiet and measured style used by George Bush. So does it follow that: 'Arabs (Saddam) watching him on television, saw an unexcitable figure who couldn't really mean what he said. Otherwise wouldn't he shout and throw in a couple of fine oaths for good measure?'

Assuming that this interpretation of different cultural styles is accurate – and this itself is an issue which requires much more detailed examination – how far can these interpersonal issues really influence the outcome of international events?

The relationship between skills, awareness and social values

One implication of my discussion of communication skills is that we *can* change our behaviour and communicate more effectively with other people. I argued that this was not simply a matter of mechanically adopting fixed, new behaviour patterns but did crucially depend upon our understanding. Effective communication depends upon our social knowledge and also upon our self-awareness. But there is also the question of values, which I tried to highlight in the discussion of assertiveness and male/female communication, and which needs further exploration.

A final prediction

In Chapter 1, I introduced the issue of the popular analysis of communication – how far are we (or should we be) influenced by the advice and analysis on human relationships which is fed to us by the media? This advice is becoming more prominent and, in some cases, more extreme. As I was putting the final touches to this book, I came across even more examples, including the so-called 'Speed Seduction' technique based on concepts drawn from NLP and marketed through books, seminars and the Internet!

My final prediction is that this deluge of advice will continue. I am not confident that it will be based on any more reliable principles than some of the present offerings!

And a final word

In Chapter 1, I did say that I was not going to discuss how we *should* communicate. In fact, I have expressed value judgements on several occasions – we cannot fully analyse our communication with other people without invoking ethical or moral judgements at some point. And perhaps this is the point on which to conclude this book. Our communication is the expression of our ideas and values. I hope that I have prompted you to explore your interpersonal communication with a more critical and more sensitive perspective.

Notes

Introduction

1 This survey was quoted in the leaflet which accompanies the 'TalkWorks' booklet published in the UK by BT (British Telecommunications plc) in 1997. This booklet aims to 'help you get more out of life through better conversations' and was distributed free of charge. BT also set up a supporting Web site: www.talkworks.co.uk. These initiatives are part of the work of the BT Forum which conducts research into the role of communication within society.

2 These quotes are from promotional fliers for courses advertised across the UK by Fred Pryor Seminars and CareerTrack respectively.

3 This quote is taken from a promotional letter concerning the 'Effective Speaking and Listening' course offered by R & W Heap (Publishing) Company Ltd. This course is widely and regularly advertised in the British press.

4 These quotes are taken from the *cover* of Susan Quilliam's book. See Quilliam, S. (1997) *Body Language Secrets*, London: Thorsons. The text itself is rather less dramatic and asks readers to remember that: 'body language will not give you power over people – they will not respond unless they want to' (page v); 'body language does not let you read everyone like a book – because everyone has his or her own personalised body language' (page v).

5 This tip comes from David Lewis's book and I shall discuss it in Chapter 9. See Lewis, D (1996) *How To Get Your Message Across: A practical guide to power communication*, London: Souvenir Press.

6 This book became an American best-seller and was also widely promoted in the UK. See Becker, Gavin De (1997) *The Gift of Fear: Survival signals that protect us from violence*, London: Bloomsbury.

7 I came across Anne Murcott's work in her article in the *Times Higher Education Supplement* (THES); see Murcott, A. (1997) 'The lost supper',

THES 31 January: 15. This is based on her chapter in the book edited by Pat Caplan; see Caplan, A. (ed.) (1997) *Food, Health and Identity*, London: Routledge.

8 Both these examples are taken from the *Daily Express*. The analysis of celebrities' body language is by Judi James.

9 The Drusilla Beyfuss column appears in the *You* magazine enclosed with the paper. In the 26 April (1998) edition, she comments that 'the habit (of using first names) has caught on in many sectors where once this would have been considered an impertinence'. She advises readers to go along with the norms of the specific workplace. On the vexed issue of juicy invitations, she says it is OK as long as they are 'up to date'.

10 The article by Tony Hazell ('Body language speaks volumes') appeared in the 'Career Mail' section of the *Daily Mail* 9 November 1995: 66. It was based on the following book by Allan Pease. See Pease, A. (1997) *Body Language: How to read others' thoughts by their gestures*, 3rd edn, London: Sheldon Press.

11 Lucy Miller's article ('Be your own shrink') appeared in the *Daily Express* 1 May 1998: 50. The book is Keel, P. (1998) *All About Me*, New York: Broadway Books.

12 Of the five books she analyses and criticises, at least two are still widely available in the UK. See Koivumaki, J. H. (1975) 'Body language taught here', *Journal of Communication* 25(1): 26–30.

13 From page 82 of Quilliam's book – see note 1 above.

14 From page 102 of Thomson, P. (1996) *The Secrets of Communication*, London: Simon & Schuster.

15 From page 107 of Willcocks, G. and Morris, S. (1996) *Putting Assertiveness to Work*, London: Pitman.

16 From page 193 of David Lewis's book – see note 5 above.

17 This quote is from page 108 of Burton, G. and Dimbleby, R. (1995) *Between Ourselves*, 2nd edn, London: Arnold. It summarises the often quoted conclusions of research by Mehrabian; see Mehrabian, A. (1971) *Silent Messages*, New York: Wadsworth.

18 David Perimutter's study of employees of the major publishers of American secondary-school social science textbooks suggested that social, marketing and commercial pressures combined to ensure that textbook editors 'create an image world that reduces the risk of controversy'. See Perimutter, D. (1997) 'Manufacturing visions of society and history in textbooks', *Journal of Communication* 47(3): 68–81.

19 Anyone who is not convinced that sexist language should be avoided both for the sake of accuracy and fairness is referred to this excellent book: Miller, C. and Swift, K. (1989) *The Handbook of Non-Sexist Writing*, 2nd edn, London: The Women's Press.

1 Defining what we mean by interpersonal communication

1 This quote is taken from an introductory text written by a sociologist. You may like to compare our different approaches. He does provide a very interesting chapter on theories and models which you may like to read after you have read Chapters 1 and 2: McQuail, D. (1984) *Communication*, 2nd edn, London: Longman.

2 The front-page story – 'Fight to save the Queen's English' – appeared in the *Sunday Express* 24 September 1995.

3 For example, see the list of definitions in the article by Dance, who goes on to discuss major differences between them: Dance, F. E. X. (1970) 'The concept of communication', *Journal of Communication* 20: 201–10. The article is also published in the collection by Porter and Roberts: Porter, L. W. and Roberts, K. H. (1977) *Communication in Organisations*, Harmondsworth: Penguin.

4 This analysis and the quotes are from one of the most interesting and challenging books on organisational communication: Clampitt, P. G. (1991) *Communicating For Managerial Effectiveness*, Newbury Park, CA: Sage.

5 Final-year dissertation by Lisa Whitaker, BA (Hons) Communication Studies, Sheffield Hallam University, June 1998.

6 For a typical example of this approach, see Stewart, J. and D'Angelo, G. (1975) *Together: Communicating Interpersonally*, Reading, MA: Addison-Wesley.

7 For a sociological analysis of these processes, see Ritzer, G. (1996) *The McDonaldisation of Society: An investigation into the changing character of contemporary social life*, Thousand Oaks, CA: Pine Forge Press.

8 See pages 135–9 of Price's book for this criticism of many interpersonal texts: Price, S. (1996) *Communication Studies*, Harlow: Addison Wesley Longman.

9 The model is based upon the very influential early work of Shannon and Weaver which is discussed (and often misquoted!) in virtually every textbook of communication. A very clear introduction to their approach and its more sophisticated development is contained in the article by Klaus Krippendorff: Krippendorff, K. (1975) 'Information theory', in G. J. Hanneman and W. J. McEwen (eds) *Communication and Behaviour*, Reading, MA: Addison-Wesley. Many popular books on communication also adopt what is effectively a linear model. For a recent example, see Chapter 1 of the book by Malcolm Peel: Peel, M. (1990) *Improving Your Communication Skills*, London: Kogan Page.

10 This quote is associated with Abraham Maslow, the very influential American psychologist who was concerned that psychologists should pay more attention to promoting the positive or healthy side of human beings. He believed that most of psychology concentrated on human weaknesses or limitations and did not provide useful information to help people develop their abilities or potential. His theory of human motivation suggests that humans have a progressive series of needs

culminating in the need to realise their potential. This has proved very popular and influential although it only has limited supporting evidence. See Maslow, A. H. (1971) *The Farther Reaches of Human Nature*, New York: Viking Press.

11 This is a specific example of a situation where someone behaves in accordance with their expectations even though they may not be consciously aware of them.

12 This quote is from D. M. McKay, who discusses this issue in the article 'Formal analysis of communicative processes' in the book by Robert Hinde which contains a number of interesting approaches: Hinde, R. A. (1972) *Nonverbal Communication*, Cambridge: Cambridge University Press.

13 I first heard this remark in a talk by Fred Herzberg, the well-known American management consultant. He was reminding managers that employees have good memories – if you treat them badly they will never forget it!

2 The process of interpersonal communication

1 This definition was first proposed by Harold Lasswell, one of the early American theorists of mass communication, in an article, 'The structure and function of communication in society' in Bryson, L. (ed.) (1948) *The Communication of Ideas*, New York: Institute for Religious and Social Studies.

2 I have given a rather superficial account of the notion of a theoretical model. Unfortunately it's not quite as simple as that as you will see if you read the following: Hawes, L. (1975) *Pragmatics of Analoguing: Theory and model construction in communication*, Reading, MA: Addison-Wesley; Black, M. (1962) *Models and Metaphors*, Ithaca, NY: Cornell University Press; Littlejohn, S. W. (1983) *Theories of Human Communication*, 2nd edn, Belmont, CA: Wadsworth.

3 As well as this example, Susan Ervin-Tripp has produced many fascinating analyses of the linguistic complexities of everyday speech. Probably the best starting point is Ervin-Tripp, S. (1972) 'On sociolinguistic rule: alteration and co-occurrence', in J. J. Gumperz and D. Hymes (eds) *Directions in Sociolinguistics: The ethnography of communication*, New York: Holt, Rinehart and Winston.

4 Sociologists who follow the ethnomethodological approach try to discover meanings which we tend to 'take for granted' in everyday interactions. This example is taken from a leading exponent of this approach: Garfinkel, H. (1967) *Studies in Ethnomethodology*, Englewood Cliffs, NJ: Prentice Hall.

5 See the excellent book by Kurt Danziger which also offers an interesting system for analysing interactions: Danziger, K. (1976) *Interpersonal Communication*, Oxford: Pergamon.

6 From page 1 of Danziger – see note 5 above.

7 From page 5 of Danziger – see note 5 above.

8 From page 11 of Danziger – see note 5 above.

9 From page 2 of Danziger – see note 5 above.

3 The skills of interpersonal communication

1 From page 117 of Argyle, M. (1994) *The Psychology of Interpersonal Behaviour*, 5th edn, Harmondsworth: Penguin.
2 Michael Argyle was one of the pioneers of this approach in the UK. Starting from his early publications in the 1960s, he has produced a series of books and articles on social skills and related topics, including perhaps the best-known paperback introduction to social behaviour referenced in note 1 above. A good example of his early influential thinking is Argyle, M. and Kendon, A. (1967) 'The experimental analysis of social performance', in L. Berkowitz (ed.) (1967) *Advances in Experimental Social Psychology*, vol. 3, New York: Academic Press.
3 See Chapter 5 of Argyle (1994) in note 1 above.
4 From page 15 of Tingley, J. C. (1996) *Say What you Mean, Get What You Want: A business person's guide to direct communication*, New York: AMACOM.
5 See Chapter 2 of Hargie, O. D. W, (1997) *The Handbook of Communication Skills*, 2nd edn, London: Routledge.
6 This approach is explained in Rackham, N. and Morgan, T. (1977) *Behaviour Analysis and Training*, London: McGraw-Hill.
7 As well as providing their own approach, the authors offer interesting comments on other methods. See Clark, N., Phillips, K and Barker, D. (1984) *Unfinished Process*, London: Gower Press.
8 For an example of how this is studied, see the chapter by Marzillir in Trower, P., Bryant, B. and Argyle, M. (1978) *Social Skills and Mental Health*, London: Methuen.
9 For recent reviews, see Hargie's *Handbook* – note 5 above – and his other main text: Hargie, O., Saunders, C. and Dickson, D. (1994) *Social Skills in Interpersonal Communication*, 3rd edn, Routledge: London.
10 See the discussion in Argyle (1994: 116ff.), note 1 above.
11 For further discussion of the practical implications of this and other forms of 'metacommunication', see pages 16ff. of Porritt. L. (1990) *Interaction Strategies: An introduction for health professionals*, 2nd edn, Melbourne: Churchill Livingstone.
12 This list is taken from the first edition of Hargie's *Handbook*, note 5 above.
13 See Hargie's other main text, note 9 above.
14 For more comprehensive surveys, see Argyle, M. (1988) *Bodily Communication*, 2nd edn, London: Methuen, and Knapp, M. L. and Hall, J. A. (1997) *Nonverbal Behaviour in Human Interaction*, Fort Worth, TX: Harcourt Brace.
15 See the discussion in Hargie *et al.*, pages 77f., note 9 above.
16 For example, see the section on interview question technique in Wright, P. L. and Taylor, D .S. (1984) *Improving Leadership Performance*, London: Prentice Hall.

17 Dickson's review of reflecting is Chapter 6 of Hargie's *Handbook*, note 5 above. For an alternative practical explanation of reflecting, see Chapter 8 of the book by Richard Nelson-Jones: Nelson-Jones, R. (1986) *Human Relationship Skills*, London: Cassell.

18 For a detailed analysis of interviewer tactics and skills, see Chapters 6 and 7 of Miller, R., Crute, V. and Hargie, O. (1992) *Professional Interviewing*, London: Routledge.

19 See pages 130ff. in Ruffner, M. and Burgoon, M. (1981) *Interpersonal Communication*, New York: Holt, Rinehart and Winston.

20 These are discussed in more detail in Bolton, R. (1986) *People Skills*, Sydney: Prentice Hall.

21 For a typical summary of the practical implications of listening, see Hayes, J. (1991) *Interpersonal Skills*, London: HarperCollins.

22 There has now been considerable research on this topic since Jourard's original texts. See Jourard, S. M. (1971) *Self-disclosure: An experimental analysis of the transparent self*, New York: John Wiley, and Jourard, S. M. (1971) *The Transparent Self.*, New York: Van Nostrand.

23 The window was introduced in Luft, J. (1969) *Of Human Interaction*, Palo Alto, CA: National Press Books.

24 For a recent review of this area, see Chapter 8 'Self-disclosure' by Charles H. Tardy and Kathryn Dindia in Hargie's *Handbook*, note 5 above.

25 Quote taken from Jourard (1971), note 22 above, and discussed by Tardy and Dindia, note 24 above.

4 Communication skills in context

1 Peter Trower and colleagues provide a survey of social skills deficits in both psychiatric and non-psychiatric contexts in Trower, P., Bryant, B. and Argyle, M. (1978) *Social Skills and Mental Health*, London: Methuen.

2 For a typical example, see pages 115ff. of Wells, G. (1986) *How to Communicate*, 2nd edn, London: McGraw-Hill.

3 This example and the quotes are taken from a fascinating book by Rackham and Morgan where they describe how they developed and refined techniques for observing how people behave in work situations. See Rackham, N. and Morgan, T. (1977) *Behaviour Analysis and Training*, London: McGraw-Hill.

4 Bales originally described IPA in his 1950 book: Bales, R. F. (1950) *Interaction Process Analysis: A method for the study of small groups*, Reading, MA: Addison-Wesley. He revised and updated it in the 1970 book, but most summaries rely on the 1950 presentation; see Bales, R. F. (1970) *Personality and Interpersonal Behaviour*, New York: Holt, Rinehart and Winston. There are summaries of the system and its applications in virtually every general textbook on social psychology – see Pennington for a British example: Pennington, D. C. (1986) *Essential Social Psychology*, London: Edward Arnold.

5 For a discussion of the implications of this type of work, see Flanders, N. A. (1991) 'Human interaction models of teaching', in Marjoribanks, K. (ed.), *The Foundations of Students' Learning*, London: Pergamon.

6 Maguire's article appears in the book edited by Carolyn Kagan, which is well worth reading even if you are not specifically interested in the nursing profession; see Kagan, C. M. (ed.) (1985) *Interpersonal Skills in Nursing*, London: Croom Helm.

7 These two quotes introduce the article by Peter Bannister and Carolyn Kagan on 'The need for research into interpersonal skills in nursing', in the book by Kagan, note 6 above.

8 To illustrate the complexity and sophistication of modern approaches, see the references cited for Chapter 3 such as the texts by Owen Hargie, or the following handbook which runs to two volumes, 565 pages and over 1,800 references: Hollin, C. R. and Trower, P. (eds) (1986) *Handbook of Social Skills Training*, Oxford: Pergamon.

9 See the article by Colin Davidson on 'The theoretical antecedents to social skills training' in Kagan, note 6 above.

10 Alan Radley expands on this criticism in the article where I found the quote: Radley, A. (1985) 'From courtesy to strategy: some old developments', *Bulletin of British Psychological Society* 38: 209–11. See also Chapter 8 of the book where he argues that 'Human relationships are not, essentially, social skills' (page 124): Radley, A. (1991) *In Social Relationships: An introduction to the social psychology of membership and intimacy*, Milton Keynes: Open University Press.

11 It is also worth considering the notion of social rules in interactions like this. See pages 271ff. of Argyle, M. and Henderson, M. (1985) *The Anatomy of Relationships*, Harmondsworth: Penguin.

12 Gorden's text offers a very detailed analysis of the skills of interviewing; see Gorden, R. L. (1987) *Interviewing: Strategies, techniques and tactics*, 4th edn, Homewood, IL: Dorsey Press.

5 The social context

1 There is a growing interest in problems of communication between cultures. For example, see Gudykunst, W. B., Ting-Toomey, S. and Nishida, T. (1996) *Communication in Personal Relationships Across Cultures*, Thousand Oaks, CA: Sage.

2 Both of these examples are taken from an article by Canter *et al.*, reprinted in Furnham, A. and Argyle, M. (eds) (1981) *The Psychology of Social Situations*, Oxford: Pergamon.

3 For an interesting analysis of environmental effects, see Chapter 10 of Argyle, M., Furnham, A. and Graham, E. J. A. (1981) *Social Situations*, Cambridge: Cambridge University Press.

4 This is a very famous experiment which is summarised in most social psychology textbooks. My favourite analysis is in Ashworth, P. (1979) *Social Interaction and Consciousness*, London: John Wiley.

5 This example is taken from the Bank Wiring Observation Room study which was part of the Hawthorne studies, one of the first systematic studies of social groups. For further details, see pages 178–87 of Buchanan, D. and Huczynski, A. (1997) *Organizational Behaviour: An introductory text*, 3rd edn, London: Prentice Hall.
6 See Chapter 5 of Hartley, P. (1997) *Group Communication*, London: Routledge.
7 See Chapter 9 of Hartley (1997), note 6 above.
8 This quote is taken from a lengthy discussion with Zimbardo in Evans, R. I. (1980) *The Making of Social Psychology: Discussions with creative contributors*, New York: John Wiley.
9 For these studies and for a general summary of research in this area, see Argyle, M. and Henderson, M. (1985) *The Anatomy of Friendships*, Harmondsworth: Penguin.
10 This view was developed in the UK by Basil Bernstein. For an accessible discussion of his work, see Montgomery, M. (1995) *An Introduction to Language and Society*, 2nd edn, London: Routledge.
11 Steve Duck has been a major researcher in these areas and he provides good introductions to the study of relationships and theories of stages in Duck, S. (1988) *Relating to Others*, Milton Keynes: Open University Press, and Duck, S. (1998) *Human Relationships*, 3rd edn. London: Sage.

6 Social identity

1 This account of personality theory is very brief and selective, as you will see if you refer to any good general textbook in the area, such as Pervin, L. A. (1990) *Handbook of Personality*, New York: Guilford Press. For an alternative and more controversial account which tries to chart the differences and similarities between different approaches, see Cook, M. (1984) *Levels of Personality*, London: Holt, Rinehart and Winston. For an alternative view which emphasises the 'social construction of personality', see Chapter 1 of Vivien Burr's book: Burr, V. (1995) *An Introduction to Social Constructionism*, London: Routledge.
2 The quotes are taken from Huczynski and Buchanan's account of the work of Hans Eysenck, who developed one of the most sophisticated theories related to these personality types. See Chapter 6, especially pages 144ff, of Buchanan, D. and Huczynski, A. (1997) *Organizational Behaviour: An introductory text*, 3rd edn, Hemel Hempstead: Prentice Hall. For a practical 'do-it-yourself' demonstration of Eysenck's ideas, see his 1975 book: Eysenck, H. J. and Wilson, G. (1975) *Know Your Own Personality*, London: Maurice Temple Smith.
3 Carl Rogers developed this theory as part of an approach to psychotherapy. See Chapter 10 of Rogers, C. (1951) *Client-centred Therapy: Its current practice, implications and theory*, Boston: Houghton Mifflin. See his 1973 book for how he applied these ideas more generally: Rogers, C. (1973) *Person to Person*, Boston: Houghton Mifflin.

4 Mead's ideas became enormously influential in sociology/social psychology, although they were not published till after his death. See Mead, G. H. (1934) *Mind, Self and Society*, University of Chicago.

5 A very rich account of how humans develop self-awareness with an important analysis of communication is contained in Markova, I. (1987) *Human Awareness*, London: Hutchinson.

6 This view was first proposed by George Kelly and then developed by researchers working with personal construct theory – see Chapter 7.

7 For a more detailed description, see Watzlawick, P., Bavelas, J. B. and Jackson, D. D. (1967) *Pragmatics of Human Communication*, New York: Norton.

8 This example comes from Ruesch, J. (1957) *Disturbed Communication*, New York: Norton. The book by Ruesch and Bateson was very influential in highlighting the possible impact of these forms of communication: Ruesch, J. and Bateson, G. (1968) *Communication: the Social Matrix of Psychiatry*, New York: Norton.

9 I overheard this in a radio interview by Anne Robinson. Unfortunately I was listening in the car and was unable to catch any more details!

10 Goffman is the most famous exponent of this perspective. Perhaps his most famous book is Goffman, E. (1969) *The Presentation of Self in Everyday Life*, London: Allen Lane.

11 Linton originally published his ideas in the 1920s. Analysis of social roles became a central concern for sociologists. For an organisational application of this approach, see Chapter 3 of: Handy, C. B. (1981) *Understanding Organisations*, 2nd edn, Harmondsworth: Penguin.

12 This recommendation in a 1926 etiquette manual is taken from the collection by Hawthorne. See Hawthorne, R. (1997) *Do's and Don'ts: An anthology of forgotten manners*, London: Pavilion Books.

13 Dahrendorf enlarges upon these distinctions in Dahrendorf, R. (1973) *Homo Sociologicus*, London: Routledge & Kegan Paul.

14 This quote is from page 21 of this sociological analysis of social identity: Jenkins, R. (1996) *Social Identity*, London: Routledge.

7 Social perception

1 Experiments like this (and my second example of the football game) are discussed in most general introductions to social psychology. For example, for an American perspective see Chapter 2 of Feldman, R. S. (1995) *Social Psychology*, Englewood Cliffs, NJ: Prentice Hall. For a British/European perspective see Chapters 5–7 of Hewstone, M., Stroebe, W. and Stephenson, G. M. (eds) (1996) *Introduction to Social Psychology: A European perspective*, 2nd edn, Oxford: Blackwell.

2 Forgas's book also provides discussion of the main issues in social perception. See Forgas, J. P. (1985) *Interpersonal Behaviour*, Oxford: Pergamon.

3 For an alternative and more detailed summary of the work on social perception and personality traits, see Chapter 6 of Pennington, D. C. (1986) *Essential Social Psychology*, London: Edward Arnold.

4 See pages 122ff. of Hewstone *et al.*, note 1 above.
5 This quote comes from one of the most interesting introductions to the repertory grid and the general approach which underpins it – the book by Bannister and Fransella. They also discuss some of the classic experiments mentioned in this book from a construct perspective – see Chapter 5 of Bannister, D. and Fransella, F. (1971) *Inquiring Man: The theory of personal constructs*, Harmondsworth: Penguin.
6 See Chapter 4 of Hogg, M. A. and Vaughan, G. M. (1995) *Social Psychology: An introduction*, Hemel Hemsptead: Prentice Hall.
7 The experiment by Dornbusch and its implications are discussed in more detail on pages 79ff. of Ashworth, P. (1979) *Social Interaction and Consciousness*, London: John Wiley.
8 For an overview of the complexities of analysing social situations, see the Introduction to Furnham, A. and Argyle, M. (eds) (1981) *The Psychology of Social Situations*, Oxford: Pergamon.
9 For a discussion of the accuracy of person perception in terms of practical implications, see Chapter 4 of Millar, R., Crute, V. and Hargie, O. (1992) *Professional Interviewing*, London: Routledge.
10 This definition comes from a very detailed analysis of the process of stereotyping in Chapter 4 of Hogg, M. A. and Abrams D. (1988) *Social Identifications*, London: Routledge.
11 For further discussion of the controversies in this area, see Chapter 10 of Brigham, J. C. (1986) *Social Psychology*, Boston: Little, Brown.
12 The battles which Gene Rodenberry fought with the TV establishment to create the *USS Enterprise* with its integrated crew (and including an alien, which was also resisted quite strongly!) are described in Whitfield, S. E. and Rodenberry, G. (1991) *The Making of Star Trek*, London: Titan.
13 The possible effects of teacher expectations upon pupils' performance are discussed by Colin Rogers in Chapter 8 of Hargreaves, D. J. and Colley, A. M. (eds) (1986) *The Psychology of Sex Roles*, London: Harper and Row. He also discusses the relevance of self-fulfilling prophecies and attribution theory.
14 For example, see Chapter 4 of Argyle, M. (1994) *The Psychology of Interpersonal Behaviour*, 5th edn, Harmondsworth: Penguin.

8 Codes 1

1 Taken from Watson, J. and Hill, A. (1984) *A Dictionary of Communication and Media Studies*, London: Edward Arnold.
2 This example comes from page 16 of Aitchison, J. (1996) *The Seeds of Speech: Language origin and evolution*, Cambridge: Cambridge University Press.
3 For an introduction to language problems in intercultural encounters, see Chapter 7 of Jandt, F. E. (1998) *Intercultural communication*, 2nd edn, Thousand Oaks, CA: Sage.
4 See page 15 of Morris, D (1994) *Bodytalk: A world guide to gestures*, London: Jonathan Cape.

5 See pages 145–6 of *Bodytalk*, note 4 above.
6 For a more detailed discussion, see Chapter 1 of Montgomery, M. (1995) *An Introduction to Language and Society*, 2nd edn, London: Routledge.
7 See Montgomery, page 71, note 6 above.
8 See Giles, H. and Robinson, W. P. (1990) *Handbook of Language and Social Psychology*, Chichester: John Wiley.
9 For a more recent development of this sort of approach, see Bhatia's work on genre: Bhatia, V. K. (1993) *Analysing Genre: Language use in professional settings*, London: Longman.
10 See note 3 above.
11 For the classic discussion of this issue see Watzlawick, P., Bavelas, J. B. and Jackson, D. D. (1967) *Pragmatics of Human Communication: A study of interactional patterns, pathologies and paradoxes*, New York: W.W. Norton. For a more recent summary, see pages 166ff. of Littlejohn, S. W. (1983) *Theories of Human Communication*, 2nd edn, Belmont, CA: Wadsworth.
12 See page 248 of Chapter 11, 'Interpersonal accounting', by Michael J. Cody and Margaret L. McLaughlin in Giles and Robinson – see note 8 above.
13 See Schiffrin, D. (1994) *Approaches to Discourse*, Cambridge, MA: Blackwell.
14 See Chapter 3 of Schiffrin, note 13 above.
15 See page 7 of of Schiffrin, note 13 above.
16 See Chapter 5 of Schiffrin, note 13 above.
17 See pages 416ff. of Schiffrin, note 13 above.

9 Using codes 2

1 See the chapter by Colin Fraser in Tajfel, H. and Fraser, C. (eds) (1978) *Introducing Social Psychology*, Harmondsworth: Penguin.
2 See Chapter 7 'Functions of non-verbal behaviour in social interaction' by Miles L. Patterson in Giles, H. and Robinson, W. P. (1990) *Handbook of Language and Social Psychology*, Chichester: John Wiley.
3 For example, see Ekman, P. and Friesen, W. V. (1982) *Unmasking the Face*, Englewood Cliffs, NJ: Prentice Hall.
4 See Ekman, P. (1985) *Telling Lies*, New York: Norton.
5 Kendon's study was published in 1967: Kendon, A. (1967) 'Some functions of gaze direction in social interaction', *Acta Psychologica* 26: 1–47. For an interesting critical review, see Chapter 1 of the book by Derek Rutter: Rutter, D. R. (1984) *Looking and Seeing: The role of visual communication in social interaction*, Chichester: John Wiley.
6 See Chapter 10, pages 181ff., of Ellis, A. and Beattie, G. (1986) *The Psychology of Language and Communication*, London: Weidenfeld and Nicholson.
7 Quoted on page 8 of the book by Rutter – see note 5 above.
8 See Argyle, M. (1988) *Bodily Communication*, 2nd edn, London: Methuen.

9 These conclusions come from the following study: Somner, R. and Somner, B. A. (1989) 'Social facilitation effects in coffeehouses', *Environment and Behaviour* 21(6): 561–6.
10 Edward T. Hall's classic texts were Hall, E. T. (1959) *The Silent Language*, New York: Doubleday, and Hall, E. T. (1966) *The Hidden Dimension*, New York: Doubleday.
11 See page 19 of Duck, S. (1998) *Human Relationships*, 3rd edn, London: Sage.
12 Reported in the *Daily Express* 2 June 1998.
13 The model by Howard S. Friedman and Joan S. Tucker is explained in their Chapter 12, 'Language and deception', in Giles and Robinson, note 2 above.
14 See page 213 of Lewis, D. (1996). *How To Get Your Message Across: A practical guide to power communication*, London: Souvenir Press.
15 See notes 4 and 5 above.
16 See Chapter 6 of *Bodily Communication*, note 8 above.
17 See Chapter 10, pages 164ff., in Ellis and Beattie, note 6 above.
18 See the quotes in the Introduction.
19 See Chapter 1 of Poyatos, F. (1983) *New Perspectives in Nonverbal Communication*, Oxford: Pergamon.
20 See pages 152–3 of Morris, D (1994) *Bodytalk: A world guide to gestures*, London: Jonathan Cape.
21 For another recent example, see Axtell, R. E. (1998) *Gestures: The do's and taboos of body language around the world*, revised and expanded edition. New York: John Wiley.

10 How useful are 'popular' models of interpersonal communication?

1 Ian Stewart provides a comprehensive review of Berne's life and thinking in Stewart, I. (1992) *Eric Berne*, London: Sage.
2 As with most of Berne's books, this is still in print. See Berne, E. (1961) *Transactional Analysis in Psychotherapy*, New York: Grove Press.
3 The 1964 original has been reprinted many times and is still widely available in paperback. See Berne, E. (1964) *Games People Play*, New York: Grove Press, or Berne, E. (1968) *Games People Play*, Harmondsworth: Penguin.
4 Quoted in Stewart, page 171, note 1 above.
5 If you just want to read one book by Eric Berne, then I would recommend his last one. See Berne, E. (1972) *What Do You Say After You Say Hello?*, New York: Grove Press, or Berne, E. (1975) *What Do You Say After You Say Hello?*, London: Corgi.
6 See Chapter 5 of the book by Ian Stewart, note 1 above, or the following book: Barnes, G. (ed.) (1977) *Transactional Analysis After Eric Berne: Teachings and practices of three TA schools*, New York: Harper's College Press.
7 See pages 22ff. of the book by Ian Stewart, note 1 above.

8 This is a typical definition taken from Berne, E. (1966) *Principles of Group Treatment*, New York: Oxford University Press.
9 Both quotes are from page 103 of Berne, E. (1971) *Sex In Human Loving*, London: Andre Deutsch.
10 See Chapter 1 of Mavis Klein's book: Klein, M. (1980) *Lives People Live: A textbook of Transactional Analysis*, Chichester: John Wiley. This quote is on page 14.
11 See pages 18–20 of Stewart, I. and Joines, V. (1987) *TA Today: A new introduction to Transactional Analysis*, Nottingham: Lifespace Publishing.
12 Most TA analysts suggest that there are two divisions to the Parent. For example, see Chapter 3 of Stewart and Joines, note 11 above.
13 From page 14 of Klein, note 10 above.
14 See the discussion in Steiner, C. (1974) *Scripts People Live: Transactional analysis of life scripts*, New York: Grove Press.
15 Obviously see *Games People Play* or Chapter 23 of Stewart. and Joines, note 11 above, for notes on how his ideas developed. Or see Chapter 12 of Hewson, J. and Turner, C. (1992) *Transactional Analysis in Management*, Chichester, John Wiley.
16 Now advertised on the cover of the 1990 British edition as the best-selling book on NLP with 'over 350,000 copies having been sold worldwide', this was the book that first introduced the main ideas. Page numbers below are from the 1990 British edition. See Bandler, R. and Grinder, J. (1979) *Frogs into Princes*, Moab, UT: Real People Press, and Bandler, R. and Grinder, J (1990) *Frogs into Princes*, Enfield: Eden Grove Editions. For a more detailed history, see pages 47ff. of Andreas, S. and Faulkner, S. (1996) *NLP: The new technology of achievement*, London: Nicholas Brealey.
17 A typical example is Alder, H. (1996) *NLP For Managers*, London: Piatkus.
18 From *Frogs Into Princes*, page 54.
19 From *Frogs Into Princes*, pages 4 and 18.
20 From *Frogs Into Princes*, page 81.
21 From *Frogs Into Princes*, page 18.
22 See page 90 of O'Connor, J. and Seymour, J. (1993) *Introducing Neuro-Linguistic Programming: Psychological skills for understanding and influencing people*, revised edition. London: The Aquarian Press.
23 See pages 7ff. of Steiner (1974), note 14 above.
24 Berne's last book is the best introduction to this – see note 5 above.

11 Do men and women communicate differently?

1 From the feature 'A degree of justice' by Catherine O'Brien, which appeared in *You* magazine, part of the *Mail on Sunday* 23 August 1998.
2 The article 'He-women?', by Ruth Sunderland and Andrew Moody, appeared in the *Financial Mail* on Sunday, 16 August 1998. It focused on the research by Andrew and Nada Kakabadse and Andrew Myers. See Kakabadse, A., Kakabadse, N. and Myers, A. (1998) 'Demographics

and leadership philosophy: exploring gender differences', *Journal of Management Development* 17: nos 5 and 6.

3 See Chapter 4 of Hudson, R. A. (1996) *Sociolinguistics*, 2nd edn, Cambridge: Cambridge University Press.

4 See Spender, D. (1980) *Man Made Language*, London: Routledge & Kegan Paul.

5 There is an interesting discussion of many of the issues raised in this chapter in Hudson, note 3 above.

6 See pages 95–105 of Hudson, note 3 above.

7 See pages 17–18 of Cameron, D. (1990) *Verbal Hygeine*, London: Routledge.

8 Lakoff's work had a major impact in the 1970s and you might like to compare Lakoff, R. (1975) *Language and Woman's Place*, New York: Harper and Row, and Lakoff, R. T. (1990) *Talking Power: The politics of language in our lives*, New York: Basic Books.

9 For a further example of her work in this area, see Holmes, J. (1989) 'Sex differences and apologies: one aspect of communicative competence', *Applied Linguistics* 10 (2): 194–213.

10 This influential study is described in Zimmerman, D. H. and West, C. (1975) 'Sex roles, interruptions and silences in conversation', in B. Thorne and N. Henley (eds) (1975) *Language and Sex: Difference and dominance*, Rowley, MA: Newbury House.

11 See pages 103ff. of Ellis, A. and Beattie, G. (1986) *The Psychology of Language and Communication*, London: Weidenfeld and Nicholson.

12 See note 11. There is also a very interesting discussion of attitudes to female communication in Chapter 5 of Cameron, D. (1995) *Verbal Hygiene*, London: Routledge.

13 See their account in Maltz, D. N. and Borker, R. (1982) 'A cultural approach to male-female communication', in J. J. Gumperz (ed.) *Language and Social Identity*, Cambridge: Cambridge University Press.

14 Deborah Tannen suggests in the Preface to her 1994 book that it is 'the third in a series'. In the first, she explains her 'framework of conversational style'; see Tannen, D. (1986) *That's Not What I Meant: How conversational style makes or breaks your relations with others*, New York: William Morrow, Ballantine. In the second, she focuses on patterns influenced by gender. In both these books she concentrates on 'one-to-one conversations between intimates and friends'; see Tannen, D. (1990) *You Just Don't Understand: Women and men in conversation*, New York: William Morrow, Ballantine. In the third, she looks at conversations at work; see Tannen, D. (1994) *Talking From 9 To 5: How women's and men's conversational styles affect who gets heard, who gets credit, and what gets done at work*, New York: William Morrow, Ballantine.

15 The most famous explanation of John Gray's ideas is his original Mars/Venus book. He has since written several sequels exploring particular situations. See Gray, J. (1993) *Men Are From Mars, Women Are From Venus: A practical guide for improving communication and getting what you want in your relationships*, London: Thorsons.

16 For example, see Tannen, D. (ed.) (1993) *Framing in Discourse*, Oxford: Oxford University Press.
17 From the Afterword, pages 311–17, of *Talking From 9 To 5*, note 14 above.
18 Quotes are taken from pages 285–6 of *Men Are From Mars, Women Are From Venus*, note 15 above.

12 Does assertiveness work?

1 From page 1 of one of the most interesting reviews of assertiveness: Wilson, K. and Gallois, C. (1993) *Assertion and its Social Context*, Oxford: Pergamon.
2 From page xiii of the Introduction to Tingley, J. C. (1996) *Say What You Mean, Get What You Want: A business person's guide to direct communication*, New York: AMACOM.
3 One of the earliest examples was by Alperti and Emmons in 1970. A recent edition is Alperti, R. and Emmons, M. (1990) *Your Perfect Right: A guide to assertive living*, 6th edn, San Luis Obispo, CA: Impact.
4 From page 2 of Wilson and Gallois, note 1 above.
5 Perhaps the most comprehensive review of the research is Rakos, R. (1991) *Assertive Behaviour: Theory, research and training*, London: Routledge.
6 From page 269 of Hargie, O., Saunders, C. and Dickson, D. (1994) *Social Skills in Interpersonal Communication*, 3rd edn, London: Routledge.
7 The full list of rights is on pages 7 and 8 of one of the best practical guides to assertiveness: Townend, A. (1991) *Developing Assertiveness*, London: Routledge.
8 From page 1 of Hargie *et al.*, note 6 above.
9 See page 271 of Hargie *et al*, note 6 above.
10 Taken from Chapter 5 of Back, K. and Back, K. with Terry Bates (1991) *Assertiveness at Work: A practical guide to handling awkward situation*, 2nd edn, London: McGraw-Hill.
11 The research evidence for the problems listed below is fully discussed in Wilson and Gallois, note 1 above.
12 From page 175 of Wilson and Gallois, note 1 above.

13 Communication and groups

1 The concept of group mind was first popularised by Gustave le Bon; see Le Bon, G. (1896) *The Crowd: A study of the popular mind*, London: T. Fisher Unwin. For a discussion of his work which also discusses the relationship between interpersonal and group behaviour see Chapter 1 in Rupert Brown's book: Brown, R. (1988) *Group Processes*, Oxford: Basil Blackwell.
2 This definition comes from the classic text on group interaction: Sherif, M. and Sherif, C. W. (1969) *Social Psychology*, New York: Harper and Row.

3 For a more extended discussion of these issues, see Tajfel, H. and Fraser, C. (1978) *Introducing Social Psychology*, Harmondsworth: Penguin.
4 For more discussion of these issues and for more detailed accounts of all the concepts introduced in this chapter, see Hartley, P. (1997) *Group Communication*, London: Routledge.
5 John Adair's text contains typical recommendations for effective teamwork; see Adair, J. (1986) *Effective Teambuilding*, London: Pan. For a more recent analysis, see the book by Michael West: West, M. (1994) *Effective Teamwork*, Leicester: BPS Books.
6 A balanced discussion of the characteristics of different types of experiential groups can be found in Blumberg, A. and Golembiewski, R. T. (1976) *Learning and Change in Groups*, Harmondsworth: Penguin.
7 For more discussion of these issues, see Chapter 12 of Hartley (1997), note 4 above.
8 This theory was first developed by Tuckman in 1965: Tuckman, B. W. (1965) 'Developmental sequences in small groups', *Psychological Bulletin* 63: 384–99.
9 For a review of alternative approaches to group development, see Chapter 4 of Hartley (1997), note 4 above.
10 This definition of conformity comes from Aronson, E. (1992) *The Social Animal*, 6th edn, San Francisco: W.H. Freeman.
11 The classic studies of obedience which distinguish it from conformity behaviour were undertaken by Stanley Milgram – the 'electric shock' experiments; see Milgram, S. (1974) *Obedience to Authority: An experimental view*, London: Harper and Row. For a more recent discussion of the implications of this work see Chapter 4 in Andrew Colman's book: Colman, A. M. (1987) *Facts, Fallacies and Frauds in Psychology*, London: Hutchinson.
12 Solomon Asch summarised his researches in *Psychological Monographs* in 1956; see Asch, S. E. (1956) 'Studies of independence and conformity: A minority of one against a unanimous majority', *Psychological Monographs: General and Applied* 70: 1–70. Whole No. 416. His earlier book on social psychology also contains very interesting discussions of group influence; see Asch, S. E. (1952) *Social Psychology*, Englewood Cliffs, NJ: Prentice Hall. Aronson provides a very readable account of the experiments (see note 11 above). For a more recent review of this work in relation to other work on social influence see the book by John Turner: Turner, J. C. (1992) *Social Influence*, Milton Keynes: Open University Press.
13 Perrin and Spencer's reworking of the Asch experiments is described in their 1981 article: Perrin, S. and Spencer, C. (1981) 'Independence or conformity in the Asch experiment as a reflection of cultural and situational factors', *British Journal of Social Psychology* 20: 20–9. Asch responded to their studies in a later edition of the same journal (1981: 223–5).
14 See Janis's 1982 book for a detailed discussion of the groupthink phenomenon: Janis, I. (1982) *Groupthink*, Boston: Houghton Mifflin.

For a typical summary, see page 255ff. of Johnson, D. W. and Johnson, F. P. (1994) *Joining Together: Group theory and group skills*, 5th edn, Needham Heights, MA: Allyn and Bacon.

15 This quote is from Rogers' own book on encounter groups, which is a good introduction to his philosophy. See Rogers, C. R. (1969) *Encounter Groups*, Harmondsworth: Penguin.

16 For further discussion, see Chapter 12 of Hartley (1997), note 4 above.

17 For a discussion of the nature of cooperation, which relates to the Sherif experiments and other lines of research, see Chapter 11 of Argyle, M. (1992) *Cooperation: The basis of sociability*, London: Routledge.

18 From the interview with Muzafer and Carolyn Sherif in Evans, R. I. (1980) *The Making of Social Psychology: Discussions with creative contributors*, New York: John Wiley.

19 To explore this area further, see Chapter 9 of Hartley (1997), note 4 above.

14 Final thoughts

1 See Eyre, E. C. (1979) *Effective Communication Made Simple*, London: W. H. Allen.

2 Also see the introduction to Herring, S. C. (ed.) (1996) *Computer-Mediated Communication: Linguistic, social and cross-cultural perspectives*, Philadelphia: John Benjamins.

3 For a full discussion of both theoretical and practical implications, see Rutter, D. R. (1984) *Looking and Seeing*, Chichester: John Wiley.

4 For an overview of more research in this area, see Lea, M. (ed.) (1992) *Contexts of Computer-mediated Communication*, London: Harvester-Wheatsheaf.

5 From page 3 of Herring, note 2 above.

6 One of the most interesting introductions to this area is the book by Sherry Turkle, especially Chapter 7: Turkle, S. (1996) *Life on the Screen: Identity in the age of the Internet*, London: Weidenfeld and Nicholson.

7 From page 482 of Hargie, O. D. W. (ed.) (1997) *The Handbook of Communication Skills*, London: Routledge.

8 This analysis appeared in the editorial column of the magazine *Cross Culture* 3(1): Spring, 1991.

Index